THE WORLD'S CLASSICS

422

FIVE ELIZABETHAN
COMEDIES

Oxford University Press, Ely House, London W. 1

GLASGOW NEW YORK TORONTO MELBOURNE WELLINGTON
CAPE TOWN IBADAN NAIROBI DAR ES SALAAM LUSAKA ADDIS ABABA
DELHI BOMBAY CALCUTTA MADRAS KARACHI LAHORE DACCA
KUALA LUMPUR SINGAPORE HONG KONG TOKYO

FIVE ELIZABETHAN COMEDIES

EDITED

WITH AN INTRODUCTION BY

A. K. McILWRAITH

LONDON

OXFORD UNIVERSITY PRESS

Five Elizabethan Comedies *was first published*
in The World's Classics *in* 1934 *and reprinted*
in 1945, 1951, 1956, 1959, 1962,
1965, 1969, *and* 1973

ISBN 0 19 250422 3

PRINTED IN GREAT BRITAIN

CONTENTS

INTRODUCTION

THIS volume is one of a series planned by the publishers to present selections from the English drama classified by period and by type. The plays in it have been chosen for their intrinsic merits, not for their historical importance, but the existence of the general scheme has imposed certain restrictions. No play is included which was not probably written during the reign of Queen Elizabeth (1558 to 1603), and Shakespeare and Jonson are not represented because they deserve separate presentation as individuals. With due regard to these limitations the editor's aim has been to select the five best comic dramatists of the period, including that prolific Elizabethan playwright Anonymous, and from the work of each to choose the best comedy written in the period. Emphasis is laid on comic merit, so that Lyly is represented by the amusing *Campaspe* and Peele by *The Old Wives' Tale* rather than by the more poetic and pastoral loveliness of the rather better-known *Endymion* and *The Arraignment of Paris*.

Dramatic activity was continuous throughout Elizabeth's reign, but the promise of a worthy comic drama which had been held out shortly before her accession by plays like *Ralph Roister Doister* and *Gammer Gurton's Needle* was not immediately fulfilled. The student finds historical interest in translations or adaptations of foreign plays like Gascoigne's *Supposes* (1566, from the Italian of Ariosto) and in native romantic plays like Richard Edwards's 'tragical comedy' of *Damon and Pythias* (1564); and indeed they are not lacking in humour and pathos, and sometimes show true feeling for characterization and dramatic structure. But it was not until Elizabeth's reign was almost half over, about 1580, that the drama which bears her name burst into full flower with a suddenness which is one of its marvels. The building of the great London theatres—the Theatre and the Curtain in 1576, and four more before the end of the century—and the permanent establishment in them of the hitherto itinerant companies of actors, created a demand for more and better plays which was eagerly met by young men who had been encouraged to perform or to watch amateur theatricals in school and university. (The new humanist theory and practice of education treated play-acting as useful training in deportment and elocution.) About the same time the Masters of the Royal Chapels and of the Grammar School of St. Paul's began to give public performances of the plays which their boys were rehearsing for presentation before the Queen, justifying the action on the grounds that their young actors gained confidence from practice in speaking before an audience, and that the charges for admission helped to defray the expenses of production.[1]

Lyly's *Campaspe*, 'Played before the Queen's Majesty on New Year's day at night, by Her Majesty's Children and the Children of Paul's', has thus an additional 'Prologue at the Blackfriars', a small private theatre of which the author was for a time a lessee. Lyly had made his name with the two parts of his novel *Euphues*, published in 1578 and 1579. In this his first play he had the good sense to modify considerably for speaking on the stage the elaborate style of his novel; the Gentlemen Readers to whom the first part of the novel is addressed might take delight, as they read *Euphues*, in the dexterity and felicity, the melodiousness and learning, of its style:

Although hitherto, Euphues, I have shrined thee in my heart for a trusty friend, I will shun thee hereafter as a

[1] There are many good histories of the drama at this time; one of the latest and best, to which the present introduction is indebted, is *An Introduction to Tudor Drama*, by F. S. Boas, Oxford, 1933.

trothless foe, and although I cannot see in thee less wit than I was wont, yet do I find less honesty. I perceive at the last (although, being deceived, it be too late) that musk, although it be sweet in the smell, is sour in the smack; that the leaf of the cedar tree, though it be fair to be seen, yet the syrup depriveth sight; that friendship, though it be plighted by shaking the hand, yet it is shaken off by fraud of the heart. But thou hast not much to boast of, for as thou hast won a fickle lady, so hast thou lost a faithful friend. How canst thou be secure of her constancy when thou hast had such trial of her lightness? How canst thou assure thyself that she will be faithful to thee, which hath been faithless to me?

Thus (with a great deal more to the same effect) Philautus to his friend Euphues, who had stolen his sweetheart Lucilla. The genuine beauty of this style is a thing to linger over and to savour at leisure; on the stage, even if its complex structure remained intelligible, its slowness would delay the action beyond the limits of the spectators' patience. There are some remnants of it in *Campaspe*, in the prologues and epilogues, which are outside the action and apart from it, and also within the play where it is dramatically appropriate, as in the arguments about love between Alexander and Hephaestion in Act II, scene ii, or in the long soliloquy of the forlorn Apelles in Act III, scene v. But these are special cases, and for the most part the dialogue moves quickly, in terse sentences and short speeches, in the brisk interplay of repartee between the rival philosophers and their witty servants.

At first sight these philosophers and their servants seem to be only slightly connected with the romantic central theme of the play; but, apart from their inherent comic value, they serve useful and necessary ends in fashioning the imagined society in which Lyly's Alexander and Campaspe and Apelles live, and in portraying the character of the hero himself, with his unsatisfied mind aspiring to perfection in all things —in wisdom as in warfare, in conduct and in character;

and they help to make Alexander's conduct more plausible and more worthy of applause by revealing it as part of an insistent and consistent quest for the ideal. Characters are portrayed with a directness and simplicity which places no strain on the understandings or abilities of the boy actors,[1] but the plain course of the story as a whole reveals Lyly's more complex idea of the character of a great man. What we lose in the reading, and what our imaginations should supply if we are to recapture the full beauty of the play, is the high, clear voices of the choir-boys (who must have enjoyed, as Boas suggests, the contests of wit) lending an ethereal beauty to the discussions of pure love.

In the logical structure of his plot, in the elevated wit of his dialogue, and in the homogeneity of his play as a whole, Lyly made a great advance upon his romantic predecessors, and the older plays were outclassed. An 'old wives' tale' is an old-fashioned romantic tale, a fairy story, told, as Peele's is supposed to be told, by a simple countrywoman before the hearth in the evening. 'A tale of an hour long were as good as an hour's sleep', says Fantastic, and he and Frolic are as eager as children in suggesting the sort of story they want ('of the Giant and the King's Daughter, and I know not what'), and in interrupting with embarrassing practical questions ('Who drest his dinner then?'); and Madge, like many a later narrator of bed-time stories, has to pull herself up and supply details she had overlooked ('O Lord, I quite forgot, there was a conjurer, and this conjurer could do anything', &c.). Peele's play is often spoken of as a delicate literary satire on the incoherent medleys of excitement contained in the old romantic plays, and in a

---

[1] Lyly further helps them out by making each character frequently speak of himself by name in the third person instead of as 'I'; the audience might not be able to tell one boy from another, but there was no excuse for them if they could not distinguish between Alexander and Hephaestion.

few places we can recognize bits of burlesque parody of earlier and contemporary literature—not only plays —as when Huanebango speaks in rumbling English imitations of the classical hexameter, and in his couplet

> O, that I might,—but I may not, woe to my destiny therefore!—
> Kiss that I clasp! but I cannot: tell me, my destiny, wherefore?

echoes Gabriel Harvey's *Encomium Lauri* (1580),

> Fain would I crave, might I so presume, some farther acquaintance:
> O, that I might! but I may not: woe to my destiny therefore!

Peele's quiet humour could turn literary absurdities of any age to his own purpose, but the tone of the induction which introduces his story is not so much satirical as affectionately apologetic, and we shall best appreciate *The Old Wives' Tale* if we succumb to its fairy-like atmosphere of enchantments and transformations, lost maidens and gallant rescuers, ghosts and marvels, of sudden changes, excitement, and wonder, bearing in mind the cosy fire-lit setting of which we are reminded from time to time by the comments of Madge and her listeners.

Lyly's play and Peele's have their sweetness and their poetic fancy in common, but they have little else. The other plays in this volume give some idea of the further variety of Elizabethan comedy—though not a complete one, since Jonson's comedy of Humours is absent, and no example of Middleton's satiric comedy of intrigue can be probably assigned to our period. But with all its variety this comedy reveals, by its repetition of certain subjects and situations, some of the popular tastes of the day. Greene's *Friar Bacon and Friar Bungay* catches up again the central idea of *Campaspe*, of the prince in love with a humble maid who gives her up to a subject whom she prefers, and returns to the calls of his higher destiny; and its

sketches of country life are as charming as those of
The Old Wives' Tale (and a good deal more extensive).
Magic and sorcery—whether actually believed in or
not—were infinitely more dreadful possibilities to
the Elizabethan audience than they are to-day, and
there was a fashion for 'conjuring' plays during the
last ten years of the century. The outstanding
example of this fashion in the tragic drama is Marlowe's *Doctor Faustus*, and it used to be confidently
assumed that it was in rivalry with Marlowe that
Greene wrote *Friar Bacon and Friar Bungay*. Evidence
recently produced[1] for dating *Doctor Faustus* rather
later than has usually been done (in the early months
of 1592 instead of in 1588 or 1589) makes this a little
more difficult to believe, since Greene died on the
3rd September, 1592, though it is still not impossible;
but whether there was really any rivalry or not, both
plays attest the popularity as a dramatic figure of the
learned sorcerer who has the devils of hell at his command, and *The Merry Devil of Edmonton* in the early
years of the next century perhaps marks the wane of
the vogue, as we shall see.

Greene exploits Friar Bacon's powers to the full
extent of their comic or thrilling possibilities in one
half of his play, with the help of the clownish servant
Miles. The other, and to us the more attractive, half
tells the idyllic love-story of Margaret, the fair maid
of Fressingfield, with her two wooers, her loyalty to her
chosen love, and the Prince's magnanimity—all lead-
ing to a suitable happy ending. To this part belong
the delightful glimpses of country life and sports,
though the oft-quoted praise of Oxford which Greene
puts into the mouth of the Emperor (at the beginning
of Act III, scene ii) belongs rather to the other.[2] The

[1] By F. S. Boas in his edition of the play in Marlowe's
Works and Life, ed. R. H. Case, 6 vols., 1930–3.
[2] Oxford men have been heard to remind themselves
that Greene's University was Cambridge when they read

two halves are rather loosely connected by the part which Friar Bacon plays in each, but each story separately is well told, the love-story proceeding through doubt and apparent disaster to its triumphant end, Bacon's achievements and repute reaching their height in the contest with Vandermast and then falling to naught through the stupidity of Miles, until the whole issues serenely in one of those compliments which the poets were never tired of paying to the Virgin Queen,

> so rich and fair a bud
> Whose brightness shall deface proud Phoebus' flower.

The Shoemaker's Holiday takes us away from fairyland and (except for a few scenes at Old Ford) from rural England to tell two love-stories set in the heart of London, the wooing and winning by Rowland Lacy[1] of the Lord Mayor's daughter Rose, and the loyalty during their long separation of Jane and her husband Ralph, with their ultimate reunion. The two stories are closely interwoven—it is easy to overlook the part Hammon plays in each—and both are legitimately connected with the 'Gentle Craft' of shoe-making in whose honour Dekker wrote, for it is thanks to the craft that Lacy is able to meet his love and that Ralph finds his lost wife. We hardly regret the missing charms of a country setting, for Dekker, a Londoner through and through, finds, within the shop of the jovial shoemaker, all the jollity and goodfellowship, the loyalty and larks, of the simple folk. Lovers or no lovers, story or none, Simon Eyre is the outstanding

that one of the charms of Oxford is 'The *mountains* full of fat and fallow deer', but then a good many Oxford men of to-day who have been to Switzerland have not walked from Horsepath to Shotover nor climbed from Hinksey to the top of Hurst Hill. Modern roads flatten gradients and modern buildings hide the country.

[1] The surname is that of Greene's hero and both belong to the family of the Earls of Lincoln, but the Christian name of Greene's Lacy was Ned.

figure of the play. Warm hearted, high spirited, he outlasts all the others in the memory, with his scolding of his wife, his jollying of his men, his astuteness and his simplicity, to the refrain of 'Prince am I none, yet am I princely born'.

He finds his counterpart in Host Blague of the George, in *The Merry Devil of Edmonton*, who serves the good Duke of Norfolk. In this anonymous play (once preposterously attributed to Shakespeare) we are back in the country again, with another story of faithful love and trusty friends, and mercenary and tyrannical parents. The intrigue is good, the friends and lovers delightful, and the outwitted elders properly ridiculous; but, as in *The Shoemaker's Holiday*, the purely comic characters bulk large: the Host himself; Smug, a character whose adventures are narrated more at large in a prose tale of the same name as the play; and the deer-stealing priest Sir John (a stock name for a priest) with his excellent morality of 'Grass and hay! we are all mortal; let's live till we die, and be merry; and there's an end'.

Magic, here, is at a discount. The Induction, in which Peter Fabell outwits the devil who comes to claim his forfeit soul, is an obvious travesty of Marlowe's terrible scene (Act v, scene ii) in *Doctor Faustus*, where Faustus in agony awaits the same fatal hour; and there is no magic or sorcery in the play itself, unless we are to suppose that the disguising of Raymond and Fabell was magically executed (which is nowhere stated and is quite unnecessary). If we are in at the death of one fashion, we catch suggestions of the birth of a new. The deer-stealing scenes here are less idyllic and more human than the country scenes of *Friar Bacon and Friar Bungay*, and in that more realistic; here, as in *The Shoemaker's Holiday*, the jolly servants and working men are closer to life than Greene's Miles, much more so than Lyly's servants. At the end of the century a vogue of realism began with Jonson's *Every*

Man in his Humour of 1598, and flourished in the comedies of satire and intrigue of Middleton, Chapman, Marston, and others; and Dekker (the only one of our dramatists who lived long into the new reign) was ready to change with the times.

The pristine freshness and innocence of English comedy finds its sweetest expression in the last twenty years of Elizabeth's reign, and it should be remembered that these years brought forth almost all of Shakespeare's comedies—all but *Measure for Measure* and the two late romances *The Winter's Tale* and *The Tempest*—as well as the Falstaff of *Henry IV*. Romance and wonder were to return again, and very soon, but never with the same happy innocence of first youth. The sweet loves of Campaspe and Margaret and Rose and Millicent were shy of reappearing in the years that followed, and the homely good-fellowship of Madge and her audience, of Eyre and his men, or of Host Blague and his companions, proved hard to recover in later days.

NOTE ON THE TEXTS

THE texts in this volume have been modernized in spelling and punctuation and, where it seemed absolutely necessary, emended, usually in silence. The scholar will need texts which preserve the original spelling and punctuation and record all variant readings: a note at the head of each play will refer such studious readers to the standard critical edition of each author on which (when there is one) the present text is based (though the reading of that edition is not necessarily adopted). A half-hearted compromise would irritate some, deceive others, and serve no useful purpose.

None of these five plays except *Campaspe* was divided into acts and scenes in the early editions. The divisions made by modern editors are harmless, and have been adopted for convenience of reference. Attempts to fix the localities of scenes in 'A Street' or in 'such and such a room of So and So's house' are useless and distracting, and have not been foisted in. When the dramatists wanted the audience to know where their characters were supposed to be, they made it clear in the dialogue. The notes occasionally suggest on what part of the Elizabethan stage the actors probably stood, and the following rough diagram will explain the terms employed:

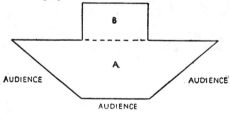

A = Outer Stage. B = Inner Stage, or 'Study' (which can be shut off by curtains along the dotted line). Above the Inner Stage is a gallery, or Upper Stage.

The notes are meant only to help readers to whom Elizabethan English is unfamiliar. They do not, except where it is necessary to their true purpose, discuss difficulties of reading or interpretation which are of interest chiefly to scholars. Those which are not original nor derived (as almost all are) either from the standard edition referred to or from the *Oxford English Dictionary* are generally ascribed to the scholar responsible for them.

Much has been left to the sagacity of the reader. The use with a plural subject of a verb which appears to be in the singular should be as familiar from any respectable edition of Shakespeare as it will become in the present volume, and it is passed over in silence except where it might cause any ambiguity. Elizabethan dramatists had as much right to mystify their unlearned readers with Latin as have modern ones with French or Italian, and indeed they generally followed a Latin phrase with an English paraphrase if they really wanted the audience to know what it meant: but once-familiar classical quotations have been translated in the notes, and a version has been given of Lacy's pidgin-Dutch in *The Shoemaker's Holiday*, which could be made by the actor to sound much less bewildering when spoken than some of it looks in print.

The engaging phraseology of the original stage directions has been retained. Most of them are quite normal, but a few range from the author's tentative suggestions to the producer, like '*Enter the* Prioress *of Cheston, with a nun or two*' to such direct imperatives to the actor as '*Sit down and knock your head*'. They preserve the flavour of the original without causing any difficulty.

CAMPASPE

BY
JOHN LYLY

JOHN LYLY (1554?–1606)

Campaspe

Acted probably in 1580 or 1581; printed in 1584.

[*Complete Works*, ed. R. W. Bond, 3 vols., Oxford, 1902. This supersedes all earlier editions for the text, but the biographical section of the introduction is in turn largely superseded by A. Feuillerat, *John Lyly*, Cambridge, 1910 (in French).]

Campaſpe,

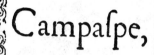

Played beefore the
Queenes Maieſtie on
newyeares day at night, by her
Maieſties Children, and the
Children of Paules.

(∴)

¶ *Imprinted at London*
for Thomas Cadman,
1584.

Dramatis Personae

ALEXANDER, *King of Macedon.*

HEPHAESTION, *his General.*

CLITUS
PARMENIO
MILECTUS } *Warriors.*
PHRYGIUS

MELIPPUS, *Chamberlain to Alexander.*

PLATO
ARISTOTLE
DIOGENES
CHRYSIPPUS
CRATES } *Philosophers.*
CLEANTHES
ANAXARCHUS
CRYSUS

APELLES, *a Painter.*

SOLINUS
SYLVIUS } *Citizens of Athens.*

PERIM
MILO } *Sons to Sylvius.*
TRICO

GRANICUS, *Servant to Plato.*

MANES, *Servant to Diogenes.*

PSYLLUS, *Apprentice to Apelles.*

Page to *Alexander.*

Citizens of Athens.

CAMPASPE
TIMOCLEA } *Theban Captives.*

LAIS, *a Courtezan.*

THE PROLOGUE AT THE BLACKFRIARS

THEY that fear the stinging of wasps make fans of peacocks' tails, whose spots are like eyes; and Lepidus, which could not sleep for the chatting of birds, set up a beast whose head was like a dragon; and we, which stand in awe of report, are compelled to set before our owl Pallas' shield, thinking by her virtue to cover the other's deformity. It was a sign of famine to Egypt when Nilus flowed less than twelve cubits or more than eighteen; and it may threaten despair unto us if we be less curious than you look for, or more cumbersome: but as Theseus, being promised to be brought to an eagle's nest, and travelling all the day found but a wren in a hedge, yet said 'This is a bird', so we hope, if the shower of our swelling mountain seem to bring forth some elephant, perform but a mouse, you will gently say 'This is a beast'. Basil, softly touched, yieldeth a sweet scent, but, chafed in the hand, a rank savour: we fear even so that our labours, slyly glanced on, will breed some content, but, examined to the proof, small commendation. The haste in performing shall be our excuse: there went two nights to the begetting of Hercules; feathers appear not on the phoenix under seven months; and the mulberry is twelve in budding; but our travails are like the hare's, who at one time bringeth forth, nourisheth, and engendreth again; or like the brood of Trochilus, whose eggs, in the same moment that they are laid, become birds. But howsoever we finish our work we crave pardon if we offend in the matter and patience if we transgress in the manners. We have mixed mirth with counsel, and discipline with delight, thinking it not amiss in the same garden to sow pot-herbs that

7 deformity] The owl was supposed to be a ludicrous monstrosity.   10 curious] careful.   14 shower] appearance.   18 slyly] casually.

we set flowers; but we hope (as harts that cast their
horns, snakes their skins, eagles their bills, become
more fresh for any other labour) so, our charge being
shaken off, we shall be fit for greater matters. But lest
like the Mindyans we make our gates greater than our
town, and that our play runs out at the preface, we
here conclude, wishing that although there be in your
precise judgements an universal mislike yet we may
enjoy by your wonted courtesies a general silence. 41

THE PROLOGUE AT THE COURT

WE are ashamed that our bird, which fluttered by
twilight seeming a swan, should be proved a bat, set
against the sun, but as Jupiter placed Silenus' ass
among the stars, and Alcibiades covered his pictures,
being owls and apes, with a curtain embroidered with
lions and eagles, so are we enforced upon a rough discourse to draw on a smooth excuse, resembling lapi-
daries who think to hide the crack in a stone by setting
it deep in gold. The gods supped once with poor
Baucis, the Persian kings sometimes shaved sticks: our
hope is, your Highness will at this time lend an ear to
an idle pastime. Appion, raising Homer from Hell,
demanded only who was his father, and we, calling
Alexander from his grave, seek only who was his love.
Whatsoever we present, we wish it may be thought
the dancing of Agrippa his shadows, who, in the
moment they were seen, were of any shape one would
conceive, or lynxes, who, having a quick sight to
discern, have a short memory to forget. With us it is
like to fare as with these torches, which giving light
to others consume themselves, and we showing delight
to others shame ourselves.　　　　　22

1–3] The obscurity of performance at the Blackfriars
contrasted with the eminence of performance at Court.

11 your Highness] Queen Elizabeth　　　20 torches]
which lit the stage; they are referred to again in the
Epilogue at Court, lines 20–1.

CAMPASPE

Actus Primus.   Scaena Prima.

Enter Clitus *and* Parmenio.

Clit. Parmenio, I cannot tell whether I should more commend in Alexander's victories courage or courtesy, in the one being a resolution without fear, in the other a liberality above custom; Thebes is rased, the people not racked; towers thrown down, bodies not thrust aside; a conquest without conflict, and a cruel war in a mild peace.   7

Par. Clitus, it becometh the son of Philip to be none other than Alexander is: therefore, seeing in the father a full perfection, who could have doubted in the son an excellency? For as the moon can borrow nothing else of the sun but light, so of a sire in whom nothing but virtue was, what could the child receive but singular? It is for turquoise to stain each other, not for diamonds: in the one to be made a difference in goodness, in the other no comparison.   16

Clit. You mistake me, Parmenio, if whilst I commend Alexander you imagine I call Philip into question—unless haply you conjecture (which none of judgement will conceive) that because I like the fruit, therefore I heave at the tree, or coveting to kiss the child, I therefore go about to poison the teat.   22

Par. Ay but Clitus I perceive you are born in the East, and never laugh but at the sun rising, which argueth, though a duty where you ought, yet no great devotion where you might.   26

Clit. We will make no controversy of that which there ought to be no question; only this shall be the opinion of us both, that none was worthy to be the father of Alexander but Philip, nor any meet to be the son of Philip but Alexander.   31

Par. Soft, Clitus! behold the spoils and prisoners! a pleasant sight to us, because profit is joined with honour; not much painful to them, because their captivity is eased by mercy.   35

Enter Timoclea, Campaspe, *with other captives, and spoils, guarded.*

Timo. Fortune, thou didst never yet deceive virtue, because virtue never yet did trust fortune. Sword and fire will never get spoil, where wisdom and fortitude bears sway. O Thebes, thy walls were raised by the sweetness of the harp, but rased by the shrillness of the trumpet. Alexander had never come so near the walls, had Epaminondas walk'd about the walls, and yet might the Thebans have been merry in their streets, if he had been to watch their towers. But destiny is seldom foreseen, never prevented; we are here now captives, whose necks are yoked by force, but whose hearts cannot yield by death. Come, Campaspe and the rest, let us not be ashamed to cast our eyes on him, on whom we feared not to cast our darts.   50

Par. Madam, you need not doubt; it is Alexander that is the conqueror.

Timo. Alexander hath overcome, not conquered.

Par. To bring all under his subjection is to conquer.

Timo. He cannot subdue that which is divine.

Par. Thebes was not.   56

Timo. Virtue is.

Clit. Alexander, as he tendreth virtue, so he will you: he drinketh not blood, but thirsteth after honour; he is greedy of victory, but never satisfied with mercy. In fight terrible, as becometh a captain, in conquest mild, as beseemeth a king. In all things, than which nothing can be greater, he is Alexander.   63

Camp. Then, if it be such a thing to be Alexander, I hope it shall be no miserable things to be a virgin;

36 deceive] disappoint.   51 doubt] fear.

for if he save our honours it is more than to restore
our goods, and rather do I wish he preserve our fame
than our lives, which if he do, we will confess there
can be no greater thing than to be Alexander.   69

Enter Alexander, Hephaestion, *and attendants.*

Alex. Clitus, are these prisoners? Of whence these
spoils?

Clit. Like your Majesty, they are prisoners, and of
Thebes.

Alex. Of what calling or reputation?

Clit. I know not, but they seem to be ladies of
honour.

Alex. I will know.—Madam, of whence you are,
I know, but who, I cannot tell.   78

Timo. Alexander, I am the sister of Theagenes who
fought a battle with thy father before the city of
Chaeronie, where he died—I say which none can
gainsay—valiantly.

Alex. Lady, there seem in your words sparks of
your brother's deeds, but worser fortune in your life
than his death: but fear not, for you shall live without
violence, enemies, or necessity. But what are you,
fair lady? Another sister to Theagenes?

Camp. No sister to Theagenes, but an humble handmaid to Alexander, born of a mean parentage but to
extreme fortune.   90

Alex. Well, ladies, (for so your virtues show you,)
whatsoever your births be, you shall be honourably
entreated. Athens shall be your Thebes, and you shall
be not as abjects of war but as subjects to Alexander.
Parmenio, conduct these honourable ladies into the
city; charge the soldiers not so much as in words to
offer them any offence, and let all wants be supplied
so far forth as shall be necessary for such persons, and
my prisoners.   [*Exeunt* Parmenio *and captives.*

72 Like your Majesty] may it please your Majesty.   81
Chaeronie] Chaeronea.   93 entreated] treated.

Alex. Hephaestion, it resteth now that we have as
great care to govern in peace as conquer in war,
that whilst arms cease arts may flourish, and, joining
letters with lances, we endeavour to be as good philosophers as soldiers, knowing it no less praise to be wise
than commendable to be valiant.   105

Heph. Your Majesty therein showeth that you have
as great desire to rule as to subdue, and needs must
that commonwealth be fortunate whose captain is a
philosopher, and whose philosopher is a captain.
                                          [*Exeunt.*

Scaena Secunda.

Enter Manes, Granicus, Psyllus.

Man. I serve, instead of a master, a mouse, whose
house is a tub, whose dinner is a crust, and whose bed
is a board.

Psyl. Then art thou in a state of life which philosophers commend: a crumb for thy supper, an hand
for thy cup, and thy clothes for thy sheets; for *Natura
paucis contenta.*   7

Gran. Manes, it is pity so proper a man should be
cast away upon a philosopher! But that Diogenes
(that dog) should have Manes (that dogbolt), it
grieveth nature and spiteth art, the one having found
thee so dissolute—absolute, I would say—in body, the
other so single—singular—in mind.   13

Man. Are you merry? It is a sign, by the trip of
your tongue and the toys of your head, that you have
done that to-day which I have not done these three
days.

Psyl. What is that?

Man. Dined.

Gran. I think Diogenes keeps but cold cheer.   20

Man. I would it were so; but he keepeth neither
hot nor cold.

10 dogbolt] worthless fool.   15 toys] trifles, fancies.

Gran. What then, lukewarm? What made Manes run from his master the other day.

Psyl. Manes had reason, for his name foretold as much.

Man. My name? How so, sir boy?

Psyl. You know that it is called *Mons, a movendo,* because it stands still.

Man. Good.   30

Psyl. And thou art named *Manes, a manendo,* because thou runnest away.

Man. Passing reasons! I did not run away, but retire.

Psyl. To a prison! Because thou wouldst have leisure to contemplate.

Man. I will prove that my body was immortal, because it was in prison.

Gran. As how?

Man. Did your masters never teach you that the soul is immortal?   41

Gran. Yes.

Man. And the body is the prison of the soul?

Gran. True.

Man. Why then, thus: to make my body immortal, I put it to prison.

Gran. Oh, bad!

Psyl. Excellent ill!

Man. You may see how dull a fasting wit is! Therefore, Psyllus, let us go to supper with Granicus; Plato is the best fellow of all philosophers. Give me him that reads in the morning in the school and at noon in the kitchen.   53

Psyl. And me.

Gran. Ah sirs, my master is a king in his parlour for the body, and a God in his study for the soul. Among all his men, he commendeth one that is an excellent musician; then stand I by, and clap another on the shoulder, and say 'This is a passing good cook'.   59

33, 59 passing] excellent.

Man. It is well done, Granicus, for give me pleasure that goes in at the mouth, not the ear; I had rather fill my guts than my brains.   62

Psyl. I serve Apelles, who feedeth me as Diogenes doth Manes; for at dinner the one preacheth abstinence, the other commendeth counterfeiting. When I would eat meat he paints a spit, and when I thirst, 'Oh,' saith he, 'is not this a fair pot?' and points to a table which contains the banquet of the Gods, where are many dishes to feed the eye, but not to fill the gut.

Gran. What dost thou then?   70

Psyl. This doth he then: bring in many examples that some have lived by savours, and proveth that much easier it is to fat by colours, and tells of birds that have been fatted by painted grapes in winter, and how many have so fed their eyes with their mistress' picture that they never desired to take food, being glutted with the delight in their favours. Then doth he show me counterfeits, such as have surfeited with their filthy and loathsome vomits, and with the riotous bacchanals of the God Bacchus and his disorderly crew, which are painted all to the life in his shop. To conclude, I fare hardly though I go richly, which maketh me, when I should begin to shadow a Lady's face, to draw a lamb's head, and sometime to set to the body of a maid a shoulder of mutton, for *semper animus meus est in patinis.*   86

Man. Thou art a God to me, for could I but see a cook's shop painted I would make mine eyes fat as butter! For I have nought but sentences to fill my maw, as *'plures occidit crapula quam gladius'*, *'musa ieiunantibus amica'*, 'repletion killeth delicately', and an old saw of abstinence, Socrates', 'the belly is the head's grave'. Thus with sayings, not with meat, he maketh a gallimaufrey.   94

Gran. But how dost thou then live?

68 table] picture.   73 fat] fatten.   94 gallimaufrey] a dish of mixed chopped meats.

Man. With fine jests, sweet air, and the dog's alms.

Gran. Well, for this time I will stanch thy gut, and among pots and platters thou shalt see what it is to serve Plato.

Psyl. For joy of Granicus, let's sing!   100

Man. My voice is as clear in the evening as in the morning.

Gran. Another commodity of emptiness!

Song

Gran.   O for a bowl of fat Canary,
        Rich Palermo, sparkling sherry,
        Some Nectar else, from Juno's dairy,
        O, these draughts would make us merry.

Psyl.   O for a wench! (I deal in faces
        And in other daintier things!)
        Tickled am I with her embraces—   110
        Fine dancing in such Fairy Rings.

Man.   O for a plump, fat leg of mutton,
        Veal, lamb, capon, pig, and coney!
        None is happy but a glutton,
        None an ass, but who wants money.

Chorus. Wines, indeed, and girls are good,
        But brave victuals feast the blood.
        For wenches, wine, and lusty cheer
        Jove would leap down to surfeit here!

                            [Exeunt.

Scaena Tertia

Enter Melippus.

Melip. I had never such ado to warn scholars to come before a king. First I came to Chrysippus, a tall, lean, old man, willing him presently to appear before Alexander: he stood staring on my face, neither moving his eyes nor his body. I urging him to give some answer, he took up a book, sat down, and said nothing. Melissa, his maid, told me it was his manner, and

96 dog's alms] 'such scraps as are thrown to dogs' (Bond).

that oftentimes she was fain to thrust meat into his mouth, for that he would rather starve than cease study. 'Well,' thought I, 'seeing bookish men are so blockish, and so great clerks such simple courtiers, I will neither be partaker of their commons nor their commendations.' From thence I came to Plato and to Aristotle, and to divers other, none refusing to come saving an old obscure fellow, who, sitting in a tub turned towards the sun, read Greek to a young boy. Him when I willed to appear before Alexander, he answered, 'If Alexander would fain see me, let him come to me; if learn of me, let him come to me; whatsoever it be, let him come to me.' 'Why,' said I, 'he is a king!' He answered, 'Why, I am a philosopher!' 'Why, but he is Alexander!' 'Ay, but I am Diogenes!' I was half angry to see one so crooked in his shape to be so crabbed in his sayings, so, going my way, I said 'Thou shalt repent it if thou comest not to Alexander.' 'Nay,' smiling answered he, 'Alexander may repent it if he come not to Diogenes; virtue must be sought not offered.' And so, turning himself to his cell, he grunted I know not what, like a pig under a tub.— But I must be gone, the philosophers are coming.   30

                                          [*Exit.*

Enter Plato, Aristotle, Cleanthes, Anaxarchus, Crates, *and* Chrysippus.

Plat. It is a difficult controversy, Aristotle, and rather to be wondered at than believed, how natural causes should work supernatural effects.

Arist. I do not so much stand upon the apparition is seen in the moon, neither the *demonium* of Socrates, as that I cannot by natural reason give any reason of the ebbing and flowing of the sea, which makes me in the depth of my studies to cry out '*O ens entium, misere mei!*'

Plat. Cleanthes and you attribute so much to Nature by searching for things which are not to be

                11 clerks] men of learning.

found that whilst you study a cause of your own you omit the occasion itself. There is no man so savage in whom resteth not this divine particle: that there is an omnipotent, eternal, and divine mover, which may be called God.   45

Clean. I am of this mind, that that first mover, which you term God, is the instrument of all the movings which we attribute to Nature. The earth, which is mass, swimmeth on the sea; seasons divided in themselves, fruits growing in themselves, the majesty of the sky, the whole firmament of the world and whatsoever else appeareth miraculous, what man almost of mean capacity but can prove it natural?

Anax. These causes shall be debated at our philosophers' feast, in which controversy I will take part with Aristotle, that there is *natura naturans* and yet not God.

Crat. And I with Plato, that there is *Deus optimus maximus* and yet not Nature.

Arist. Here cometh Alexander.   59

Enter Alexander, Hephaestion, Parmenio, *and* Clitus.

Alex. I see, Hephaestion, that these philosophers are here attending for us.

Heph. They were not philosophers if they knew not their duties.

Alex. But I much marvel Diogenes should be so dogged.

Heph. I do not think but his excuse will be better than Melippus' message.   67

Alex. I will go see him, Hephaestion, because I long to see him that would command Alexander to come (to whom all the world is like to come.)— Aristotle and the rest, sithence my coming from Thebes to Athens, from a place of conquest to a palace of quiet, I have resolved with myself, in my Court to have as many philosophers as I had in my Camp

61 attending] waiting.   73 resolved] decided.

soldiers. My court shall be a school wherein I will have used as great doctrine in peace as I did in war discipline.   77

Arist. We are all here ready to be commanded, and glad we are that we are commanded, for that nothing better becometh kings than literature, which maketh them come as near to the gods in wisdom as they do in dignity.

Alex. It is so, Aristotle; but yet there is among you, yea and of your bringing up, that sought to destroy Alexander: Calisthenes, Aristotle, whose treasons against his Prince shall not be borne out with the reasons of his philosophy.   87

Arist. If ever mischief entered into the heart of Calisthenes, let Calisthenes suffer for it; but that Aristotle ever imagined any such thing of Calisthenes, Aristotle doth deny.

Alex. Well Aristotle, kindred may blind thee, and affection me, but in kings' causes I will not stand to scholars' arguments. This meeting shall be for a commandment that you all frequent my court; instruct the young with rules, confirm the old with reasons; let your lives be answerable to your learnings lest my proceedings be contrary to my promises.   98

Heph. You said you would ask every one of them a question which yesternight none of us could answer.

Alex. I will.—Plato, of all beasts which is the subtilest?

Plat. That which man hitherto never knew.

Alex. Aristotle, how should a man be thought a god?

Arist. In doing a thing unpossible for a man.

Alex. Chrysippus, which was first, the day or the night?

Chrys. The day, by a day.   109

Alex. Indeed strange questions must have strange

93 affection] the fact that I am personally affected (Bond).   97 answerable] appropriate.

answers. Cleanthes, what say you, is life or death the stronger?

Clean. Life, that suffereth so many troubles.

Alex. Crates, how long should a man live?

Crat. Till he think it better to die than live.

Alex. Anaxarchus, whether doth the sea or the earth bring forth most creatures?

Anax. The earth, for the sea is but a part of the earth.   119

Alex. Hephaestion, methinks they have answered all well, and in such questions I mean often to try them.

Heph. It is better to have in your court a wise man than in your ground a golden mine; therefore would I leave war to study wisdom, were I Alexander.

Alex. So would I, were I Hephaestion. But come, let us go and give release, as I promised, to our Theban thralls.

[*Exeunt* Alexander, Hephaestion, Parmenio, *and* Clitus.

Plat. Thou art fortunate, Aristotle, that Alexander is thy scholar.   129

Arist. And you happy that he is your sovereign.

Chrys. I could like the man well, if he could be contented to be but a man.

Arist. He seeketh to draw near to the gods in knowledge, not to be a god.

Enter Diogenes.

Plat. Let us question a little with Diogenes, why he went not with us to Alexander.—Diogenes, thou didst forget thy duty, that thou went'st not with us to the king.   138

Diog. And you your profession, that you went to the king.

134 stage direction] The original has no stage direction here; probably the curtains of the inner stage opened to reveal Diogenes. The audience may have been expected to imagine that he was in his tub.

135 question] discuss.

Plat. Thou takest as great pride to be peevish as others do glory to be virtuous.

Diog. And thou as great honour, being a philosopher, to be thought courtlike, as others shame, that be courtiers, to be accounted philosophers.

Arist. These austere manners set aside, it is well known that thou didst counterfeit money.

Diog. And thou thy manners, in that thou didst not counterfeit money.   149

Arist. Thou hast reason to contemn the court, being both in body and mind too crooked for a courtier.

Diog. As good be crooked and endeavour to make myself straight, from the court, as to be straight, and learn to be crooked at the court.

Crat. Thou thinkest it a grace to be opposite against Alexander.

Diog. And thou to be jump with Alexander.

Anax. Let us go, for in contemning him we shall better please him than in wondering at him.   160

Arist. Plato, what dost thou think of Diogenes?

Plat. To be Socrates furious. Let us go.

                                        [*Exeunt philosophers.*

Actus Secundus. Scaena Prima.

Enter on one side Diogenes *with a lantern; on the other* Psyllus, Manes, Granicus.

Psyl. Behold, Manes, where thy master is, seeking either for bones for his dinner or pins for his sleeves. I will go salute him.

Man. Do so, but mum! not a word you saw Manes!

Gran. Then stay thou behind, and I will go with Psyllus.

Psyl. All hail, Diogenes, to your proper person!

Diog. All hate to thy peevish conditions!

Gran. O dog!

158 jump with] in accord with.   162 furious] mad.

Psyl. What dost thou seek for here?   10

Diog. For a man and a beast.

Gran. That is easy, without a light, to be found; be not all these men?

Diog. Called men.

Gran. What beast is it thou lookest for?

Diog. The beast my man, Manes.

Psyl. He is a beast indeed that will serve thee!

Diog. So is he that begat thee!

Gran. What wouldst thou do if thou shouldst find Manes?   20

Diog. Give him leave to do as he hath done before.

Gran. What's that?

Diog. To run away.

Psyl. Why, hast thou no need of Manes?

Diog. It were a shame for Diogenes to have need of Manes and for Manes to have no need of Diogenes.

Gran. But put the case he were gone, wouldst thou entertain any of us two?

Diog. Upon condition.

Psyl. What?   30

Diog. That you should tell me wherefor any of you both were good.

Gran. Why, I am a scholar, and well seen in philosophy!

Psyl. And I a prentice, and well seen in painting!

Diog. Well then, Granicus, be thou a painter to amend thine ill face, and thou, Psyllus, a philosopher to correct thine evil manners. But who is that? Manes?

Man. I care not who I were, so I were not Manes.

Gran. You are taken tardy!   41

Psyl. Let us slip aside, Granicus, to see the salutation between Manes and his master.

Diog. Manes, thou knowest the last day I threw away my dish, to drink in my hand, because it was

27 put the case] suppose.   28 any] either.   31 wherefor] for what.   33, 35 well seen] experienced, expert.

superfluous; now I am determined to put away my
man and serve myself, *quia non egeo tui vel te.*

Man. Master, you know a while ago I ran away;
so do I mean to do again, *quia scio tibi non esse argentum.*

Diog. I know I have no money, neither will I have
ever a man, for I was resolved long sithence to put
away both my slaves, money and Manes.   52

Man. So was I determined to shake off both my
dogs, hunger and Diogenes.

Psyl. O sweet consent, between a crowd and a Jew's
Harp!

Gran. Come, let us reconcile them!

Psyl. It shall not need, for this is their use; now do
they dine one upon another!   [*Exit* Diogenes.

Gran. How now, Manes, art thou gone from thy
master?   61

Man. No, I did but now bind myself to him!

Psyl. Why, you were at mortal jars!

Man. In faith, no; we brake a bitter jest one upon
another.

Gran. Why, thou art as dogged as he!

Psyl. My father knew them both little whelps.

Man. Well, I will hie me after my master.

Gran. Why? is it supper time with Diogenes?

Man. Ay, with him at all times when he hath meat.

Psyl. Why then every man to his home, and let us
steal out again anon.   72

Gran. Where shall we meet?

Psyl. Why, at *Alae vendibili suspensa haedera non est
opus.*

Man. O Psyllus, *habeo te loco parentis.* Thou blessest
me.   [*Exeunt.*

Scaena Secunda.

Enter Alexander, Hephaestion, *and a Page.*

Alex. Stand aside, sir boy, till you be called.—

55 consent] harmony.   crowd] fiddle.   58 use]
custom.   63 jars] quarrels.

Hephaestion, how do ye like the sweet face of Campaspe?

Heph. I cannot but commend the stout courage of Timoclea.

Alex. Without doubt Campaspe had some great man to her father.

Heph. You know Timoclea had Theagenes to her brother.

Alex. 'Timoclea' still in thy mouth! Art thou not in love?   11

Heph. Not I!

Alex. Not with Timoclea, you mean; wherein you resemble the lapwing, who crieth most where her nest is not: and so, to lead me from espying your love with Campaspe, you cry 'Timoclea!'

Heph. Could I as well subdue kingdoms as I can my thoughts, or were I as far from ambition as I am from love, all the world would account me as valiant in arms as I know myself moderate in affection.   20

Alex. Is love a vice?

Heph. It is no virtue.

Alex. Well, now shalt thou see what small difference I make between Alexander and Hephaestion, and sith thou hast been always partaker of my triumphs thou shalt be partaker of my torments. I love, Hephaestion, I love! I love Campaspe, a thing far unfit for a Macedonian, for a king, for Alexander! Why hangest thou down thy head, Hephaestion? Blushing to hear that which I am not ashamed to tell?   31

Heph. Might my words crave pardon and my counsel credit, I would both discharge the duty of a subject (for so I am) and the office of a friend (for so I will).

Alex. Speak, Hephaestion; for, whatsoever is spoken, Hephaestion speaketh to Alexander.   37

Heph. I cannot tell, Alexander, whether the report be more shameful to be heard or the cause sorrowful

to be believed. What! is the son of Philip, King of
Macedon, become the subject of Campaspe, the captive of Thebes? Is that mind whose greatness the
world could not contain drawn within the compass of
an idle alluring eye? Will you handle the spindle with
Hercules, when you should shake the spear with
Achilles? Is the warlike sound of drum and trump
turned to the soft noise of lyre and lute? the neighing
of barbed steeds, whose loudness filled the air with
terror and whose breaths dimmed the sun with smoke,
converted to delicate tunes and amorous glances?
O Alexander, that soft and yielding mind should not be
in him whose hard and unconquered heart hath made
so many yield! But you love; ah, grief! But whom?
Campaspe; ah, shame! A maid, forsooth, unknown,
unnoble, and who can tell whether immodest?
Whose eyes are framed by art to enamour, and whose
heart was made by nature to enchant. Ay, but she is
beautiful; yea, but not therefore chaste. Ay, but she
is comely in all parts of the body; yea, but she may
be crooked in some part of the mind. Ay, but she
is wise; yea, but she is a woman! Beauty is like
the blackberry, which seemeth red when it is not ripe,
resembling precious stones that are polished with
honey, which, the smoother they look, the sooner they
break. It is thought wonderful among the seamen that
mugil, of all fishes the swiftest, is found in the belly
of the bret, of all the slowest, and shall it not seem
monstrous to wise men that the heart of the greatest
conqueror of the world should be found in the hands
of the weakest creature of nature—of a woman, of a
captive? Ermines have fair skins but foul livers,
sepulchres fresh colours but rotten bones, women fair
faces but false hearts. Remember, Alexander, thou
hast a camp to govern, not a chamber; fall not from
the armour of Mars to the arms of Venus, from the

66 mugil] mullet.   67 bret] ray.

fiery assaults of war to the maidenly skirmishes of
love, from displaying the eagle in thine ensign, to set
down the sparrow. I sigh, Alexander, that where fortune could not conquer folly should overcome! But
behold all the perfection that may be in Campaspe:
a hair curling by nature not art, sweet alluring eyes, a
fair face made in despite of Venus and a stately port in
disdain of Juno, a wit apt to conceive and quick to
answer, a skin as soft as silk and as smooth as jet, a long,
white hand, a fine, little foot—to conclude, all parts
answerable to the best part—what of this? Though
she have heavenly gifts, virtue and beauty, is she not
of earthly metal, flesh and blood? You, Alexander,
that would be a god, show yourself in this worse than
a man, so soon to be overseen and overtaken in a
woman, whose false tears know their true times,
whose smooth words wound deeper than sharp swords.
There is no surfeit so dangerous as that of honey, nor
any poison so deadly as that of love: in the one physic
cannot prevail, nor in the other counsel.   95

Alex. My case were light, Hephaestion, and not
worthy to be called love, if reason were a remedy, or
sentences could salve that sense cannot conceive.
Little do you know (and therefore slightly do you
regard) the dead embers in a private person or live
coals in a great prince, whose passions and thoughts
do as far exceed others in extremity as their callings
do in majesty. An eclipse in the sun is more than
the falling of a star! None can conceive the torments
of a king unless he be a king, whose desires are
not inferior to their dignities. And then, judge,
Hephaestion, if the agonies of love be dangerous in a
subject, whether they be not more than deadly unto
Alexander, whose deep and not-to-be-conceived sighs
cleave the heart in shivers, whose wounded thoughts
can neither be expressed nor endured. Cease then,

82 port] bearing.   90 overseen] hoodwinked.
overtaken] captivated.   98 that] that which.

Hephaestion, with arguments to seek to refel that which with their deity the gods cannot resist, and let this suffice to answer thee, that it is a king that loveth, and Alexander—whose affections are not to be measured by reason, being immortal, nor (I fear me) to be borne, being intolerable.   117

Heph. I must needs yield, when neither reason nor counsel can be heard.

Alex. Yield, Hephaestion, for Alexander doth love, and therefore must obtain.

Heph. Suppose she loves not you? Affection cometh not by appointment or birth, and then as good hated as enforced.   124

Alex. I am a king, and will command.

Heph. You may—to yield to lust, by force; but to consent to love, by fear, you cannot.

Alex. Why, what is that which Alexander may not conquer as he list?

Heph. Why, that which you say the gods cannot resist—love!   131

Alex. I am a conqueror, she a captive; I as fortunate as she fair; my greatness may answer her wants, and the gifts of my mind the modesty of hers. Is it not likely then that she should love? Is it not reasonable?

Heph. You say that in love there is no reason, and therefore there can be no likelihood.   137

Alex. No more, Hephaestion! In this case I will use mine own counsel, and in all other thine advice. Thou mayst be a good soldier, but never a good lover. —Call my page.—Sirrha, go presently to Apelles, and will him to come to me without either delay or excuse.

Page. I go.   [*Exit.*

Enter Diogenes.

Alex. In the mean season, to recreate my spirits,

112 refel] subdue.   143 stage direction] As before (I. iii. 134) the original has no indication of Diogenes' entry; once more, he was probably revealed by the drawing of the curtains of the inner stage.

being so near, we will go see Diogenes.—And see where his tub is!—Diogenes?

Diog. Who calleth?

Alex. Alexander! How happened it that you would not come out of your tub to my palace?

Diog. Because it was as far from my tub to your palace as from your palace to my tub.   151

Alex. Why, then, dost thou owe no reverence to kings?

Diog. No.

Alex. Why so?

Diog. Because they be no gods.

Alex. They be gods of the earth.

Diog. Yea, gods of earth!

Alex. Plato is not of thy mind.

Diog. I am glad of it.

Alex. Why?   160

Diog. Because I would have none of Diogenes' mind but Diogenes.

Alex. If Alexander have anything that may pleasure Diogenes, let me know, and take it.

Diog. Then take not from me that you cannot give me, the light of the world.

Alex. What dost thou want?

Diog. Nothing that you have.

Alex. I have the world at command.

Diog. And I in contempt.   170

Alex. Thou shalt live no longer than I will.

Diog. But I will die whether you will or no.

Alex. How should one learn to be content?

Diog. Unlearn to covet.

Alex. Hephaestion, were I not Alexander, I would wish to be Diogenes.

Heph. He is dogged, but discreet; I cannot tell how sharp, with a kind of sweetness; full of wit, yet too, too wayward.

Alex. Diogenes, when I come this way again I will both see thee and confer with thee.   181

165 that] that which.

Diog. Do.

Enter Apelles.

Alex. But here cometh Apelles.—How now, Apelles, is Venus' face yet finished?

Apel. Not yet; beauty is not so soon shadowed, whose perfection cometh not within the compass either of cunning or of colour.

Alex. Well, let it rest unperfect, and come you with me, where I will show you that finished by nature that you have been trifling about by art.   [*Exeunt.*

Actus Tertius. Scaena Prima.

Enter Apelles, Campaspe, *and* Psyllus.

Apel. Lady, I doubt whether there be any colour so fresh that may shadow a countenance so fair.

Camp. Sir, I had thought you had been commanded to paint with your hand not to gloss with your tongue! But, as I have heard, it is the hardest thing, in painting, to set down a hard favour, which maketh you to despair of my face. And then shall you have as great thanks to spare your labour as to discredit your art.

Apel. Mistress, you neither differ from yourself nor your sex! For, knowing your own perfection, you seem to dispraise that which men most commend, drawing them by that mean into an admiration, where feeding themselves they fall into an ecstasy! Your modesty being the cause of the one, and of the other your affections.   15

Camp. I am too young to understand your speech, though old enough to withstand your device. You have been so long used to colours, you can do nothing but colour.

Apel. [*aside*]. Indeed, the colours I see, I fear, will alter the colour I have!—But come, madam, will you

185 shadowed] painted.   6 hard favour] ugly face.
15 affections] disposition.   19 colour] a pun: (1) paint,
(2) pretend.

draw near? For Alexander will be here anon.—
Psyllus, stay you here at the window; if any inquire for
me, answer '*Non lubet esse domi.*'   [*Exeunt.*

Scaena Secunda.

Psyllus *remains behind.*

Psyl. It is always my master's fashion when any
fair gentlewoman is to be drawn within, to make me
stay without. But if he should paint Jupiter—like a
bull, like a swan, like an eagle—then must Psyllus
with one hand grind colours and with the other hold
the candle. But let him alone; the better he shadows
her face the more will he burn his own heart!—And
now if a man could meet with Manes, who I dare say
looks as lean as if Diogenes dropped out of his nose—

Enter Manes.

Man. And here comes Manes, who hath as much
meat in his maw as thou hast honesty in thy head.

Psyl. Then I hope thou art very hungry.   12

Man. They that know thee, know that!

Psyl. But dost thou not remember that we have
certain liquor to confer withal?

Man. Ay, but I have business; I must go cry a thing.

Psyl. Why, what hast thou lost?

Man. That which I never had: my dinner.

Psyl. Foul lubber! wilt thou cry for thy dinner?

Man. I mean, I must *cry.* Not as one would say *cry,*
but *cry*—that is, make a noise.   21

Psyl. Why, fool! that is all one: for if thou cry thou
must needs make a noise.

Man. Boy, thou art deceived. 'Cry' hath divers
significations, and may be alluded to many things;
'knave' but one, and can be applied but to thee.

Scaena Secunda] Apelles and Campaspe have with-
drawn to the inner stage leaving Psyllus on the outer
stage. 6 shadows] paints.   15 confer] discuss together.
25 alluded to] used in reference to.

Psyl. Profound, Manes!

Man. We cynics are mad fellows! Didst thou not
find I did quip thee?

Psyl. No, verily! why, what is a quip?   30

Man. We great girders call it a short saying of a
sharp wit, with a bitter sense in a sweet word.

Psyl. How canst thou thus divine, divide, define,
dispute, and all, on the sudden?

Man. Wit will have his swing! I am bewitch'd,
inspir'd, inflamed, infected!

Psyl. Well, then will I not tempt thy gibing spirit.

Man. Do not, Psyllus; for thy dull head will be but
a grindstone for my quick wit, which if thou whet
with overthwarts, *periisti! actum est de te!* I have drawn
blood at one's brains with a bitter bob!   41

Psyl. Let me cross myself, for I die if I cross thee.

Man. Let me do my business; I myself am afraid
lest my wit should wax warm, and then must it needs
consume some hard head with fine and pretty jests.
I am sometimes in such a vein that for want of some
dull-pate to work on I begin to gird myself!

Psyl. The gods shield me from such a fine fellow,
whose words melt wits like wax!

Man. Well, then, let us to the matter; in faith, my
master meaneth, to-morrow, to fly.   51

Psyl. It is a jest!

Man. Is it a jest to fly? Shouldst thou fly so, soon
thou shouldst repent it in earnest.

Psyl. Well, I will be the crier.

Man. and Psyl. [*one after another*]. Oyez! Oyez!
Oyez! All manner of men, women, or children, that
will come to-morrow into the market place, between
the hours of nine and ten, shall see Diogenes the
Cynic fly!   60

Psyl. I do not think he will fly.

31 girders] jokers.   40 overthwarts] retorts.   41 bob]
taunt.   60–1] When Psyllus's turn comes to say 'fly'
he hesitates.

Man. Tush! Say 'fly'.

Psyl. Fly.

Man. Now let us go, for I will not see him again till midnight.—I have a back way into his tub!

Psyl. Which way callest thou the 'back way', when every way is open?

Man. I mean, to come in at his back.

Psyl. Well, let us go away, that we may return speedily.   [*Exeunt.*

Scaena Tertia.

Enter Apelles *and* Campaspe.

Apel. I shall never draw your eyes well, because they blind mine.

Camp. Why then paint me without eyes, for I am blind.

Apel. Were you ever shadowed before of any?

Camp. No; and would you could so now shadow me that I might not be perceived of any!

Apel. It were pity but that so absolute a face should furnish Venus' temple, amongst these pictures.

Camp. What are these pictures?   10

Apel. This is Leda, whom Jove deceived in likeness of a swan.

Camp. A fair woman, but a foul deceit!

Apel. This is Alcmena, unto whom Jove came in shape of Amphytrion, her husband, and begat Hercules.

Camp. A famous son but an infamous fact!

Apel. He might do it, because he was a god.

Camp. Nay, therefore it was evil done, because he was a god!   20

Apel. This is Danae, into whose prison Jupiter drizzled a golden shower, and obtained his desire.

Camp. What gold can make one yield to desire?

Scaena Tertia] Inner stage.   8 absolute] perfect.
17 fact] deed.

Apel. This is Europa, whom Jupiter ravished; this, Antiopa.

Camp. Were all the gods like this Jupiter?

Apel. There were many gods in this like Jupiter!

Camp. I think, in those days, love was well ratified among men on earth, when lust was so full authorized by the gods in heaven!   30

Apel. Nay, you may imagine there were women passing amiable, when there were gods exceeding amorous!

Camp. Were women never so fair, men would be false.

Apel. Were women never so false, men would be fond.

Camp. What counterfeit is this, Apelles?

Apel. This is Venus, the goddess of love.

Camp. What! Be there also loving goddesses?   40

Apel. This is she that hath power to command the very affections of the heart.

Camp. How is she hired? By prayer, by sacrifice, or bribes?

Apel. By prayer, sacrifice, and bribes.

Camp. What prayer?

Apel. Vows irrevocable.

Camp. What sacrifice?

Apel. Hearts ever sighing, never dissembling.

Camp. What bribes?   50

Apel. Roses and kisses. But were you never in love?

Camp. No, nor love in me!

Apel. Then have you injuried many!

Camp. How so?

Apel. Because you have been loved of many.

Camp. Flattered, perchance, of some!

Apel. It is not possible that a face so fair and a wit so sharp, both without comparison, should not be apt to love.   59

Camp. If you begin to tip your tongue with cunning,

28 ratified] esteemed.   27 fond] foolish.

I pray dip your pencil in colours, and fall to that you
must do, not that you would do.   [*Exeunt.*

Scaena Quarta.

Enter Clitus *and* Parmenio.

Clit. Parmenio, I cannot tell how it cometh to pass
that in Alexander, nowadays, there groweth an un-
patient kind of life: in the morning he is melancholy,
at noon solemn; at all times either more sour or severe
than he was accustomed.

Parm. In kings' causes I rather love to doubt than
conjecture, and think it better to be ignorant than
inquisitive. They have long ears and stretched arms,
in whose heads suspicion is a proof, and to be accused
is to be condemned.   10

Clit. Yet between us there can be no danger to find
out the cause, for that there is no malice to withstand
it. It may be an unquenchable thirst of conquering
maketh him unquiet; it is not unlikely his long ease
hath altered his humour; that he should be in love
is not impossible.   16

Parm. In love, Clitus! No, no, it is as far from his
thought as treason in ours! He, whose ever waking
eye, whose never tired heart, whose body patient of
labour, whose mind unsatiable of victory, hath always
been noted, cannot so soon be melted into the weak
conceits of love. Aristotle told him there were many
worlds, and that he hath not conquered one, that
gapeth for all, galleth Alexander.—But here he
cometh.   25

Enter Alexander *and* Hephaestion.

Alex. Parmenio and Clitus, I would have you both
ready to go into Persia about an embassage no less
profitable to me than to yourselves honourable.

Clit. We are ready at all commands, wishing
nothing else but continually to be commanded.   30

Alex. Well then, withdraw yourselves till I have further considered of this matter.

[*Exeunt* Clitus *and* Parmenio.

Alex. Now we will see how Apelles goeth forward. I doubt me that nature hath overcome art, and her countenance his cunning.

Heph. You love, and therefore think anything!

Alex. But not so far in love with Campaspe as with Bucephalus, if occasion serve either of conflict or of conquest!   39

Heph. Occasion cannot want if will do not. Behold all Persia swelling in the pride of their own power, the Scythians careless what courage or fortune can do, the Egyptians dreaming in the soothsayings of their augurs and gaping over the smoke of their beasts' entrails! All these, Alexander, are to be subdued, if that world be not slipped out of your head, which you have sworn to conquer with that hand.   47

Alex. I confess the labours fit for Alexander, and yet recreation necessary, among so many assaults, bloody wounds, intolerable troubles. Give me leave a little, if not to sit, yet to breathe; and doubt not but Alexander can, when he will, throw affections as far from him as cowardice.

Enter Diogenes *and* Crysus.

Alex. But behold Diogenes talking with one at his tub!

Crys. One penny, Diogenes! I am a cynic.

Diog. He made thee a beggar, that first gave thee anything!

Crys. Why, if thou wilt give nothing, nobody will give thee!   60

Diog. I want nothing, till the springs dry and the earth perish.

Crys. I gather for the gods.

38 Bucephalus] Alexander's horse.   60 give thee] give to thee.

Diog. And I care not for those gods which want money.

Crys. Thou art a right cynic, that will give nothing!

Diog. Thou art not, that will beg anything!

Crys. Alexander, King Alexander, give a poor cynic a groat!

Alex. It is not for a king to give a groat.   70

Crys. Then give me a talent.

Alex. It is not for a beggar to ask a talent. Away!— Apelles?

Apelles and Campaspe *discovered in the studio.*

Apel. Here!

Alex. Now, Gentlewoman, doth not your beauty put the painter to his trump?

Camp. Yes, my Lord; seeing so disordered a countenance, he feareth he shall shadow a deformed counterfeit.   79

Alex. Would he could colour the life with the feature! And methinketh, Apelles, were you as cunning as report saith you are, you may paint flowers as well with sweet smells as fresh colours, observing in your mixture such things as should draw near to their savours.

Apel. Your majesty must know it is no less hard to paint savours than virtues; colours can neither speak nor think.

Alex. Where do you first begin when you draw any picture?   90

Apel. The proposition of the face in just compass, as I can.

Alex. I would begin with the eye, as a light to all the rest.

66 right] complete.   73] The stage direction is not in the Quarto.   76 put . . . to his trump] make him play his trump card, i.e. push him to his last resource (Keltie). 78–9 shadow . . . counterfeit] paint . . . picture.   91 proposition] shape   just compass] accurate proportions.

Apel. If you will paint as you are a king, your majesty may begin where you please, but as you would be a painter you must begin with the face.

Alex. Aurelius would in one hour colour four faces.

Apel. I marvel in half an hour he did not four!

Alex. Why? Is it so easy?   100

Apel. No, but he doth it so homely!

Alex. When will you finish Campaspe?

Apel. Never *finish!* for always, in absolute beauty, there is somewhat above art.

Alex. Why should not I, by labour, be as cunning as Apelles?

Apel. God shield you should have cause to be so cunning as Apelles!

Alex. Methinketh four colours are sufficient to shadow any countenance, and so it was, in the time of Phidias.   111

Apel. Then had men fewer fancies and women not so many favours. For now, if the hair of her eyebrows be black, yet must the hair of her head be yellow; the attire of her head must be different from the habit of her body, else must the picture seem like the blason of ancient armory, not like the sweet delight of new-found amiableness. For, as in garden knots diversity of odours make a more sweet savour, or as in music divers strings cause a more delicate consent, so, in painting, the more colours the better counterfeit, observing black for a ground and the rest for grace.

Alex. Lend me thy pencil, Apelles; I will paint, and thou shalt judge.   124

Apel. Here.

Alex. The coal breaks.

Apel. You lean too hard.

111 Phidias] the celebrated Attic painter, about 500–431 B.C.   115 habit] dress.   116–17 blason of ancient armory] description of an old (and therefore crude) coat of arms.   118 knots] flower-beds.   120 consent] harmony.   126 coal] charcoal (of the painter's pencil).

Alex. Now it blacks not.

Apel. You lean too soft.

Alex. This is awry.   130

Apel. Your eye goeth not with your hand.

Alex. Now it is worse!

Apel. Your hand goeth not with your mind.

Alex. Nay, if all be too hard or soft, so many rules and regards, that one's hand, one's eye, one's mind, must all draw together, I had rather be setting of a battle than blotting of a board! But how have I done here?

Apel. Like a king!   138

Alex. I think so; but nothing more unlike a painter! Well, Apelles, Campaspe is finished as I wish; dismiss her, and bring presently her counterfeit after me.

Apel. I will.

       [Alexander *and* Hephaestion *come from the studio.*

Alex. Now, Hephaestion, doth not this matter cotton as I would? Campaspe looketh pleasantly; liberty will increase her beauty, and my love shall advance her honour.   146

Heph. I will not contrary your majesty; for time must wear out that love hath wrought, and reason wean what appetite nursed.

       [Campaspe *comes from the studio.*

Alex. How stately she passeth by! Yet how soberly! A sweet consent in her countenance, with a chaste disdain, desire mingled with coyness, and—I cannot tell how to term it—a curs'd yielding modesty!   153

Heph. Let her pass!

Alex. So she shall, for the fairest on earth!

       [*Exeunt.*

Scaena Quinta.

Enter Psyllus *and* Manes.

Psyl. I shall be hanged for tarrying so long.

139 more unlike] *sc.* could be more unlike.   142,
151, Scaena Quinta] The stage directions are not in the
Quarto. The 'studio' is the inner stage.

Man. I pray God my master be not flown before I come.

Psyl. Away, Manes! My master doth come.

        [*Exit* Manes. Apelles *comes from the studio.*

Apel. Where have you been all this while?

Psyl. Nowhere but here.

Apel. Who was here since my coming?

Psyl. Nobody.

Apel. Ungracious wag, I perceive you have been loitering! Was Alexander nobody?   10

Psyl. He was a King; I meant no mean body.

Apel. I will cudgel your body for it, and then I will say it was 'no body' because it was no honest body! Away, in!   [*Exit* Psyllus.

Apel. Unfortunate Apelles! And therefore unfortunate, because Apelles! Hast thou by drawing her beauty brought to pass that thou canst scarce draw thine own breath? And by so much the more hast thou increased thy care, by how much the more thou hast showed thy cunning! Was it not sufficient to behold the fire and warm thee but, with Satyrus, thou must kiss the fire and burn thee? O, Campaspe, Campaspe! Art must yield to nature, reason to appetite, wisdom to affection! Could Pygmalion entreat by prayer to have his ivory turned into flesh, and cannot Apelles obtain by plaints to have the picture of his love changed to life? Is painting so far inferior to carving? Or dost thou, Venus, more delight to be hewed with chisels than shadowed with colours? What Pygmalion or what Pyrgoteles or what Lysippus is he that ever made thy face so fair, or spread thy fame so far, as I?—Unless, Venus, in this thou enviest mine art, that in colouring my sweet Campaspe I have left no place by cunning to make thee so amiable! But, alas, she is the paramour to a prince! Alexander, the monarch of the earth, hath both her body and affection! For what is it that kings cannot obtain, by prayers, threats, and promises? Will not she think it better to

sit under a cloth of estate like a queen than in a poor
shop like a housewife, and esteem it sweeter to be
the concubine of the lord of the world than spouse to
a painter in Athens? Yes, yes, Apelles, thou mayest
swim against the stream with the crab, and feed
against the wind with the deer, and peck against the
steel with the cockatrice! Stars are to be looked at
not reached at, princes to be yielded unto not con-
tended with, Campaspe to be honoured not obtained,
to be painted not possessed of thee. O fair face!
O unhappy hand, and why didst thou draw it so fair
a face! O beautiful countenance, the express image of
Venus, but somewhat fresher; the only pattern of that
eternity which Jupiter, dreaming of asleep, could not
conceive again waking! Blush, Venus, for I am
ashamed to end thee! Now must I paint things unpossible for mine art but agreeable with my affections: deep and hollow sighs, sad and melancholy
thoughts, wounds and slaughters of conceits! A life
posting to death, a death galloping from life, a waver-
ing constancy, an unsettled resolution, and what not,
Apelles! And what but, Apelles? But as they that are
shaken with a fever are to be warmed with clothes not
groans, and as he that melteth in a consumption is to
be recured by cullises not conceits, so the feeding
canker of my care, the never-dying worm of my heart,   -
is to be killed by counsel not cries, by applying of
remedies not by replying of reasons; and, sith in cases
desperate there must be used medicines that are
extreme, I will hazard that little life that is left to
restore the greater part that is lost. And this shall be
my first practice (for wit must work where authority
is not): As soon as Alexander hath viewed this portrai-
ture I will, by device, give it a blemish, that by that

39 cloth of estate] canopy of state.   60 what but]
what else.   63 recured] cured.   cullises] strong broths,
strengthening fare for invalids.   conceits] witticisms.
70 practice] scheme.   72 device] deliberate trick.

means she may come again to my shop; and then as
good it were to utter my love and die with denial, as
conceal it and live in despair. 75

Song by Apelles.

Cupid and my Campaspe play'd
At cards for kisses: Cupid pay'd.
He stakes his quiver, bow, and arrows,
His mother's doves and team of sparrows,
Loses them too: then down he throws
The coral of his lip, the rose
Growing on 's cheek (but none knows how);
With these, the crystal of his brow,
And then the dimple of his chin:
All these did my Campaspe win.
At last he set her both his eyes:
She won, and Cupid blind did rise.
O Love, has she done this to thee? 88
What shall, alas, become of me! [*Exit.*

Actus Quartus. Scaena Prima.

Enter Solinus, Psyllus, Granicus.

Soli. This is the place, the day, the time, that
Diogenes hath appointed to fly.

Psyl. I will not lose the flight of so fair a fowl as
Diogenes is, though my master cudgel my no-body
as he threatened.

Gran. What, Psyllus, will the beast wag his wings
to-day?

Psyl. We shall hear, for here cometh Manes.

Enter Manes.

Psyl. Manes, will it be?

Man. Be? He were best be as cunning **as a** bee,
or else shortly he will not be at all! 11

Gran. How is he furnished to fly? Hath he feathers?

74 denial] rejection.   86 set] bet.

Man. Thou art an ass! Capons, geese, and owls have feathers. He hath found Daedalus' old waxen wings, and hath been piecing them this month, he is so broad in the shoulders. O, you shall see him cut the air even like a tortoise!

Sol. Methinks so wise a man should not be so mad! His body must needs be too heavy.   19

Man. Why, he hath eaten nothing this sevennight but cork and feathers!

Psyl. Touch him, Manes!

Man. He is so light that he can scarce keep him from flying at midnight!

Citizens enter.

Man. See, they begin to flock. And behold, my master bustles himself to fly.   26

Enter Diogenes.

Diog. Ye wicked and bewitched Athenians, whose bodies make the earth to groan and whose breaths infect the air with stench! Come ye to see Diogenes fly? Diogenes cometh to see you sink! Ye call me dog: so I am, for I long to gnaw the bones in your skins. Ye term me an hater of men: no, I am a hater of your manners. Your lives dissolute, not fearing death, will prove your deaths desperate, not hoping for life. What do you else in Athens but sleep in the day and surfeit in the night? Back gods in the morning, with pride, in the evening, belly gods with gluttony! You flatter kings, and call them gods: speak truth of yourselves, and confess you are devils! From the bee you have not taken the honey but the wax to make your reli-

---

15 piecing] patching.   16–17 O, ... tortoise] alluding to Bidpai's fable of one carried through the air hanging on a stick which birds supported (Bond). Or does Manes confuse the tortoise with the turtle (*sc.* turtle-dove)?   22 Touch him] Ridicule him (*sc.* Diogenes).   36–7 Back gods ... belly gods] worshipping fine clothes by day and rich food by night.

gion, framing it to the time not to the truth! Your filthy lust you colour under a courtly colour of love, injuries abroad under the title of policies at home, and secret malice creepeth under the name of public justice! You have caused Alexander to dry up springs and plant vines, to sow rocket and weed endive, to shear sheep and shrine foxes. All conscience is sealed at Athens. Swearing cometh of a hot metal, lying of a quick wit, flattery of a flowing tongue, undecent talk of a merry disposition. All things are lawful at Athens. Either you think there are no gods, or I must think ye are no men. You build as though you should live for ever, and surfeit as though you should die to-morrow. None teacheth true philosophy but Aristotle, because he was the king's schoolmaster! O times! O men! O corruption in manners! Remember that green grass must turn to dry hay! When you sleep, you are not sure to wake, and when you rise, not certain to lie down; look you never so high, your heads must lie level with your feet. Thus have I flown over your disordered lives, and if you will not amend your manners I will study to fly further from you, that I may be nearer to honesty.   63

Sol. Thou ravest, Diogenes, for thy life is different from thy words. Did not I see thee come out of a brothel-house! Was it not a shame!

Diog. It was no shame to go out, but a shame to go in.

Gran. It were a good deed, Manes, to beat thy master.   70

Man. You were as good eat my master!

One of the people. Hast thou made us all fools, and wilt thou not fly?

Diog. I tell thee, unless thou be honest, I will fly!

People. Dog! Dog! Take a bone!

42 colour] disguise.   46 rocket . . . endive] 'the seedes of the Rockatte . . . breede incontinencie' (Lyly, *Euphues*). Endive is used in wholesome salads.   47 sealed] blinded.

Diog. Thy father need fear no dogs, but dogs thy father!

People. We will tell Alexander that thou reprovest him behind his back.

Diog. And I will tell him that you flatter him before his face!   81

People. We will cause all the boys in the street to hiss at thee.

Diog. Indeed I think the Athenians have their children ready for any vice, because they be Athenians.

Man. Why, master, mean you not to fly?

Diog. No, Manes, not without wings.

Man. Everybody will account you a liar.

Diog. No, I warrant you, for I will always say the Athenians are mischievous.   90

Psyl. I care not; it was sport enough for me to see these old huddles hit home.

Gran. Nor I.

Psyl. Come, let us go; and hereafter when I mean to rail upon anybody openly it shall be given out I will fly.   [*Exeunt.*

Scaena Secunda.

Campaspe *alone.*

Camp. Campaspe, it is hard to judge whether thy choice be more unwise, or the chance unfortunate! Dost thou prefer—but stay! utter not that in words which maketh thine ears to glow with thoughts! Tush! Better thy tongue wag than thy heart break! Hath a painter crept further into thy mind than a prince, Apelles than Alexander? Fond wench, the baseness of thy mind bewrays the meanness of thy birth. But, alas, affection is a fire which kindleth as well in the bramble as in the oak, and catcheth hold where it first lighteth, not where it may best burn. Larks that mount aloof in the air build their nests

92 huddles] decrepit old men.   hit home] scored off.

7 fond] foolish.   12 aloof] aloft.

below in the earth, and women that cast their eyes
upon kings may place their hearts upon vassals.
A needle will become thy fingers better than a lute,
and a distaff is fitter for thy hand than a sceptre: ants
live safely till they have gotten wings, and juniper is
not blown up till it hath gotten an high top: the mean
estate is without care, as long as it continueth without
pride.—But here cometh Apelles, in whom I would
there were the like affection.   21

Enter Apelles.

Apel. Gentlewoman, the misfortune I had with
your picture will put you to some pains to sit again
to be painted.

Camp. It is small pains for me to sit still, but infinite
for you to draw still.

Apel. No, Madam! To paint Venus was a pleasure,
but to shadow the sweet face of Campaspe . . . it is a
heaven!   29

Camp. If your tongue were made of the same flesh
that your heart is, your words would be as your
thoughts are, but such a common thing it is amongst
you to commend that oftentimes for fashion sake you
call them beautiful, whom you know black!

Apel. What might men do to be believed?

Camp. Whet their tongues on their hearts.

Apel. So they do, and speak as they think.

Camp. I would they did!

Apel. I would they did not!

Camp. Why? Would you have them dissemble?   40

Apel. Not in love, but their love. . . . But will you
give me leave to ask you a question, without offence?

Camp. So that you will answer me another, without
excuse.

Apel. Whom do you love best in the world?

Camp. He that made me last in the world.

18 blown up] uprooted by the wind.   34 black] uglv.
43 So that] on condition that.

Apel. That was a god.

Camp. I had thought it had been a man. But whom do you honour most, Apelles?

Apel. The thing that is likest you, Campaspe.   50

Camp. My picture?

Apel. I dare not venture upon your person. But come, let us go in; for Alexander will think it long till we return.   *Exeunt.*

Scaena Tertia.

Enter Clitus, Parmenio.

Clit. We hear nothing of our embassage; a colour, belike, to blear our eyes, or tickle our ears, or inflame our hearts. But what doth Alexander in the mean season but use for 'Tantara', 'sol fa la', for his hard couch, down beds, for his handful of water, his standing cup of wine?   6

Par. Clitus, I mislike this new delicacy and pleasing peace; for what else do we see now than a kind of softness in every man's mind: bees to make their hives in soldiers' helmets, our steeds furnished with footcloths of gold instead of saddles of steel, more time to be required to scour the rust off our weapons than there was wont to be in subduing the countries of our enemies! Sithence Alexander fell from his hard armour to his soft robes, behold the face of his court! Youths that were wont to carry devices of victory in their shields engrave now posies of love in their rings, they that were accustomed on trotting horses to charge the enemy with a lance now in easy coaches ride up and down to court ladies, instead of sword and target to hazard their lives use pen and paper to paint their loves . . . yea, such a fear and faintness is grown in the court that they wish rather to hear the blowing of a

1 colour] pretence.   4 Tantara] martial music.   **sol fa la**] amorous music.   10 footcloths] decorative trappings unsuited for war.   16 devices] emblems.   **20 target**] shield.

horn to hunt than the sound of a trumpet to fight! O
Philip, wert thou alive to see this alteration, thy men
turned to women, thy soldiers to lovers, gloves worn
in velvet caps instead of plumes in graven helmets,
thou wouldst either die among them for sorrow or
confound them for anger!   29

Clit. Cease, Parmenio, lest in speaking what becometh thee not thou feel what liketh thee not! Truth
is never without a scratch'd face, whose tongue, although it cannot be cut out, yet must it be tied up.

Par. It grieveth me not a little for Hephaestion,
who thirsteth for honour not ease; but such is his fortune and nearness in friendship to Alexander that he
must lay a pillow under his head when he would put
a target in his hand. But let us draw in to see how
well it becomes them to tread the measures in a dance
that were wont to settle the order for a march.

                                       [*Exeunt.*

Scaena Quarta.

Apelles, Campaspe, *discovered.*

Apel. I have now, Campaspe, almost made an end.

Camp. You told me, Apelles, you would never end.

Apel. Never end my love, for it shall be eternal.

Camp. That is, neither to have beginning nor ending.

Apel. You are disposed to mistake! I hope you do
not mistrust.

Camp. What will you say if Alexander perceive
your love?

Apel. I will say it is no treason to love.

Camp. But how if he will not suffer thee to see my
person?   11

31 liketh] pleaseth.   Sc. iv, v] The scene opens on the
inner stage (representing Apelles' studio). At l. 22 Campaspe comes on to the outer stage to soliloquize, and at the
end of the scene goes off. At the beginning of the next
scene Apelles comes from the inner to the outer stage, and
there meets the page.

Apel. Then will I gaze continually on thy picture.

Camp. That will not feed thy heart.

Apel. Yet shall it fill mine eye! Besides, the sweet thoughts, the sure hopes, thy protested faith, will cause me to embrace thy shadow continually in mine arms, of the which, by strong imagination, I will make a substance.

Camp. Well, I must be gone; but this assure yourself, that I had rather be in thy shop grinding colours than in Alexander's court following higher fortunes!   22

Campaspe, *alone.*

Camp. Foolish wench, what hast thou done? That, alas, which cannot be undone, and therefore I fear me undone! But content is such a life, I care not for abundance. O, Apelles, thy love cometh from the heart, but Alexander's from the mouth. The love of kings is like the blowing of winds, which whistle sometimes gently among the leaves and straightways turn the trees up by the roots; or fire, which warmeth afar off and burneth near at hand; or the sea, which maketh men hoise their sails in a flattering calm and to cut their masts in a rough storm. They place affection by times, by policy, by appointment. If they frown, who dares call them unconstant? If bewray secrets, who will term them untrue? If fall to other loves, who trembles not if he call them unfaithful? In kings there can be no love but to queens, for as near must they meet in majesty as they do in affection. It is requisite to stand aloof from kings' love, Jove, and lightning.   [*Exit.*

Scaena Quinta.

Apelles *comes forward.*

Apel. Now, Apelles, gather thy wits together! Campaspe is no less wise than fair: thyself must be no less

32 hoise] hoist.

cunning than faithful. It is no small matter to be rival
with Alexander.

Enter a Page.

Page. Apelles, you must come away quickly with
the picture; the king thinketh that now you have
painted it, you play with it.

Apel. If I would play with pictures I have enough
at home.

Page. None, perhaps, you like so well!   10

Apel. It may be I have painted none so well.

Page. I have known many fairer faces.

Apel. And I many better boys.   [*Exeunt.*

Actus Quintus. Scaena Prima.

Enter Diogenes, Silvius, Perim, Milo, Trico,
Manes.

Silv. I have brought my sons, Diogenes, to be
taught of thee.

Diog. What can thy sons do?

Silv. You shall see their qualities; dance, sirrah!

Then Perim *danceth.*

Silv. How like you this? Doth he well?

Diog. The better the worser.

Silv. The music very good!

Diog. The musicians very bad, who only study to
have their strings in tune, never framing their manners
to order.   10

Silv. Now shall you see the other; tumble, sirrah!

Milo tumbleth.

Silv. How like you this? Why do you laugh?

Diog. To see a wag, that was born to break his neck
by destiny, to practise it by art.

Milo. This dog will bite me! I will not be with him.

Diog. Fear not, boy, dogs eat no thistles.

Perim. I marvel what dog thou art, if thou be a dog.

Diog. When I am hungry, a mastiff, and when my
belly is full, a spaniel.

Silv. Dost thou believe that there are any gods, that
thou art so dogged? 21

Diog. I must needs believe there are gods, for I
think thee an enemy to them.

Silv. Why so?

Diog. Because thou hast taught one of thy sons to
rule his legs and not to follow learning, the other to
bend his body every way and his mind no way.

Perim. Thou dost nothing but snarl and bark like
a dog.

Diog. It is the next way to drive away a thief. 30

Silv. Now shall you hear the third, who sings like
a nightingale.

Diog. I care not, for I have heard a nightingale
sing herself.

Silv. Sing, sirrah!

Trico *singeth.*

What bird so sings, yet so does wail?
Oh, 'tis the ravish'd Nightingale.
Jug, jug, jug, jug, tereu, she cries,
And still her woes at midnight rise.
Brave prick-song! Who is't now we hear? 40
None but the lark, so shrill and clear:
Now at heaven's gates she claps her wings,
The morn not waking till she sings!
Hark, hark, with what a pretty throat
Poor robin redbreast tunes his note!
Hark how the jolly cuckoos sing
'Cuckoo', to welcome in the spring!
Cuckoo, to welcome in the spring.

Silv. Lo, Diogenes, I am sure thou canst not do so
much! 50

21 dogged] cantankerous; cf. line 29.   30 next] quickest.
40 prick-song] written (and hence regularly and artistically
composed) music, with a punning allusion to the legend
that the nightingale pricks her breast against a thorn to
inspire her lamenting song.

Diog. But there is never a thrush but can.

Silv. What hast thou taught Manes, thy man?

Diog. To be as unlike as may be thy sons.

Man. He hath taught me to fast, lie hard, and run away.

Silv. How sayest thou, Perim, wilt thou be with him?

Perim. Ay, so he will teach me first to run away.

Diog. Thou needest not be taught, thy legs are so nimble. 60

Silv. How sayest thou, Milo, wilt thou be with him?

Diog. Nay, hold your peace! He shall not.

Silv. Why?

Diog. There is not room enough for him and me both to tumble in one tub.

Silv. Well, Diogenes, I perceive my sons brook not thy manners. 67

Diog. I thought no less, when they knew my virtues.

Silv. Farewell, Diogenes; thou needest not have scraped roots if thou wouldst have followed Alexander.

Diog. Nor thou have followed Alexander if thou hadst scraped roots. [*Exeunt.*

Scaena Secunda.

Enter Apelles.

Apel. I fear me, Apelles, that thine eyes have blabbed that which thy tongue durst not. What little regard hadst thou! Whilst Alexander viewed the counterfeit of Campaspe, thou stoodest gazing on her countenance! If he espy, or but suspect, thou must needs twice perish, with his hate and thine own love. Thy pale looks when he blushed, thy sad countenance when he smiled, thy sighs when he questioned, may breed in him a jealousy, perchance a frenzy. O love, I never before knew what thou wert, and now hast

58 so] on the condition that.   66 brook] bear.   2–3 What little regard hadst thou!] How careless you were!

thou made me that I know not what myself am! Only
this I know, that I must endure intolerable passions
for unknown pleasures! Dispute not the cause,
wretch, but yield to it! For better it is to melt with
desire than wrestle with love. Cast thyself on thy careful bed, be content to live unknown and die unfound.
O Campaspe, I have painted thee in my heart!
Painted? nay, contrary to mine art, imprinted, and
that in such deep characters that nothing can rase it
out unless it rub my heart out.   [*Exit.*

Scaena Tertia.

Enter Milectus, Phrygius, Lais, *to* Diogenes
in his tub.

Mil. It shall go hard but this peace shall bring us
some pleasure.

Phryg. Down with arms and up with legs! This is
a world for the nonce.

Lais. Sweet youths, if you knew what it were to
save your sweet blood, you would not so foolishly
go about to spend it. What delight can there be in
gashing, to make foul scars in fair faces and crooked
maims in straight legs, as though men being born
goodly by nature would of purpose become deformed
by folly? And all for a new-found term called 'valiant', a word which breedeth more quarrels than sense
can commendation!   13

Mil. It is true, Lais; a feather bed hath no fellow,
good drink makes good blood, and shall pelting words
spill it?

Phryg. I mean to enjoy the world, and to draw out
my life at the wire-drawer's, not to curtail it off at the
cutler's.   19

Lais. You may talk of war, speak big, conquer
worlds with great words; but stay at home, where

15–16 careful] full of care.   3 arms] of war.   legs]
in a dance.   15 pelting] petty.

instead of alarums you shall have dances, for hot
battles with fierce men, gentle skirmishes with fair
women. These pewter coats can never sit so well as
satin doublets. Believe me, you cannot conceive the
pleasure of peace unless you despise the rudeness of
war.

Mil. It is so.—But see Diogenes prying over his
tub!—Diogenes, what sayest thou to such a morsel?

Diog. I say I would spit it out of my mouth because
it should not poison my stomach.   31

Phryg. Thou speakest as thou art! It is no meat for
dogs.

Diog. I am a dog, and philosophy rates me from
carrion.

Lais. Uncivil wretch, whose manners are answerable to thy calling! The time was thou wouldst have
had my company, had it not been, as thou saidst, too
dear.   39

Diog. I remember there was a thing that I repented
me of, and now thou hast told it; indeed, it was too
dear of nothing, and thou dear to nobody!

Lais. Down, villain, or I will have thy head broken!

Mil. Will you couch?

Phryg. Avaunt, cur! Come, sweet Lais, let us go
to some place and possess peace.—But first let us sing;
there is more pleasure in tuning of a voice than in a
volley of shot.   48

Song.

Mil. Now let us make haste, lest Alexander find us
here.   [*Exeunt.*

---

24 pewter coats] armour.   28 prying] peering. Apparently the Tub is on the stage with Diogenes inside
looking out over the top. Cf. line 43.   29 such a morsel]
'Lais' was traditionally a name of a prostitute.   30 be-
cause] so that.   36–7 answerable] suitable.   42 of] at
the price of.   44 couch] lie down.   49 Song.] This
song is not preserved.

Scaena Quarta.

Enter Alexander, Hephaestion, *and a Page.*

Alex. Methinketh, Hephaestion, you are more melancholy than you were accustomed; but I perceive it is all for Alexander. You can neither brook this peace nor my pleasure. Be of good cheer! Though I wink, I sleep not.

Heph. Melancholy I am not, nor well content, for, I know not how, there is such a rust crept into my bones with this long ease that I fear I shall not scour it out with infinite labours.   9

Alex. Yes, yes, if all the travails of conquering the world will set either thy body or mine in tune, we will undertake them! But what think you of Apelles? Did ye ever see any so perplexed? He neither answered directly to any question, nor looked steadfastly upon anything. I hold my life the painter is in love.

Heph. It may be, for commonly we see it incident in artificers to be enamoured of their own works, as Archidamus of his wooden dove, Pygmalion of his ivory image, Arachne of his wooden swan; especially painters, who, playing with their own conceits, now coveting to draw a glancing eye, then a rolling, now a winking, still mending it, never ending it, till they be caught with it;—and then, poor souls, they kiss the colours with their lips with which before they were loth to taint their fingers!   25

Alex. I will find it out!—Page, go speedily for Apelles; will him to come hither, and, when you see us earnestly in talk, suddenly cry out 'Apelles' shop is on fire!'

Page. It shall be done.   30

Alex. Forget not your lesson.   [*Exit Page.*

Heph. I marvel what your device shall be.

---

3 brook] bear.   5 wink] doze.   15 hold] bet.
20 conceits] imaginations, fancies.   32 device] design.

Alex. The event shall prove.

Heph. I pity the poor painter, if he be in love.

Alex. Pity him not, I pray thee! That severe gravity set aside, what do you think of love?

Heph. As the Macedonians do of their herb *beet*, which, looking yellow in the ground and black in the hand, think it better seen than touch'd.

Alex. But what do you imagine it to be?   40

Heph. A word by superstition thought a god, by use turned to an humour, by self-will made a flattering madness.

Alex. You are too hard-hearted, to think so of love. Let us go to Diogenes.

Diogenes *is discovered.*

Alex. Diogenes, thou mayest think it somewhat that Alexander cometh to thee again so soon.

Diog. If you come to learn you could not come soon enough; if to laugh, you be come too soon.

Heph. It would better become thee to be more courteous, and frame thyself to please.   51

Diog. And you better to be less, if you durst displease.

Alex. What dost thou think of the time we have here?

Diog. That we have little and lose much.

Alex. If one be sick, what wouldst thou have him do?

Diog. Be sure that he make not his physician his heir.   60

Alex. If thou mightest have thy will, how much ground would content thee?

Diog. As much as you, in the end, must be contented withal.

Alex. What, a world?

Diog. No, the length of my body.

46 somewhat] something (*sc.* something noteworthy).

Alex. Hephaestion, shall I be a little pleasant with him?

Heph. You may, but he will be very perverse with you.   70

Alex. It skilleth not, I cannot be angry with him.— Diogenes, I pray thee, what dost thou think of love?

Diog. A little worser than I can of hate.

Alex. And why?

Diog. Because it is better to hate the things which make to love, than to love the things which give occasion of hate.

Alex. Why, be not women the best creatures in the world?

Diog. Next men and bees.   80

Alex. What dost thou dislike chiefly in a woman?

Diog. One thing.

Alex. What?

Diog. That she is a woman.

Alex. In mine opinion thou wert never born of a woman, that thou thinkest so hardly of women.—But now cometh Apelles, who, I am sure, is as far from thy thought as thou art from his cunning. Diogenes, I will have thy cabin removed nearer to my court, because I will be a philosopher.   90

Diog. And when you have done so I pray you remove your court further from my cabin, because I will not be a courtier.

Enter Apelles.

Alex. But here cometh Apelles.—Apelles, what piece of work have you in hand?

Apel. None in hand, if it like your majesty, but I am devising a platform in my head.

Alex. I think your hand put it in your head! Is it nothing about Venus?

67 be a little pleasant] humour a little.   71 skilleth not] does not matter.   96 like] please.   97 platform] ground-plan, picture-scheme (Bond).

Apel. No, but something about Venus!   100

Enter the Page.

Page. Apelles! Apelles! Look about you! Your shop is on fire!

Apel. Ay me! If the picture of Campaspe be burnt, I am undone!

Alex. Stay, Apelles, no haste! It is your heart is on fire, not your shop, and if Campaspe hang there I would she were burnt! But have you the picture of Campaspe? Belike you love her well, that you care not though all be lost, so she be safe.   109

Apel. Not love her, but your Majesty knows that painters in their last works are said to excel themselves, and in this I have so much pleased myself that the shadow as much delighteth me being an artificer as the substance doth others that are amorous.

Alex. You lay your colours grossly; though I could not paint in your days, I can spy into your excuse. Be not ashamed, Apelles; it is a gentleman's sport to be in love!—Call hither Campaspe.—Methinks I might have been made privy to your affection; though my counsel had not been necessary, yet my countenance might have been thought requisite. But Apelles, forsooth, loveth underhand, yea, and under Alexander's nose! And—but I say no more.   123

Apel. Apelles loveth not so, but he liveth to do as Alexander will.

Enter Campaspe.

Alex. Campaspe, here is news! Apelles is in love with you.

Camp. It pleaseth your Majesty to say so.

Alex. [*aside*]. Hephaestion, I will try her, too.—Campaspe, for the good qualities I know in Apelles, and the virtue I see in you, I am determined you shall enjoy one another. How say you, Campaspe? Would you say 'Ay'?   133

120 countenance] approval.

Camp. Your handmaid must obey, if you command.—

Alex. Think you not, Hephaestion, that she would fain be commanded?

Heph. I am no thought-catcher but I guess unhappily.—

Alex. I will not enforce marriage, where I cannot compel love.   141

Camp. But your Majesty may move a question, where you be willing to have a match.—

Alex. Believe, me, Hephaestion, these parties are agreed: they would have me both priest and witness! —Apelles, take Campaspe! Why move ye not? Campaspe, take Apelles! Will it not be? If you be ashamed one of the other, by my consent you shall never come together. But dissemble not, Campaspe; do you love Apelles?   150

Camp. Pardon, my Lord, I love Apelles.

Alex. Apelles, it were a shame for you, being loved so openly of so fair a virgin, to say the contrary. Do you love Campaspe?

Apel. Only Campaspe!

Alex. Two loving worms, Hephaestion! I perceive Alexander cannot subdue the affections of men, though he conquer their countries. Love falleth like dew as well upon the low grass as upon the high cedar; sparks have their heat, ants their gall, flies their spleen. Well, enjoy one another; I give her thee frankly, Apelles. Thou shalt see that Alexander maketh but a toy of love, and leadeth affection in fetters, using fancy as a fool to make him sport or a minstrel to make him merry. It is not the amorous glance of an eye can settle an idle thought in the heart; no, no, it is children's game, a life for seamsters and scholars: the

138–9 unhappily] Apparently Hephaestion still believes Alexander to be in love with Campaspe and considers Apelles as an unwelcome rival.   156 worms] a not uncommon term of affectionate contempt.   163 toy] trifle.

one, pricking in clouts, have nothing else to think on,
the other, picking fancies out of books, have little else
to marvel at.—Go, Apelles, take with you your Campaspe; Alexander is cloyed with looking on that which
thou wonderest at.   172

Apel. Thanks to your Majesty, on bended knee;
you have honoured Apelles.

Camp. Thanks with bowed heart; you have blessed
Campaspe.   [*Exeunt* Apelles *and* Campaspe.

Alex. Page, go warn Clitus and Parmenio and the
other Lords to be in readiness; let the trumpet sound,
strike up the drum, and I will presently into Persia.
—How now, Hephaestion, is Alexander able to resist
love as he list?   181

Heph. The conquering of Thebes was not so honourable as the subduing of these thoughts.

Alex. It were a shame Alexander should desire to
command the world, if he could not command himself. But come, let us go; I will try whether I can better bear my hand with my heart than I could with
mine eye. And, good Hephaestion, when all the
world is won, and every country is thine and mine,
either find me out another to subdue or, of my word,
I will fall in love.   [*Exeunt.*

THE EPILOGUE AT THE BLACK-FRIARS

WHERE the rainbow toucheth the tree no caterpillars
will hang on the leaves, where the glow-worm creepeth
in the night no adder will go in the day: we hope in the
ears where our travails be lodged no carping shall harbour in those tongues. Our exercises must be as your
judgement is, resembling water, which is always of the
same colour into what it runneth.   7

168 pricking in clouts] sewing clothes.   **7 into what]**
as that into which.

In the Trojan horse lay couched soldiers with
children, and in heaps of many words, we fear, divers
unfit among some allowable; but as Demosthenes
with often breathing up the hill amended his stam-
mering, so we hope with sundry labours against the
hair to correct our studies. If the tree be blasted that
blossoms, the fault is in the wind and not in the root;
and if our pastimes be misliked, that have been
allowed, you must impute it to the malice of others
and not our endeavour. And so we rest in good case if
you rest well content.   18

THE EPILOGUE AT THE COURT

WE cannot tell whether we are fallen among
Diomedes' birds or his horses; the one received some
men with sweet notes, the other bit all men with sharp
teeth. But, as Homer's gods conveyed them into
clouds whom they would have kept from curses, and
as Venus, lest Adonis should be pricked with the
stings of adders, covered his face with the wings of
swans, so we hope, being shielded with your Highness'
countenance, we shall, though hear the neighing,
yet not feel the kicking, of those jades, and receive,
though no praise (which we cannot deserve) yet a
pardon, which in all humility we desire. As yet we
cannot tell what we should term our labours, iron
or bullion: only it belongeth to your Majesty to make
them fit either for the forge or the mint, current by the
stamp or counterfeit by the anvil; for as nothing is to
be called white unless it had been named white by
the first creator, so can there be nothing thought
good in the opinion of others unless it be christened

12–13 against the hair] against the grain (as of an animal
rubbed the wrong way) (Bond).   17 case] fortune.
Epilogue at the Court. 14 only . . . to your Majesty] to
your Majesty alone.

good by the judgement of yourself. For ourselves,
again we are those torches' wax, of which, being in
your Highness' hands, you may make doves or vul-
tures, roses or nettles, laurel for a garland or elder for
a disgrace.   24

21 again] Cf. the prologue at the Court, lines 19–22.
23–4 elder for a disgrace] because Judas is said to have
hung himself on an elder-tree (Collier).

FINIS.

THE OLD WIVES' TALE

BY

GEORGE PEELE

GEORGE PEELE (1557–1598)

The Old Wives' Tale

Acted probably after 1589; printed in 1595.

[*Complete Works*, ed. A. H. Bullen, 2 vols., 1888,
is scarce, costly, and modernized. A type-
facsimile of *The Old Wives' Tale* was issued by
the Malone Society in 1908.]

THE
Old Wiues Tale.

A pleasant conceited Come-
die, played by the Queenes Maieſties players.

Written by *G. Peele*

Printed at London by *Iohn Danter*, and are to
be ſold by *Raph Hancocke*, and *Iohn*
Hardie. 1 5 9 5.

Dramatis Personae

SACRAPANT.
First Brother, named CALY-
   PHA.
Second Brother, named
   THELEA.
EUMENIDES.
ERESTUS.
LAMPRISCUS.
HUANEBANGO.
COREBUS.
WIGGEN.
Churchwarden.
Sexton.
Ghost of JACK.

Friar, Harvest-men, Furies
   Fiddlers, &c.
DELIA, *sister to Calypha and
   Thelea.*
VENELIA, *betrothed to Erestus.*
ZANTIPPA, } *daughters to*
CELANTA, } *Lampriscus.*
Hostess.

ANTIC.
FROLIC.
FANTASTIC.
CLUNCH, *a smith.*
MADGE, *his wife.*

THE OLD WIVES' TALE

Enter Antic, Frolic, *and* Fantastic.

Ant. How now, fellow Frolic, what, all amort? doth this sadness become thy madness? What though we have lost our way in the woods, yet never hang the head, as though thou hadst no hope to live till to-morrow: for Fantastic and I will warrant thy life to-night for twenty in the hundred.

Frol. Antic and Fantastic, as I am frolic franion, never in all my life was I so dead slain. What! to lose our way in the wood, without either fire or candle, so uncomfortable! *O coelum! O terra! O maria!* O Neptune! 11

Fant. Why makes thou it so strange, seeing Cupid hath led our young master to the fair lady, and she is the only saint that he hath sworn to serve?

Frol. What resteth then but we commit him to his wench, and each of us take his stand up in a tree, and sing out our ill fortune to the tune of *O man in desperation*?

Ant. Desperately spoken, fellow Frolic, in the dark: but seeing it falls out thus, let us rehearse the old proverb: 21

> Three merry men, and three merry men,
> And three merry men be we;
> I in the wood, and thou on the ground,
> And Jack sleeps in the tree.

Fant. Hush! a dog in the wood, or a wooden dog! O comfortable hearing! I had even as lief the chamberlain of the White Horse had called me up to bed. 29

1 all amort] dejected.   7 franion] idler.   12 makes] makest.   17-18 *O man in desperation*] a well-known popular tune.   26 wooden] mad.

Frol. Either hath this trotting cur gone out of his circuit, or else are we near some village, which should not be far off, for I perceive the glimmering of a glow-worm, a candle, or a cat's eye, my life for a halfpenny! In the name of my own father, be thou ox or ass that appearest, tell us what thou art.

Enter Clunch *with a lanthorn and candle.*

Clunch. What am I? why I am Clunch the smith. What are you? what make you in my territories at this time of the night?   39

Ant. What do we make, dost thou ask? why, we make faces for fear; such as if thy mortal eyes could behold, would make thee water the long seams of thy side slops, smith.

Frol. And in faith sir, unless your hospitality do relieve us, we are like to wander with a sorrowful heigh-ho, among the owlets and hobgoblins of the forest. Good Vulcan, for Cupid's sake that hath cozened us all, befriend us as thou mayst; and command us howsoever, wheresoever, whensoever, in whatsoever, for ever and ever.   50

Clunch. Well masters, it seems to me you have lost your way in the wood: in consideration whereof, if you will go with Clunch to his cottage, you shall have house-room and a good fire to sit by, although we have no bedding to put you in.

All. O blessed smith, O bountiful Clunch!   56

Clunch. For your further entertainment, it shall be as it may be, so and so.   [*Here a dog barks.* Hark! this is Ball my dog, that bids you all welcome in his own language. Come, take heed for stumbling on the threshold.—Open door, Madge; take in guests.

Enter Madge.

Madge. Welcome Clunch, and good fellows all, that come with my good-man; for my good-man's sake,

40 make] pun on (*a*) do (as in l. 38) and (*b*) make (faces).
43 side slops] wide breeches.   47 Vulcan] smith.

come on, sit down: here is a piece of cheese, and a pudding of my own making.

Ant. Thanks, gammer: a good example for the wives of our town.

Frol. Gammer, thou and thy good-man sit lovingly together; we come to chat and not to eat.   69

Clunch. Well masters, if you will eat nothing, take away. Come, what do we to pass away the time? Lay a crab in the fire to roast for lamb's-wool. What, shall we have a game at trump or ruff to drive away the time? how say you?

Fant. This smith leads a life as merry as a king with Madge his wife. Sirrah Frolic, I am sure thou art not without some round or other: no doubt but Clunch can bear his part.   78

Frol. Else think you me ill brought up, so set to it when you will.   [*They sing.*

Song.

> When as the rye reach to the chin,
> And chopcherry, chopcherry ripe within,
> Strawberries swimming in the cream,
> And school-boys playing in the stream;
> Then O, then O, then O, my true love said,
> Till that time come again,
> She could not live a maid.

Ant. This sport does well; but methinks, gammer, a merry winter's tale would drive away the time trimly: come, I am sure you are not without a score.   90

Fant. I' faith, gammer, a tale of an hour long were as good as an hour's sleep.

Frol. Look you, gammer, of the Giant and the King's Daughter, and I know not what: I have seen the day, when I was a little one, you might have drawn me a mile after you with such a discourse.

66 gammer] old woman (lit. 'grandmother').   72 lamb's-wool] drink made of beer and roast crab-apples. 73 trump . . . ruff] card games.   77 round] round song.

Madge. Well, since you be so importunate, my good-man shall fill the pot and get him to bed; they that ply their work must keep good hours: one of you go lie with him; he is a clean-skinned man I tell you, without either spavin or wind-gall: so I am content to drive away the time with an old wives' winter's tale.

Fant. No better hay in Devonshire, o' my word gammer, I'll be one of your audience.   104

Frol. And I another, that's flat.

Ant. Then must I to bed with the good-man.— *Bona nox*, gammer, God night, Frolic.

Clunch. Come on my lad, thou shalt take thy un-natural rest with me.   [*Exeunt* Antic *and* Clunch.

Frol. Yet this vantage shall we have of them in the morning, to be ready at the sight thereof extempore.

Madge. Now this bargain, my masters, must I make with you, that you will say hum and ha to my tale, so shall I know you are awake.

Both. Content gammer, that will we do.   115

Madge. Once upon a time there was a king, or a lord, or a duke, that had a fair daughter, the fairest that ever was; as white as snow, and as red as blood: and once upon a time his daughter was stolen away, and he sent all his men to seek out his daughter, and he sent so long, that he sent all his men out of his land.

Frol. Who drest his dinner then?

Madge. Nay, either hear my tale, or kiss my tail.

Fant. Well said! on with your tale, gammer.   124

Madge. O Lord, I quite forgot, there was a conjurer, and this conjurer could do anything, and he turned himself into a great dragon, and carried the king's daughter away in his mouth to a castle that he made of stone, and there he kept her I know not how long, till at last all the king's men went out so long, that her

103 No better hay in Devonshire] 'hay' may be either a country dance or an abbreviation of 'have you', but I do not understand this in either case.   107 God night] good night.   125 conjurer] magician.

two brothers went to seek her. O, I forget: she (he, I would say,) turned a proper young man to a bear in the night, and a man in the day, and keeps by a cross that parts three several ways, and he made his lady run mad—Gods me bones, who comes here?

Enter the Two Brothers.

Frol. Soft gammer, here some come to tell your tale for you.

Fant. Let them alone, let us hear what they will say.

1st Bro. Upon these chalky cliffs of Albion
We are arrived now with tedious toil,   140
And compassing the wide world round about
To seek our sister, to seek fair Delia forth,
Yet cannot we so much as hear of her.

2nd Bro. O fortune cruel, cruel and unkind!
Unkind in that we cannot find our sister,
Our sister, hapless in her cruel chance—
Soft! who have we here?

Enter Erestus *at the Cross, stooping to gather.*

1st Bro. Now, father, God be your speed! what do you gather there?

Erest. Hips and haws, and sticks and straws, and things that I gather on the ground, my son.   151

1st Bro. Hips and haws, and sticks and straws! why, is that all your food, father?

Erest. Yea, son.

2nd Bro. Father, here is an alms penny for me, and if I speed in that I go for, I will give thee as good a gown of grey as ever thou didst wear.

1st Bro. And father, here is another alms penny for me, and if I speed in my journey, I will give thee a palmer's staff of ivory, and a scallop shell of beaten gold.

Erest. Was she fair?   161

132 proper] handsome.   133 keeps] lives (*sc.* the young man does).   161 Was she fair?] some speeches must be lost in which the brothers told Erestus of their search for their sister.

2nd Bro. Ay, the fairest for white, and the purest
for red, as the blood of the deer, or the driven
snow.

Erest. Then hark well, and mark well, my old spell:
Be not afraid of every stranger,
Start not aside at every danger:
Things that seem are not the same,
Blow a blast at every flame:
For when one flame of fire goes out,   170
Then comes your wishes well about:
If any ask who told you this good,
Say, the White Bear of England's Wood.

1st Bro. Brother, heard you not what the old man
said?
Be not afraid of every stranger,
Start not aside for every danger:
Things that seem are not the same,
Blow a blast at every flame:
If any ask who told you this good,   180
Say, the White Bear of England's Wood.

2nd Bro. Well, if this do us any good,
Well fare the White Bear of England's Wood!
                        [*Exeunt the* Two Brothers.

Erest. Now sit thee here and tell a heavy tale.
Sad in thy mood, and sober in thy cheer,
Here sit thee now, and to thyself relate
The hard mishap of thy most wretched state.
In Thessaly I liv'd in sweet content,
Until that fortune wrought my overthrow;
For there I wedded was unto a dame,   190
That liv'd in honour, virtue, love, and fame:
But Sacrapant, that cursed sorcerer,
Being besotted with my beauteous love—
My dearest love, my true betrothed wife—
Did seek the means to rid me of my life.
But worse than this, he with his chanting spells

185 cheer] bearing, deportment.   196 chanting
spells] incantations.

Did turn me straight unto an ugly bear;
And when the sun doth settle in the west,
Then I begin to don my ugly hide:
And all the day I sit, as now you see,   200
And speak in riddles, all inspir'd with rage,
Seeming an old and miserable man:
And yet I am in April of my age.

Enter Venelia, *his Lady, mad; and goes in again.*

See where Venelia, my betrothed love,
Runs madding, all enrag'd, about the woods,
All by his cursed and enchanting spells.

Enter Lampriscus *with a pot of honey.*

But here comes Lampriscus, my discontented neighbour. How now, neighbour, you look toward the
ground as well as I! you muse on something.   209
Lamp. Neighbour, on nothing, but on the matter
I so often moved to you: if you do anything for charity,
help me; if for neighbourhood or brotherhood, help
me: never was one so cumbered as is poor Lampriscus:
and to begin, I pray receive this pot of honey to mend
your fare.
Erest. Thanks, neighbour, set it down; honey is
always welcome to the bear.—And now neighbour,
let me hear the cause of your coming.
Lamp. I am (as you know, neighbour) a man un-
married, and lived so unquietly with my two wives,
that I keep every year holy the day wherein I buried
them both; the first was on Saint Andrew's day, the
other on Saint Luke's.   223
Erest. And now neighbour, you of this country say
'your custom is out.' But on with your tale, neighbour.
Lamp. By my first wife, whose tongue wearied me
alive, and sounded in my ears like the clapper of a
great bell, whose talk was a continual torment to all

208–9 toward the ground] downcast.   211 moved]
propounded.

that dwelt by her, or lived nigh her, you have heard
me say I had a handsome daughter.   231

Erest. True, neighbour.

Lamp. She it is that afflicts me with her continual
clamours, and hangs on me like a bur: poor she is, and
proud she is; as poor as a sheep new shorn, and
as proud of her hopes, as a peacock of her tail well
grown.

Erest. Well said, Lampriscus! you speak it like an
Englishman.   239

Lamp. As curst as a wasp, and as froward as a child
new taken from the mother's teat; she is to my age,
as smoke to the eyes, or as vinegar to the teeth.

Erest. Holily praised, neighbour. As much for the
next.

Lamp. By my other wife I had a daughter so hard-
favoured, so foul, and ill-faced, that I think a grove
full of golden trees, and the leaves of rubies and diamonds, would not be a dowry answerable to her
deformity.   249

Erest. Well, neighbour, now you have spoke, hear
me speak; send them to the well for the water of life:
there shall they find their fortunes unlooked for.
Neighbour, farewell.   [*Exit.*

Lamp. Farewell, and a thousand. And now goeth
poor Lampriscus to put in execution this excellent
counsel.   [*Exit.*

Frol. Why, this goes round without a fiddling-
stick; but do you hear, gammer, was this the man that
was a bear in the night and a man in the day?   259

Madge. Ay, this is he; and this man that came to
him was a beggar, and dwelt upon a green. But soft!
who comes here? O, these are the harvest-men; ten
to one they sing a song of mowing.

240 curst] bad-tempered.   246 foul] ugly.   248
answerable to] fit compensation for.   257-8 without a
fiddling-stick] the tune plays itself (?).

Enter the Harvest-men *a-singing, with this song double repeated.*

> All ye that lovely lovers be,
> Pray you for me:
> Lo, here we come a-sowing, a-sowing,
> And sow sweet fruits of love;
> In your sweet hearts well may it prove!

> [*Exeunt.*

Enter Huanebango *with his two-hand sword, and* Corebus.

Fant. Gammer, what is he?

Madge. O, this is one that is going to the conjurer: let him alone, hear what he says.   271

Huan. Now by Mars and Mercury, Jupiter and Janus, Sol and Saturnus, Venus and Vesta, Pallas and Proserpina, and by the honour of my house Poli-mackeroeplacidus, it is a wonder to see what this love will make silly fellows adventure, even in the wane of their wits and infancy of their discretion. Alas, my friend, what fortune calls thee forth to seek thy fortune among brazen gates, enchanted towers, fire and brimstone, thunder and lightning? Beauty, I tell thee, is peerless, and she precious whom thou affectest: do off these desires, good countryman, good friend, run away from thyself, and, so soon as thou canst, forget her,—whom none must inherit but he that can monsters tame, labours achieve, riddles absolve, loose enchantments, murder magic, and kill conjuring— and that is the great and mighty Huanebango.   287

Cor. Hark you, sir, hark you. First know I have here the flirting feather, and have given the parish the start for the long stock: now sir, if it be no more but running through a little lightning and thunder, and 'riddle me, riddle me, what's this?' I'll have the wench from the conjurer, if he were ten conjurers.   293

Huan. I have abandoned the court and honourable

---

281 affectest] lovest.   290 long stock] long stocking; he is boasting of his new fashions (Bullen).

company, to do my devoir against this sore sorcerer and mighty magician: if this lady be so fair as she is said to be, she is mine, she is mine—*meus, mea, meum, in contemptum omnium grammaticorum.*

Cor. O *falsum Latinum!* The fair maid is *minum, cum apurtinantibus gibletis* and all.   300

Huan. If she be mine, as I assure myself the heavens will do somewhat to reward my worthiness, she shall be allied to none of the meanest gods, but be invested in the most famous stock of Huanebango—Polimacke-roeplacidus my grandfather, my father Pergopolineo, my mother Dionora de Sardinia, famously descended.

Cor. Do you hear, sir, had not you a cousin that was called Gustecceridis?

Huan. Indeed, I had a cousin that sometime followed the court infortunately, and his name Buste-gustecceridis.   311

Cor. O Lord, I know him well: he is the knight of the neat's-feet.

Huan. O, he loved no capon better! he hath often-times deceived his boy of his dinner; that was his fault, good Bustegustecceridis.

Cor. Come, shall we go along?

Enter Erestus.

Soft! here is an old man at the cross, let us ask him the way thither.—Ho, you gaffer, I pray you tell where the wise man the conjurer dwells.   320

Huan. Where that earthly goddess keepeth her abode, the commander of my thoughts, and fair mistress of my heart.

Erest. Fair enough, and far enough from thy fingering, son.

Huan. I will follow my fortune after mine own fancy, and do according to mine own discretion.

Erest. Yet give something to an old man before you go.

319 gaffer] old man (lit. 'grandfather').

Huan. Father, methinks a piece of this cake might
serve your turn.   331

Erest. Yea, son.

Huan. Huanebango giveth no cakes for alms: ask
of them that give gifts for poor beggars.—Fair lady,
if thou wert once shrined in this bosom, I would
buckler thee haratantara.   [*Exit.*

Cor. Father, do you see this man? you little think
he'll run a mile or two for such a cake, or pass for a
pudding! I tell you, father, he has kept such a begging of me for a piece of this cake! Whoo! he comes
upon me with a 'superfantial substance, and the foison
of the earth', that I know not what he means. If he
came to me thus, and said, 'My friend Booby,' or so,
why I could spare him a piece with all my heart; but
when he tells me how God hath enriched me above
other fellows with a cake, why he makes me blind and
deaf at once. Yet, father, here is a piece of cake for
you, as hard as the world goes.   *Cake.*

Erest. Thanks, son, but list to me;
He shall be deaf when thou shalt not see.   350
Farewell, my son: things may so hit,
Thou mayst have wealth to mend thy wit.

Cor. Farewell, father, farewell; for I must make
haste after my two-hand sword that is gone before.

                                                [*Exeunt.*

Enter Sacrapant *in his study.*

Sac. The day is clear, the welkin bright and gray,
The lark is merry and records her notes;
Each thing rejoiceth underneath the sky,
But only I, whom heaven hath in hate,
Wretched and miserable Sacrapant.

336 buckler] protect.   338 pass] care.   341
superfantial] the *Oxford English Dictionary* shares Corebus's
ignorance of this word.   foison] plenty.   343
Booby] Corebus; the Quarto sometimes calls him so even
in stage directions.   348 as hard . . . goes] though
times are hard.   s. d. *Cake*] sc. he gives him some.

In Thessaly was I born and brought up;   360
My mother Meroe hight, a famous witch,
And by her cunning I of her did learn
To change and alter shapes of mortal men.
There did I turn myself into a dragon,
And stole away the daughter to the king,
Fair Delia, the mistress of my heart,
And brought her hither to revive the man
That seemeth young and pleasant to behold
And yet is aged, crooked, weak and numb.
Thus by enchanting spells I do deceive   370
Those that behold and look upon my face;
But well may I bid youthful years adieu.

Enter Delia *with a pot in her hand.*

See where she comes from whence my sorrows grow!
How now, fair Delia, where have you been?

Del. At the foot of the rock for running water, and
gathering roots for your dinner, sir.

Sac. Ah, Delia, fairer art thou than the running
water, yet harder far than steel or adamant!

Del. Will it please you to sit down, sir?

Sac. Ay, Delia, sit and ask me what thou wilt, thou
shalt have it brought into thy lap.   381

Del. Then, I pray you, sir, let me have the best
meat from the King of England's table, and the best
wine in all France, brought in by the veriest knave in
all Spain.

Sac. Delia, I am glad to see you so pleasant! Well,
sit thee down.—
Spread, table, spread; meat, drink and bread,
Ever may I have, what I ever crave,
               When I am spread,   390
For meat for my black cock, and meat for my red.

Enter a Friar *with a chine of beef and a pot of wine.*

Here, Delia, will ye fall to?

361 hight] was called.

Del. Is this the best meat in England?

Sac. Yea.

Del. What is it?

Sac. A chine of English beef, meat for a king and a king's followers.

Del. Is this the best wine in France?

Sac. Yea.

Del. What wine is it?   400

Sac. A cup of neat wine of Orleans, that never came near the brewers in England.

Del. Is this the veriest knave in all Spain?

Sac. Yea.

Del. What is he, a friar?

Sac. Yea, a friar indefinite, and a knave infinite.

Del. Then, I pray ye, Sir Friar, tell me before you go, which is the most greediest Englishman?

Fri. The miserable and most covetous usurer.

Sac. Hold thee there, friar. [*Exit Friar.*] But, soft! Who have we here? Delia, away, be gone!   411

Enter the Two Brothers.

Delia, away! for beset are we.—
But heaven or hell shall rescue her for me.
                    [*Exeunt* Delia *and* Sacrapant.

1st Bro. Brother, was not that Delia, did appear,
Or was it but her shadow that was here?

2nd Bro. Sister, where art thou? Delia, come again!
He calls, that of thy absence doth complain.—
Call out, Calypha, that she may hear,
And cry aloud, for Delia is near.

Echo. Near.   420

1st Bro. Near! O, where? hast thou any tidings?

Echo. Tidings.

2nd Bro. Which way is Delia, then? or that, or this?

Echo. This.

1st Bro. And may we safely come where Delia is?

415 shadow] image.

Echo. Yes.

2nd Bro. Brother, remember you the White Bear of England's Wood?

    'Start not aside for every danger,   430
      Be not afear'd of every stranger;
      Things that seem are not the same.'

1st Bro. Brother, why do we not, then, courageously enter?

2nd Bro. Then, brother, draw thy sword and follow me.

Enter Sacrapant; *it lightens and thunders; the* 2nd Brother *falls down.*

    1st Bro. What, brother, dost thou fall?

    Sac. Ay, and thou too, Calypha.

                    [*The* 1st Brother *falls down.*

Adeste, daemones!

                Enter Two Furies.

                Away with them: 440
Go carry them straight to Sacrapanto's cell,
There in despair and torture for to dwell.

          [*Exeunt* Furies *with the* Two Brothers.
These are Thenores' sons of Thessaly,
That come to seek Delia their sister forth:
But, with a potion I to her have given,
My arts have made her to forget herself.

         [*He removes a turf, and shows a light in a glass.*
See here the thing which doth prolong my life—
With this enchantment I do anything;
And till this fade, my skill shall still endure,
And never none shall break this little glass,   450
But she that 's neither wife, widow, nor maid:
Then cheer thyself; this is thy destiny,
Never to die but by a dead man's hand.   [*Exit.*

Enter Eumenides, *the wandering Knight, and* Erestus, *at the Cross.*

    Eum. Tell me, Time,

Tell me, just Time, when shall I Delia see?
When shall I see the loadstar of my life?
When shall my wandering course end with her sight,
Or I but view my hope, my heart's delight?
Father, God speed! If you tell fortunes, I pray, good
father, tell me mine.   460

Erest. Son, I do see in thy face
Thy blessed fortune work apace;
I do perceive that thou hast wit;
Beg of thy fate to govern it,
For wisdom govern'd by advise,
Makes many fortunate and wise.
Bestow thy alms, give more than all,
Till dead men's bones come at thy call.
Farewell, my son: dream of no rest,
Till thou repent that thou didst best.   [*Exit.*

Eum. This man hath left me in a labyrinth: 471
He biddeth me give more than all,
'Till dead men's bones come at thy call:'
He biddeth me dream of no rest,
Till I repent that I do best.   [*Lies down and sleeps.*

Enter Wiggen, Corebus, Churchwarden, *and* Sexton.

Wig. You may be ashamed, you whoreson scald
Sexton and Churchwarden, if you had any shame in
those shameless faces of yours, to let a poor man lie so
long above ground unburied. A rot on you all, that
have no more compassion of a good fellow when he
is gone!   481

Church. What, would you have us to bury him, and
to answer it ourselves to the parish?

Sex. Parish me no parishes; pay me my fees, and
let the rest run on in the quarter's accounts, and put
it down for one of your good deeds, o' God's name!
for I am not one that curiously stands upon merits.

Cor. You whoreson, sodden-headed sheep's-face,

465 advise] thought.   476 scald] scurvy.   483
answer] answer for.

shall a good fellow do less service and more honesty to the parish, and will you not, when he is dead, let him have Christmas burial?   491

Wig. Peace, Corebus! as sure as Jack was Jack, the frolic'st franion amongst you, and I, Wiggen, his sweet sworn brother, Jack shall have his funerals, or some of them shall lie on God's dear earth for it, that's once.

Church. Wiggen, I hope thou wilt do no more than thou darest answer.

Wig. Sir, sir, dare or dare not, more or less, answer or not answer, do this, or have this.

Sex. Help, help, help! Wiggen sets upon the parish with a pike-staff!   501

[*Eumenides awakes and comes to them.*

Eum. Hold thy hands, good fellow.

Cor. Can you blame him, sir, if he take Jack's part against this shake-rotten parish that will not bury Jack?

Eum. Why, what was that Jack?

Cor. Who, Jack, sir? who, our Jack, sir? as good a fellow as ever trod upon neat's-leather.

Wig. Look you, sir; he gave fourscore and nineteen mourning gowns to the parish when he died, and because he would not make them up a full hundred, they would not bury him; was not this good dealing!

Church. O Lord, sir, how he lies! he was not worth a halfpenny, and drunk out every penny: and now his fellows, his drunken companions, would have us to bury him at the charge of the parish. An we make many such matches, we may pull down the steeple, sell the bells, and thatch the chancel: he shall lie above ground till he dance a galliard about the church-yard, for Steeven Loach.   519

Wig. Sic argumentaris, Domine Loach,—'An we make many such matches, we may pull down the steeple, sell the bells, and thatch the chancel?' In good time,

491 Christmas] Christian   493 frolic'st franion] merriest idler.   517 thatch the chancel] *sc.* after selling the lead of its roof.

sir, and hang yourselves in the bell-ropes when you
have done. *Domine, opponens praepono tibi hanc quae-
stionem,* whether will you have the ground broken or
your pates broken first? for one of them shall be done
presently, and to begin mine, I'll seal it upon your
coxcomb.

Eum. Hold thy hands! I pray thee, good fellow, be
not too hasty.   530

Cor. You capon's face, we shall have you turned out
of the parish one of these days with never a tatter to
your arse; then you are in worse taking than Jack.

Eum. Faith and he is bad enough. This fellow does
but the part of a friend, to seek to bury his friend; how
much will bury him?

Wig. Faith, about some fifteen or sixteen shillings
will bestow him honestly.

Sex. Ay, even thereabouts, sir.   539

Eum. Here, hold it, then: —[*aside*] and I have left
me but one poor three-half-pence; now do I remember
the words the old man spake at the cross: 'Bestow all
thou hast,' and this is all, 'till dead men's bones come
at thy call:'—here, hold it [*gives money*]; and so farewell.

Wig. God, and all good, be with you, sir!
                                         [*Exit* Eumenides.
Nay, you cormorants, I'll bestow one peal of Jack at
mine own proper costs and charges.

Cor. You may thank God the long staff and the
bilbo-blade crossed not your coxcomb.—Well, we'll
to the church-stile and have a pot, and so trill-lill.
                                         [*Exit with* Wiggen.

Church., Sex. Come, let's go.   [*Exeunt.*

Fant. But, hark you, gammer, methinks this Jack
bore a great sway in the parish.   553

Madge. O, this Jack was a marvellous fellow! he
was but a poor man, but very well beloved: you shall
see anon what this Jack will come to.

527 mine] *sc.* my argument.   538 honestly] decently.
546 of] on.

Enter the Harvest-men *singing, with women in their hands.*

Frol. Soft! who have we here? our amorous harvesters.

Fant. Ay, ay, let us sit still, and let them alone.

> *Here the* Harvest-men *sing, the song doubled.*

> Lo, here we come a-reaping, a-reaping,   560
> To reap our harvest-fruit!
> And thus we pass the year so long,
> And never be we mute.

> [*Exeunt the* Harvest-men.

Enter Huanebango, *and* Corebus *the clown.*

Frol. Soft! who have we here?

Madge. O, this is a choleric gentleman! All you that love your lives, keep out of the smell of his two-hand sword: now goes he to the conjurer.

Fant. Methinks the conjurer should put the fool into a juggling-box.

Huan.   Fee, fa, fum,
    Here is the Englishman,—
    Conquer him that can,—
    Came for his lady bright,
    To prove himself a knight,
    And win her love in fight.

Cor. Who-haw, Master Bango, are you here? hear you, you had best sit down here, and beg an alms with me.

Huan. Hence, base cullion! here is he that commandeth ingress and egress with his weapon, and will enter at his voluntary, whosoever saith no.   581

A Voice and flame of fire: Huanebango *falleth down.*

Voice. No!

Madge. So with that they kissed, and spoiled the edge of as good a two-hand sword as ever God put life in. Now goes Corebus in, spite of the conjurer.

556 s.d. *in their hands*] hand in hand.

Enter Sacrapant *and strike* Corebus *blind.*

Sac. Away with him into the open fields,
To be a ravening prey to crows and kites:

[*Huanebango* is carried out.

And for this villain, let him wander up and down,
In naught but darkness and eternal night.   589

Cor. Here hast thou slain Huan, a slashing knight,
And robbed poor Corebus of his sight.   [*Exit.*

Sac. Hence, villain, hence!—Now I have unto Delia
Given a potion of forgetfulness,
That, when she comes, she shall not know her brothers.
Lo, where they labour, like to country-slaves,
With spade and mattock, on this enchanted ground!
Now will I call her by another name;
For never shall she know herself again,
Until that Sacrapant hath breath'd his last.
See where she comes.   600

Enter Delia.

Come hither, Delia, take this goad; here hard
At hand two slaves do work and dig for gold:
Gore them with this, and thou shalt have enough.

[*He gives her a goad.*

Del. Good sir, I know not what you mean.

Sac. [*aside.*] She hath forgotten to be Delia,
But not forgot the same she should forget;
But I will change her name.—
Fair Berecynthia, so this country calls you,
Go ply these strangers, wench; they dig for gold.

[*Exit.*

Del. O heavens, how   610
Am I beholding to this fair young man!
But I must ply these strangers to their work.
See where they come.

Enter the Two Brothers *in their shirts, with spades, digging.*

1st Bro. O brother, see where Delia is!

611 beholding] grateful.

2nd Bro. O Delia, happy are we to see thee here!

Del. What tell you me of Delia, prating swains?
I know no Delia, nor know I what you mean.
Ply you your work, or else you are like to smart.

    1st Bro. Why, Delia, know'st thou not thy brothers
      here?
We come from Thessaly to seek thee forth,   620
And thou deceiv'st thyself, for thou art Delia.

    Del. Yet more of Delia?   then take this, and smart:
                                [*Pricks them with the goad.*
What, feign you shifts for to defer your labour?
Work, villains, work; it is for gold you dig.

    2nd Bro. Peace, brother, peace: this vild enchanter
Hath ravish'd Delia of her senses clean,
And she forgets that she is Delia.

    1st Bro. Leave, cruel thou, to hurt the miserable.—
Dig, brother, dig, for she is hard as steel.   629

Here they dig, and descry the light under a little hill.

    2nd Bro. Stay, brother; what hast thou descried?

    Del. Away, and touch it not; it is something that
my lord hath hidden there.   [*She covers it again.*

Enter Sacrapant.

    Sac. Well said! thou plyest these pioners well.—Go
get you in, you labouring slaves.
Come, Berecynthia, let us in likewise,
And hear the nightingale record her notes.   [*Exeunt.*

Enter Zantippa, *the curst daughter, to the Well, with a
pot in her hand.*

    Zan. Now for a husband, house, and home: God
send a good one or none, I pray God! My father hath
sent me to the well for the water of life, and tells me,
if I give fair words, I shall have a husband.   640

---

625 vild] vile.   633 Well said] well done.   plyest
these pioners] keepest these diggers at their task.

Enter Celanta, *the foul wench, to the Well for water, with a pot in her hand.*

But here comes Celanta my sweet sister: I'll stand by and hear what she says.

Cel. My father hath sent me to the well for water, and he tells me, if I speak fair, I shall have a husband, and none of the worst. Well, though I am black, I am sure all the world will not forsake me, and, as the old proverb is, 'though I am black, I am not the devil.' 647

Zan. Marry gup with a murren, I know wherefore thou speakest that, but go thy ways home as wise as thou camest, or I'll set thee home with a wanion.

Here she strikes her pitcher against her sister's, and breaks them both, and goes her way.

Cel. I think this be the curstest quean in the world: you see what she is, a little fair, but as proud as the devil, and the veriest vixen that lives upon God's earth. Well, I'll let her alone, and go home and get another pitcher, and, for all this, get me to the well for water.   [*Exit.*

Enter two Furies out of Sacrapant's *Cell and lays* Huanebango *by the Well of Life.*

Enter Zantippa *with a pitcher to the Well.*

Zan. Once again for a husband; and, in faith, Celanta, I have got the start of you; belike husbands grow by the well-side. Now my father says I must rule my tongue: why, alas, what am I, then? a woman without a tongue is as a soldier without his weapon; but I'll have my water, and be gone.   662

Here she offers to dip her pitcher in, and a Head *speaks in the Well.*

Head. Gently dip, but not too deep,

647 black] dark-haired.   648 gup] meaningless expression of remonstrance.   650 wanion] vengeance.
651 curstest] worst-tempered.   quean] wench.

For fear you make the golden beard to weep.
Fair maiden, white and red,
Stroke me smooth, and comb my head,
And thou shalt have some cockle-bread.

   Zan. What is this?
'Fair maiden, white and red,
Comb me smooth, and stroke my head,   670
And thou shalt have some cockle-bread?'
'Cockle' callest thou it, boy? faith, I'll give you
cockle-bread.

She breaks her pitcher upon the Head: *then it thunders and
lightens, and* Huanebango *rises up:* Huanebango *is deaf
and cannot hear.*

   Huan. Philida, phileridos, pamphilida, florida,
flortos:
Dub dub-a-dub, bounce, quoth the guns, with a sul-
phurous huff-snuff:
Wak'd with a wench! Pretty peat, pretty love, and
my sweet pretty pigsnie,
Just by thy side shall sit surnamed great Huanebango:
Safe in my arms will I keep thee, threat Mars, or
thunder Olympus.   678
   Zan. [*aside.*] Foh, what greasy groom have we here?
He looks as though he crept out of the backside of the
well, and speaks like a drum perished at the west end.
   Huan. O, that I might,—but I may not, woe to my
destiny therefore!—
Kiss that I clasp! but I cannot: tell me, my destiny,
wherefore?
   Zan. [*aside.*] Whoop! now I have my dream. Did
you never hear so great a wonder as this, 'Three blue
beans in a blue bladder, rattle, bladder, rattle?'   686
   Huan. [*aside.*] I'll now set my countenance, and to
her in prose; it may be, this rim-ram-ruff is too rude

   667 cockle-bread] used as a love charm.   674
Philida &c.] Huanebango thunders in English hexameters.
676 peat] pet   687–8 to her] address myself to her.

an encounter.—Let me, fair lady, if you be at leisure,
revel with your sweetness, and rail upon that cowardly
conjurer, that hath cast me, or congealed me rather,
into an unkind sleep, and polluted my carcass.   692

Zan. [*aside*]. Laugh, laugh, Zantippa; thou hast thy
fortune, a fool and a husband under one.

Huan. Truly, sweet-heart, as I seem, about some
twenty years, the very April of mine age.

Zan. [*aside*]. Why, what a prating ass is this!

Huan.   Her coral lips, her crimson chin,
            Her silver teeth so white within,
            Her golden locks, her rolling eye,   700
            Her pretty parts, let them go by,
            Heigh-ho, hath wounded me,
            That I must die this day to see!

Zan. By Gog's bones, thou art a flouting knave:
'her coral lips, her crimson chin!' ka, wilshaw!

Huan. True, my own, and my own because mine,
and mine because mine, ha, ha! above a thousand
pounds in possibility, and things fitting thy desire in
possession.   709

Zan. [*aside*]. The sot thinks I ask of his lands. Lob
be your comfort, and cuckold be your destiny!—Hear
you, sir; an if you will have us, you had best say so
betime.

Huan. True, sweet-heart, and will royalize thy
progeny with my pedigree.   [*Exeunt.*

Enter Eumenides, *the wandering Knight.*

Eum. Wretched Eumenides, still unfortunate,
Envied by fortune and forlorn by fate,
Here pine and die, wretched Eumenides,—
Die in the spring, the April of my age!—
Here sit thee down, repent what thou hast done: 720
I would to God that it were ne'er begun!

705 ka, wilshaw] 'ka' means 'quoth'; 'wilshaw' is not
explained.   710 Lob] Lob's pound was the thraldom of
the hen-pecked husband (Bullen).

Enter Jack.

Jack. You are well overtaken, sir.

Eum. Who 's that?

Jack. You are heartily well met, sir.

Eum. Forbear, I say: who is that which pincheth
me?　　　　　　　　　　　　　　　　　726

Jack. Trusting in God, good Master Eumenides,
that you are in so good health as all your friends were
at the making hereof,—God give you good morrow,
sir! Lack you not a neat, handsome, and cleanly
young lad, about the age of fifteen or sixteen years,
that can run by your horse, and, for a need, make
your mastership's shoes as black as ink? how say you,
sir?

Eum. Alas, pretty lad, I know not how to keep
myself, and much less a servant, my pretty boy, my
state is so bad.　　　　　　　　　　　737

Jack. Content yourself, you shall not be so ill a
master but I'll be as bad a servant. Tut, sir, I know
you, though you know not me: are not you the man,
sir, deny it if you can, sir, that came from a strange
place in the land of Catita, where Jack-an-apes flies
with his tail in his mouth, to seek out a lady as white
as snow and as red as blood? ha, ha! have I touched
you now?

Eum. [*aside*]. I think this boy be a spirit.—How
knowest thou all this?　　　　　　　　747

Jack. Tut, are not you the man, sir, deny it if you
can, sir, that gave all the money you had to the burying of a poor man, and but one three-half-pence left
in your purse? Content you, sir, I'll serve you, that
is flat.

Eum. Well, my lad, since thou art so importunate,
I am content to entertain thee, not as a servant, but
a copartner in my journey. But whither shall we go?
for I have not any money more than one bare three-
half-pence.　　　　　　　　　　　757

742 Jack-an-apes] ape.

Jack. Well, master, content yourself, for if my divination be not out, that shall be spent at the next inn or alehouse we come to; for, master, I know you are passing hungry; therefore I'll go before and provide dinner until that you come; no doubt but you'll come fair and softly after.

Eum. Ay, go before; I'll follow thee.

Jack. But do you hear, master? do you know my name?

Eum. No, I promise thee, not yet.

Jack. Why, I am Jack.   [*Exit.*

Eum. Jack! why, be it so, then.   769

Enter the Hostess *and* Jack, *setting meat on the table; and* Fiddlers *come to play.* Eumenides *walketh up and down, and will eat no meat.*

Host. How say you, sir, do you please to sit down?

Eum. Hostess, I thank you, I have no great stomach.

Host. Pray, sir, what is the reason your master is so strange? doth not this meat please him?

Jack. Yes, hostess, but it is my master's fashion to pay before he eats; therefore, a reckoning, good hostess.   777

Host. Marry, shall you, sir, presently.   [*Exit.*

Eum. Why, Jack, what dost thou mean? thou knowest I have not any money: therefore, sweet Jack, tell me what shall I do?

Jack. Well, master, look in your purse.

Eum. Why, faith, it is a folly, for I have no money.

Jack. Why, look you, master; do so much for me.

Eum. Alas, Jack, my purse is full of money!

Jack. 'Alas,' master! does that word belong to this accident? why, methinks I should have seen you cast away your cloak, and in a bravado danced a galliard round about the chamber! why, master, your man can teach you more wit than this. Come, hostess, cheer up my master.   791

Enter Hostess.

Host. You are heartily welcome; and if it please you
to eat of a fat capon, a fairer bird, a finer bird, a
sweeter bird, a crisper bird, a neater bird, your
worship never ate of.

Eum. Thanks, my fine, eloquent hostess.

Jack. But hear you, master, one word by the way:
are you content I shall be halves in all you get in your
journey?

Eum. I am, Jack, here is my hand.   800

Jack. Enough, master, I ask no more.

Eum. Come, hostess, receive your money; and I
thank you for my good entertainment.

Host. You are heartily welcome, sir.

Eum. Come, Jack, whither go we now?

Jack. Marry, master, to the conjurer's presently.

Eum. Content, Jack.—Hostess, farewell. [*Exeunt.*

Enter Corebus *and* Celanta, *the foul wench, to the Well
for water.*

Cor. Come, my duck, come: I have now got a wife:
thou art fair, art thou not?

Cel. My Corebus, the fairest alive; make no doubt
of that.   811

Cor. Come, wench, are we almost at the well?

Cel. Ay, Corebus, we are almost at the well now.
I'll go fetch some water: sit down while I dip my
pitcher in.

A Head *comes up with ears of corn, and she combs them in
her lap.*

Head. Gently dip, but not too deep,
For fear you make the golden beard to weep.
Fair maiden, white and red,
Comb me smooth, and stroke my head,
And thou shalt have some cockle-bread.   820

809 art thou not?] Corebus is blind, see line 585 s.d.

A Head *comes up full of gold: she combs it into her lap.*

2nd Head. Gently dip, but not too deep,
For fear thou make the golden beard to weep.
Fair maid, white and red,
Comb me smooth, and stroke my head,
And every hair a sheaf shall be,
And every sheaf a golden tree.

Cel. O, see, Corebus, I have combed a great deal
of gold into my lap, and a great deal of corn!   828

Cor. Well said, wench! now we shall have just
enough: God send us coiners to coin our gold. But
come, shall we go home, sweetheart?

Cel. Nay, come, Corebus, I will lead you.

Cor. So, Corebus, things have well hit;
Thou hast gotten wealth to mend thy wit.   [*Exeunt.*

Enter Jack *and* Eumenides.

Jack. Come away, master, come.

Eum. Go along, Jack, I'll follow thee. Jack, they
say it is good to go cross-legged, and say his prayers
backward; how sayest thou?   838

Jack. Tut, never fear, master! Let me alone: here
sit you still; speak not a word; and because you shall
not be enticed with his enchanting speeches, with this
same wool I'll stop your ears——and so, master, sit still,
for I must to the conjurer.   [*Exit.*

Enter Sacrapant.

Sac. How now! what man art thou, that sits
    so sad?
Why dost thou gaze upon these stately trees
Without the leave and will of Sacrapant?
What, not a word, but mum?
Then, Sacrapant, thou art betrayed.

829 just] the word is probably wrong; some copies read
'tost', and editors have suggested 'grist', 'toast'.   839
Let me alone] trust me.   840 because] so that.

Enter Jack *invisible, and taketh off* Sacrapant's *wreath from his head, and his sword out of his hand.*

What hand invades the head of Sacrapant?
What hateful Fury doth envy my happy state?   850
Then, Sacrapant, these are thy latest days.
Alas, my veins are numb'd, my sinews shrink,
My blood is pierc'd, my breath fleeting away,
And now my timeless date is come to end!
He in whose life his actions hath been so foul,
Now in his death to hell descends his soul.   [*He dieth.*

Jack. O, sir, are you gone? now I hope we shall have some other coil.—Now, master, how like you this? the conjurer is dead, and vows never to trouble us more: now get you to your fair lady, and see what you can do with her.—Alas, he heareth me not all this while! but I will help that.   862
                    [*He pulls the wool out of his ears.*

Eum. How now, Jack! what news?

Jack. Here, master, take this sword, and dig with it at the foot of this hill.   [*He digs, and spies a light.*

Eum. How now, Jack! what is this?

Jack. Master, without this the conjurer could do nothing, and so long as this light lasts, so long doth his art endure, and this being out, then doth his art decay.   870

Eum. Why, then, Jack, I will soon put out this light.

Jack. Ay, master, how?

Eum. Why, with a stone I'll break the glass, and then blow it out.

Jack. No, master, you may as soon break the smith's anvil as this little vial; nor the biggest blast that ever Boreas blew out this little light; but she that is neither maid, wife, nor widow. Master, wind this horn, and see what will happen.   879
                    [*He winds the horn.*

858 coil] bustle, excitement.   869 his art] *sc.* the enchantments he has performed.   877 Boreas] the North Wind.

Here enters Venelia, *and breaks the glass, and blows out the
light, and goeth in again.*

Jack. So, master, how like you this? this is she that
ran madding in the woods, his betrothed love that
keeps the cross; and now, this light being out, all are
restored to their former liberty: and now, master, to
the lady that you have so long looked for.

He draweth a curtain, and there Delia *sitteth asleep.*

Eum. God speed, fair maid, sitting alone,—there is
once; God speed, fair maid,—there is twice; God
speed, fair maid,—that is thrice.

Del. Not so, good sir, for you are by.　　888

Jack. Enough, master, she hath spoke, now I will
leave her with you.　　　　　　　　　　　　[*Exit.*

Eum. Thou fairest flower of these western parts,
Whose beauty so reflecteth in my sight
As doth a crystal mirror in the sun,
For thy sweet sake I have cross'd the frozen Rhine;
Leaving fair Po, I sail'd up Danuby,
As far as Saba, whose enhancing streams
Cut twixt the Tartars and the Russians:
These have I cross'd for thee, fair Delia:
Then grant me that which I have su'd for long.　899

Del. Thou gentle knight, whose fortune is so good
To find me out and set my brothers free,
My faith, my heart, my hand I give to thee.

Eum. Thanks, gentle madam: but here comes Jack;
thank him, for he is the best friend that we have.

Enter Jack, *with a head in his hand.*

How now, Jack! what hast thou there?

Jack. Marry, master, the head of the conjurer.

Eum. Why, Jack, that is impossible; he was a young
man.　　　　　　　　　　　　　　　　　　908

Jack. Ah, master, so he deceived them that beheld
him! but he was a miserable, old, and crooked man,
though to each man's eye he seemed young and fresh;
for, master, this conjurer took the shape of the old

man that kept the cross, and that old man was in the likeness of the conjurer. But now, master, wind your horn.

He winds his horn. Enter Venelia, *the* Two Brothers, *and* Erestus.

Eum. Welcome, Erestus! welcome, fair Venelia! Welcome, Thelea and Calypha both!
Now have I her that I so long have sought;
So saith fair Delia, if we have your consent.

1st Bro. Valiant Eumenides, thou well deservest
To have our favours: so let us rejoice   921
That by thy means we are at liberty:
Here may we joy each in other's sight,
And this fair lady have her wandering knight.

Jack. So, master, now ye think you have done; but I must have a saying to you: you know you and I were partners, I to have half in all you got.

Eum. Why, so thou shalt, Jack.

Jack. Why, then, master, draw your sword, part your lady, let me have half of her presently.   930

Eum. Why, I hope, Jack, thou dost but jest: I promised thee half I got, but not half my lady.

Jack. But what else, master? have you not gotten her? therefore divide her straight, for I will have half —there is no remedy.

Eum. Well, ere I will falsify my word unto my friend, take her all: here, Jack, I'll give her thee.

Jack. Nay, neither more nor less, master, but even just half.

Eum. Before I will falsify my faith unto my friend, I will divide her: Jack, thou shalt have half.   941

1st Bro. Be not so cruel unto our sister, gentle knight.

2nd Bro. O, spare fair Delia! she deserves no death.

Eum. Content yourselves; my word is passed to him. Therefore prepare thyself, Delia, for thou must die.

923 Here] two syllables.

Del. Then farewell, world! adieu, Eumenides!

    He offers to strike, and Jack *stays him.*

Jack. Stay, master; it is sufficient I have tried your constancy. Do you now remember since you paid for the burying of a poor fellow?   950

Eum. Ay, very well, Jack.

Jack. Then, master, thank that good deed for this good turn: and so God be with you all!

               [Jack *leaps down in the ground.*

Eum. Jack, what, art thou gone?—then farewell, Jack!—

Come, brothers, and my beauteous Delia,

Erestus, and thy dear Venelia,

We will to Thessaly with joyful hearts.

All. Agreed: we follow thee and Delia.

    [*Exeunt all except* Frolic, Fantastic, *and* Madge.

Fant. What gammer, asleep?

Madge. By the mass, son, 'tis almost day, and my windows shut at the cock's-crow!   961

Frol. Do you hear, gammer? methinks this Jack bore a great sway amongst them.

Madge. O, man, this was the ghost of the poor man that they kept such a coil to bury, and that makes him to help the wandering knight so much. But come, let us in: we will have a cup of ale and a toast this morning, and so depart.

Fant. Then you have made an end of your tale, gammer?   970

Madge. Yes, faith: when this was done, I took a piece of bread and cheese, and came my way; and so shall you have, too, before you go, to your breakfast.

---

953 s.d. *in*] into.   965 coil] bustle.   968 depart] part.   973 to] for.

FINIS.

Printed at London by John Danter, for Ralph
Hancock, and John Hardie, and are to
be sold at the shop over against
Saint Giles his Church without Cripplegate.
1595.

The colophon of the first quarto.

FRIAR BACON AND FRIAR BUNGAY

BY

ROBERT GREENE

ROBERT GREENE (1558–1592)

Friar Bacon and Friar Bungay

Acted probably in 1590 or 1591; printed in 1594.

[*Complete Works*, ed. A. B. Grosart, 15 vols., 1881–6, is scarce, costly, and not very reliable; *Plays and Poems*, ed. J. C. Collins, 2 vols., Oxford, 1905, is rather more trustworthy. A type-facsimile of *Friar Bacon and Friar Bungay* was issued by the Malone Society in 1926.]

THE
HONORABLE HISTORIE
of frier Bacon, and frier Bongay.

As it was plaid by her Maiesties seruants.

Made by *Robert Greene* Maister of Arts.

LONDON,

Printed for Edward White, and are to be sold at his shop, at
the little North dore of Poules, at the signe of
the Gun. 1594.

Dramatis Personae

KING HENRY THE THIRD.

EDWARD, PRINCE OF WALES, *his son.*

EMPEROR OF GERMANY.

KING OF CASTILE.

DUKE OF SAXONY.

LACY, *Earl of Lincoln.*

WARREN, *Earl of Sussex.*

ERMSBY, *a Gentleman.*

RALPH SIMNEL, *the King's Fool.*

FRIAR BACON.

MILES, *Friar Bacon's poor scholar.*

FRIAR BUNGAY.

JAQUES VANDERMAST.

BURDEN,
MASON,   } *Doctors of Oxford.*
CLEMENT,

LAMBERT,
SERLSBY, } *Gentlemen.*

Two Scholars, *their sons.*

Keeper.

Keeper's Friend.

THOMAS,
RICHARD, } *Clowns.*

Constable.

A Post.

Lords, Clowns, &c.

ELINOR, *daughter to the King of Castile.*

MARGARET, *the Keeper's daughter.*

JOAN, *a country wench.*

Hostess of the Bell at Henley.

A Devil.

Spirit in the shape of HERCULES.

THE HONOURABLE HISTORY OF FRIAR BACON AND FRIAR BUNGAY

Act I. Scene I.

Enter Edward the First, *malcontented, with* Lacy, *Earl of Lincoln,* John Warren, *Earl of Sussex, and* Ermsby, *gentleman:* Ralph Simnel, *the King's Fool.*

Lacy. Why looks my lord like to a troubled sky
When heaven's bright shine is shadowed with a fog?
Alate we ran the deer, and through the lawnds
Stripp'd with our nags the lofty frolic bucks
That scudded 'fore the teisers like the wind:
Ne'er was the deer of merry Fressingfield
So lustily pull'd down by jolly mates,
Nor shar'd the farmers such fat venison,
So frankly dealt, this hundred years before;
Nor have I seen my lord more frolic in the chase,   10
And now chang'd to a melancholy dump.

War. After the prince got to the keeper's lodge,
And had been jocand in the house awhile,
Tossing off ale and milk in country cans;
Whether it was the country's sweet content,
Or else the bonny damsel fill'd us drink,
That seem'd so stately in her stammel red,
Or that a qualm did cross his stomach then,
But straight he fell into his passions.

Erms. Sirrah Ralph, what say you to your master,
Shall he thus all amort live malcontent?   21

4 Stripp'd] outstripped.   5 teisers] deerhounds.
11 dump] dejection.   13 jocand] joking, making
merry.   17 stammel] coarse woollen cloth.   21 all
amort] dejected.

Ralph. Hearest thou, Ned?—Nay, look if he will speak to me!

Edw. What say'st thou to me, fool?

Ralph. I prithee, tell me, Ned, art thou in love with the Keeper's daughter?

Edw. How if I be, what then?

Ralph. Why then, sirrah, I'll teach thee how to deceive love.

Edw. How, Ralph?   30

Ralph. Marry, Sirrah Ned, thou shalt put on my cap and my coat and my dagger, and I will put on thy clothes and thy sword; and so thou shalt be my fool.

Edw. And what of this?

Ralph. Why, so thou shalt beguile Love, for Love is such a proud scab, that he will never meddle with fools nor children. Is not Ralph's counsel good, Ned?

Edw. Tell me, Ned Lacy, didst thou mark the maid,
How lively in her country weeds she look'd?
A bonnier wench all Suffolk cannot yield:—   40
All Suffolk! nay, all England holds none such.

Ralph. Sirrah Will Ermsby, Ned is deceived.

Erms. Why, Ralph?

Ralph. He says all England hath no such, and I say, and I'll stand to it, there is one better in Warwickshire.

War. How provest thou that, Ralph?

Ralph. Why, is not the abbot a learned man, and hath read many books, and thinkest thou he hath not more learning than thou to choose a bonny wench? yes, I warrant thee, by his whole grammar.   50

Erms. A good reason, Ralph.

Edw. I tell thee, Lacy, that her sparkling eyes
Do lighten forth sweet love's alluring fire,
And in her tresses she doth fold the looks
Of such as gaze upon her golden hair;
Her bashful white, mix'd with the morning's red,

53 lighten forth] give forth like lightning.

Luna doth boast upon her lovely cheeks;
Her front is beauty's table, where she paints
The glories of her gorgeous excellence;
Her teeth are shelves of precious margarites,   60
Richly enclos'd with ruddy coral cleeves.
Tush, Lacy, she is beauty's over-match,
If thou survey'st her curious imagery.

    Lacy. I grant, my lord, the damsel is as fair
As simple Suffolk's homely towns can yield;
But in the court be quainter dames than she,
Whose faces are enrich'd with honour's taint,
Whose beauties stand upon the stage of fame,
And vaunt their trophies in the courts of love.

    Edw. Ah, Ned, but hadst thou watch'd her as myself,   70
And seen the secret beauties of the maid,
Their courtly coyness were but foolery.

    Erms. Why, how watch'd you her, my lord?

    Edw. Whenas she swept like Venus through the house,—
And in her shape fast folded up my thoughts,—
Into the milk-house went I with the maid,
And there amongst the cream-bowls she did shine
As Pallas 'mongst her princely huswifery:
She turn'd her smock over her lily arms,
And div'd them into milk to run her cheese;   80
But whiter than the milk her crystal skin,
Checked with lines of azure, made her blush,
That art or nature durst bring for compare—
Ermsby, if thou hadst seen, as I did note it well,
How beauty play'd the huswife, how this girl
Like Lucrece laid her fingers to the work,
Thou wouldst, with Tarquin, hazard Rome and all
To win the lovely maid of Fressingfield.

58 front] forehead.   table] tablet, sketch-book.   60
margarites] pearls.   61 cleeves] cliffs.   66 quainter]
more exquisite.   74 Whenas] when.   82 her] *sc.*
any other woman.   83 compare] comparison.

Ralph. Sirrah Ned, wouldst fain have her?

Edw. Ay, Ralph.   90

Ralph. Why, Ned, I have laid the plot in my head, thou shalt have her already!

Edw. I'll give thee a new coat, an learn me that.

Ralph. Why, Sirrah Ned, we'll ride to Oxford to Friar Bacon: O, he is a brave scholar, sirrah, they say he is a brave necromancer, that he can make women of devils, and he can juggle cats into costermongers.

Edw. And how then, Ralph?

Ralp. Marry, Sirrah, thou shalt go to him, and because thy father Harry shall not miss thee, he shall turn me into thee; and I'll to the court, and I'll prince it out, and he shall make thee either a silken purse, full of gold, or else a fine wrought smock.   103

Edw. But how shall I have the maid?

Ralph. Marry, sirrah, if thou be'st a silken purse full of gold, then on Sundays she'll hang thee by her side, and you must not say a word. Now, sir, when she comes into a great prease of people, for fear of the cut-purse, on a sudden she'll swap thee into her plackerd; then, sirrah, being there, you may plead for yourself.

Erms. Excellent policy!   111

Edw. But how if I be a wrought smock?

Ralph. Then she'll put thee into her chest and lay thee into lavender, and upon some good day she'll put thee on, and at night when you go to bed, then being turned from a smock to a man, you may make up the match.

Lacy. Wonderfully wisely counselled, Ralph.

Edw. Ralph shall have a new coat.

Ralph. God thank you when I have it on my back, Ned.   121

Edw. Lacy, the fool hath laid a perfect plot; For why our country Margaret is so coy,

93 an learn] if you will teach.   95 brave] fine.   100 because] so that.   108 prease] press.   109 plackerd] placket; opening in the front of skirt or petticoat.

And stands so much upon her honest points,
That marriage or no market with the maid:
Ermsby, it must be necromantic spells
And charms of art that must enchain her love,
Or else shall Edward never win the girl.
Therefore, my wags, we'll horse us in the morn,
And post to Oxford to this jolly friar: 130
Bacon shall by his magic do this deed.

   War. Content, my lord; and that's a speedy way
To wean these headstrong puppies from the teat.

   Edw. I am unknown, not taken for the prince;
They only deem us frolic courtiers,
That revel thus among our liege's game:
Therefore I have devis'd a policy.
Lacy, thou know'st next Friday is Saint James',
And then the country flocks to Harleston Fair:
Then will the Keeper's daughter frolic there,   140
And over-shine the troop of all the maids,
That come to see and to be seen that day.
Haunt thee disguis'd among the country-swains,
Feign th'art a farmer's son, not far from thence,
Espy her loves, and who she liketh best;
Cote him, and court her to control the clown;
Say that the courtier 'tired all in green,
That help'd her handsomely to run her cheese,
And fill'd her father's lodge with venison,
Commends him, and sends fairings to herself.   150
Buy something worthy of her parentage,
Not worth her beauty; for, Lacy, then the Fair
Affords no jewel fitting for the maid:
And when thou talk'st of me, note if she blush:
O, then she loves; but if her cheeks wax pale,
Disdain it is. Lacy, send how she fares,
And spare no time nor cost to win her loves.

   Lacy. I will, my lord, so execute this charge,
As if that Lacy were in love with her.

   146 Cote] surpass.   control the clown] put the clown
in his place.   150 fairings] presents at fair-time.

Edw. Send letters speedily to Oxford of the news. 160

Ralph. And, Sirrah Lacy, buy me a thousand thousand million of fine bells.

Lacy. What wilt thou do with them, Ralph?

Ralph. Marry, every time that Ned sighs for the Keeper's daughter, I'll tie a bell about him, and so within three or four days I will send word to his father Harry, that his son and my master Ned, is become Love's morris-dance.

Edw. Well, Lacy, look with care unto thy charge,
And I will haste to Oxford to the friar,   170
That he by art, and thou by secret gifts,
Mayst make me lord of merry Fressingfield.

Lacy. God send your honour your heart's desire.

[*Exeunt.*

Scene II.

Enter Friar Bacon, *with* Miles *his poor scholar with books under his arm; with them* Burden, Mason, Clement, *three doctors.*

Bacon. Miles, where are you?

Miles. *Hic sum, doctissime et reverendissime doctor.*

Bacon. *Attulisti nos libros meos de necromantia?*

Miles. *Ecce quam bonum et quam jucundum habitares libros in vnum!*

Bacon. Now, masters of our academic state,
That rule in Oxford, viceroys in your place,
Whose heads contain maps of the liberal arts,
Spending your time in depth of learned skill,
Why flock you thus to Bacon's secret cell,   10
A friar newly stall'd in Brazen-nose?
Say what's your mind, that I may make reply.

2 &c. No translation could reproduce the ineptitude of Miles's Latin here and throughout the play.   11 stall'd] installed.   Brazen-nose] Greene's spelling of Brasenose indicates his pronunciation, which the metre requires; the College did not exist in Bacon's day.

Burd. Bacon, we hear, that long we have suspect,
That thou art read in magic's mystery,
In pyromancy to divine by flames,
To tell by hydromantic ebbs and tides,
By aeromancy to discover doubts,
To plain out questions as Apollo did.

Bacon. Well, Master Burden, what of all this?

Miles. Marry, sir, he doth but fulfil, by rehearsing of
these names, the fable of the Fox and the Grapes: that
which is above us pertains nothing to us.   22

Burd. I tell thee, Bacon, Oxford makes report,
Nay, England, and the court of Henry says
Th'art making of a brazen head by art,
Which shall unfold strange doubts and aphorisms,
And read a lecture in philosophy;
And, by the help of devils and ghastly fiends,
Thou mean'st ere many years or days be past
To compass England with a wall of brass.   30

Bacon. And what of this?

Miles. What of this, master! why he doth speak
mystically for he knows if your skill fail to make a
brazen head yet Mother Waters' strong ale will fit his
turn to make him have a copper nose.

Clem. Bacon, we come not grieving at thy skill,
But joying that our academy yields
A man suppos'd the wonder of the world;
For if thy cunning work these miracles,
England and Europe shall admire thy fame,   40
And Oxford shall in characters of brass,
And statues, such as were built up in Rome,
Eternize Friar Bacon for his art.

Mason. Then, gentle friar, tell us thy intent.

Bacon. Seeing you come as friends unto the friar,
Resolve you, doctors, Bacon can by books
Make storming Boreas thunder from his cave,
And dim fair Luna to a dark eclipse.

37 academy] here (and usually) pronounced acadÉmy.
46 Resolve you] learn.

The great arch-ruler, potentate of hell,
Trembles when Bacon bids him, or his fiends,   50
Bow to the force of his pentageron.
What art can work, the frolic friar knows;
And therefore will I turn my magic books,
And strain out necromancy to the deep.
I have contriv'd and fram'd a head of brass
(I made Belcephon hammer out the stuff),
And that by art shall read philosophy;
And I will strengthen England by my skill,
That if ten Caesars liv'd and reign'd in Rome,
With all the legions Europe doth contain,   60
They should not touch a grass of English ground;
The work that Ninus rear'd at Babylon,
The brazen walls fram'd by Semiramis,
Carved out like to the portal of the sun,
Shall not be such as rings the English strand
From Dover to the market-place of Rye.

Burd. Is this possible?

Miles. I'll bring ye two or three witnesses.

Burd. What be those?

Miles. Marry, sir, three or four as honest devils and
good companions as any be in hell.   71

Mason. No doubt but magic may do much in this,
For he that reads but mathematic rules
Shall find conclusions that avail to work
Wonders that pass the common sense of men.

Burd. But Bacon roves a bow beyond his reach,
And tells of more than magic can perform;
Thinking to get a fame by fooleries.
Have I not pass'd as far in state of schools,
And read of many secrets? yet to think   80
That heads of brass can utter any voice,
Or more, to tell of deep philosophy,
This is a fable Æsop had forgot.

51 pentageron] pentagonon, the magical five-pointed
star.   76 roves a bow] shoots an arrow at long range,
with oblique trajectory.

Bacon. Burden, thou wrong'st me in detracting thus;
Bacon loves not to stuff himself with lies:
But tell me 'fore these doctors, if thou dare,
Of certain questions I shall move to thee.

Burd. I will: ask what thou can.

Miles. Marry, sir, he'll straight be on your pick-
pack, to know whether the feminine or the masculine
gender be most worthy.   91

Bacon. Were you not yesterday, Master Burden, at
Henley upon the Thames?

Burd. I was, what then?

Bacon. What book studied you there on all night?

Burd. I! none at all; I read not there a line.

Bacon. Then, doctors, Friar Bacon's art knows
naught.

Clem. What say you to this, Master Burden? doth
he not touch you?

Burd. I pass not of his frivolous speeches.   100

Miles. Nay, Master Burden, my master, ere he hath
done with you, will turn you from a doctor to a dunce,
and shake you so small, that he will leave no more
learning in you than is in Balaam's ass.

Bacon. Masters, for that learned Burden's skill is
    deep,
And sore he doubts of Bacon's cabalism,
I'll show you why he haunts to Henley oft:
Not, doctors, for to taste the fragrant air,
But there to spend the night in alchemy,
To multiply with secret spells of art;   110
Thus private steals he learning from us all.
To prove my sayings true, I'll show you straight
The book he keeps at Henley for himself.

Miles. Nay, now my master goes to conjuration,
take heed.

Bacon. Masters, stand still, fear not, I'll show you
but his book.

89–90 pick-pack] pick-a-back.   100 pass not] take no
heed.

Here he conjures.

Per omnes deos infernales, Belcephon! 118

Enter Hostess *with a shoulder of mutton on a
spit, and a* Devil.

Miles. O, master, cease your conjuration, or you
spoil all, for here's a she-devil come with a shoulder of
mutton on a spit: you have marred the devil's supper;
but no doubt he thinks our college fare is slender, and
so hath sent you his cook with a shoulder of mutton, to
make it exceed.

Hostess. O, where am I, or what's become of me?

Bacon. What art thou?

Hostess. Hostess at Henley, mistress of the Bell.

Bacon. How camest thou here?

Hostess. As I was in the kitchen 'mongst the maids,
Spitting the meat against supper for my guess, 130
A motion moved me to look forth of door.
No sooner had I pried into the yard,
But straight a whirlwind hoisted me from thence,
And mounted me aloft unto the clouds.
As in a trance I thought nor feared naught,
Nor know I where or whither I was ta'en,
Nor where I am, nor what these persons be.

Bacon. No? know you not Master Burden?

Hostess. O, yes, good sir, he is my daily guest.—
What, Master Burden! 'twas but yesternight 140
That you and I at Henley play'd at cards.

Burd. I know not what we did.—A pox of all conjuring friars!

Clem. Now, jolly friar, tell us, is this the book
That Burden is so careful to look on?

Bacon. It is.—But, Burden, tell me now,
Thinkest thou that Bacon's necromantic skill
Cannot perform his head and wall of brass,
When he can fetch thine hostess in such post?

Miles. I'll warrant you, master, if Master Burden

124 exceed] form holiday fare. 130 guess] guests.

could conjure as well as you, he would have his book
every night from Henley to study on at Oxford.   152

   Mason. Burden, what, are you mated by this frolic
     friar?—
Look how he droops; his guilty conscience
Drives him to bash and makes his hostess blush.

   Bacon. Well, mistress, for I will not have you miss'd,
You shall to Henley to cheer up your guests
'Fore supper gin.—Burden, bid her adieu,
Say farewell to your hostess 'fore she goes.—
Sirrah, away, and set her safe at home.   160

   Hostess. Master Burden, when shall we see you at
Henley?   [*Exeunt* Hostess *and the* Devil.

   Burd. The devil take thee and Henley too.

   Miles. Master, shall I make a good motion?

   Bacon. What's that?

   Miles. Marry, sir, now that my hostess is gone to
provide supper, conjure up another spirit, and send
Doctor Burden flying after.

   Bacon. Thus, rulers of our academic state,
You have seen the friar frame his art by proof;   170
And as the college called Brazen-nose
Is under him, and he the master there,
So surely shall this head of brass be fram'd,
And yield forth strange and uncouth aphorisms;
And hell and Hecate shall fail the friar,
But I will circle England round with brass.

   Miles. So be it, *et nunc et semper;* amen.   [*Exeunt.*

Scene III.

Enter Margaret *the fair maid of Fressingfield, with* Thomas
   and Joan, *and other Clowns,* Lacy *disguised in country*
   apparel.

   Thom. By my troth, Margaret, here's a weather is
able to make a man call his father 'whoreson': if this

153 mated] amazed.   155 bash] quail.   156
for] because.   158 gin] begin.

weather hold we shall have hay good cheap and butter
and cheese at Harleston will bear no price.

Mar.   Thomas, maids when they come to see the fair
Count not to make a cope for dearth of hay;
When we have turn'd our butter to the salt,
And set our cheese safely upon the racks,
Then let our fathers price it as they please.
We country sluts of merry Fressingfield   10
Come to buy needless naughts to make us fine,
And look that young men should be frank this day,
And court us with such fairings as they can.
Phoebus is blithe, and frolic looks from heaven,
As when he courted lovely Semele,
Swearing the pedlers shall have empty packs,
If that fair weather may make chapmen buy.

Lacy.   But, lovely Peggy, Semele is dead,
And therefore Phoebus from his palace pries,
And, seeing such a sweet and seemly saint,   20
Shows all his glories for to court yourself.

Mar.   This is a fairing, gentle sir, indeed,
To soothe me up with such smooth flattery!
But, learn of me, your scoff's too broad before.—
Well, Joan, our beauties must abide their jests;
We serve the turn in jolly Fressingfield.

Joan.   Margaret, a farmer's daughter for a farmer's
son:
I warrant you, the meanest of us both
Shall have a mate to lead us from the church.—
But, Thomas, what's the news? what, in a dump! 30
Give me your hand, we are near a pedler's shop;
Out with your purse, we must have fairings now.

Thom.   Faith, Joan, and shall: I'll bestow a fairing
on you, and then we will to the tavern, and snap off
a pint of wine or two.

All this while Lacy *whispers* Margaret *in the ear.*

6 cope] bargain.   13 &c. fairings] presents at fair-
time.   14–15 Phoebus . . . Semele] *sc.* the sun is golden.

Mar. Whence are you, sir? of Suffolk? for your terms
Are finer than the common sort of men.

   Lacy. Faith, lovely girl, I am of Beccles by,
Your neighbour, not above six miles from hence,
A farmer's son, that never was so quaint   40
But that he could do courtesy to such dames!
But trust me, Margaret, I am sent in charge,
From him that revell'd in your father's house,
And fill'd his lodge with cheer and venison,
'Tired in green: he sent you this rich purse:
His token, that he help'd you run your cheese,
And in the milkhouse chatted with yourself.

   Mar. To me? you forget yourself.

   Lacy. Women are often weak in memory.

   Mar. O, pardon, sir, I call to mind the man: 50
'Twere little manners to refuse his gift,
And yet I hope he sends it not for love:
For we have little leisure to debate of that.

   Joan. What, Margaret, blush not! maids must have
     their loves.

   Thom. Nay, by the mass, she looks pale as if she
were angry.

   Rich. Sirrah, are you of Beccles? I pray, how doth
Goodman Cob? my father bought a horse of him.—I'll
tell you, Margaret, 'a were good to be a gentleman's
jade, for of all things the foul hilding could not abide
a dung-cart.   61

   Mar. [*aside*]. How different is this farmer from the
     rest,
That erst as yet hath pleas'd my wandering sight!
His words are witty, quickened with a smile,
His courtesy gentle, smelling of the court,
Facile and debonair in all his deeds,
Proportion'd as was Paris, when, in gray,
He courted Aenon in the vale by Troy.
Great lords have come and pleaded for my love:

46 His token, that] his token is this, that.   59 'a]
he.   60 hilding] jade.   67 gray] shepherd's garb.

Who but the Keeper's lass of Fressingfield?   70
And yet methinks this farmer's jolly son
Passeth the proudest that hath pleas'd mine eye.
But, Peg, disclose not that thou art in love,
And show as yet no sign of love to him,
Although thou well wouldst wish him for thy love:
Keep that to thee till time doth serve thy turn,
To show the grief wherein thy heart doth burn.—
Come, Joan and Thomas, shall we to the fair?—
You Beccles man, will not forsake us now.

    Lacy. Not whilst I may have such quaint girls as
      you.   80

    Mar. Well, if you chance to come by Fressingfield,
Make but a step into the Keeper's lodge,
And such poor fare as woodmen can afford,
Butter and cheese, cream, and fat venison,
You shall have store, and welcome therewithal.

    Lacy. Gramercies, Peggy; look for me ere long.

                            [Exeunt.

Act II. Scene I.

Enter Henry the Third, *the* Emperor, *the* King of
    Castile, Elinor *his daughter*, Jaques Vandermast,
    a German.

    Hen. Great men of Europe, monarchs of the West,
Ring'd with the walls of old Oceanus,
Whose lofty surges like the battlements
That compass'd high-built Babel in with towers,

    *   *   *   *   *

Welcome, my lords, welcome, brave western kings,
To England's shore, whose promontory-cleeves
Shows Albion is another little world;
Welcome says English Henry to you all,
Chiefly unto the lovely Elinor,
Who dar'd for Edward's sake cut through the seas,   10

    85 store] plenty.   Heading. Emperor] *sc.* of Germany.
4–5] There seems to be a line missing; Dickinson reads
'surge is' for 'surges' in line 3.   6 cleeves] cliffs.

And venture as Agenor's damsel through the deep,
To get the love of Henry's wanton son.

  Cast. England's rich monarch, brave Plantagenet,
The Pyren Mounts swelling above the clouds,
That ward the wealthy Castile in with walls,
Could not detain the beauteous Elinor;
But hearing of the fame of Edward's youth,
She dar'd to brook Neptunus' haughty pride,
And bide the brunt of froward Æolus:
Then may fair England welcome her the more.   20

  Elin. After that English Henry by his lords
Had sent Prince Edward's lovely counterfeit,
A present to the Castile Elinor,
The comely portrait of so brave a man,
The virtuous fame discoursed of his deeds,
Edward's courageous resolution,
Done at the Holy Land 'fore Damas' walls,
Led both mine eye and thoughts in equal links
To like so of the English monarch's son,
That I attempted perils for his sake.   30

  Emp. Where is the prince, my lord?

  Hen. He posted down, not long since, from the court,
To Suffolk side, to merry Framlingham,
To sport himself amongst my fallow deer:
From thence, by packets sent to Hampton House,
We hear the prince is ridden, with his lords,
To Oxford, in the academy there
To hear dispute amongst the learned men.
But we will send forth letters for my son,
To will him come from Oxford to the court.   40

  Emp. Nay, rather, Henry, let us, as we be,
Ride for to visit Oxford with our train:
Fain would I see your universities,
And what learn'd men your academy yields.

11 Agenor's damsel] Agenor's daughter, Europa, whom
Jupiter, transformed into a bull, carried on his back across
the sea to Crete.   27 Damas'] of Damascus.

From Hapsburg have I brought a learned clerk,
To hold dispute with English orators.
This doctor, surnam'd Jaques Vandermast,
A German born, pass'd into Padua,
To Florence and to fair Bologna,
To Paris, Rheims, and stately Orleans,   50
And, talking there with men of art, put down
The chiefest of them all in aphorisms,
In magic, and the mathematic rules;
Now let us, Henry, try him in your schools.

   Hen. He shall, my lord; this motion likes me well.
We'll progress straight to Oxford with our trains,
And see what men our academy brings.—
And, wonder Vandermast, welcome to me:
In Oxford shalt thou find a jolly friar,
Call'd Friar Bacon, England's only flower: 60
Set him but non-plus in his magic spells,
And make him yield in mathematic rules,
And for thy glory I will bind thy brows,
Not with a poet's garland made of bays,
But with a coronet of choicest gold.
Whilst then we flit to Oxford with our troops,
Let's in and banquet in our English court. [*Exeunt.*

Scene II.

Enter Ralph Simnel *in* Edward's *apparel;* Edward,
      Warren, Ermsby *disguised.*

   Ralph. Where be these vacabond knaves, that they
attend no better on their master?

   Edw. If it please your honour, we are all ready at
an inch.

   Ralph. Sirrah Ned, I'll have no more post-horse
to ride on: I'll have another fetch.

   Erms. I pray you, how is that, my lord?

51 put down] worsted.   55 likes] pleases.   **66**
Whilst] till.   1 vacabond] vagabond.

Ralph. Marry, sir, I'll send to the Isle of Ely for four
or five dozen of geese, and I'll have them tied six and
six together with whip-cord: now upon their backs
will I have a fair field-bed, with a canopy; and so,
when it is my pleasure, I'll flee into what place I please.
This will be easy.   13

War. Your honour hath said well; but shall we to
Brazen-nose College before we pull off our boots?

Erms. Warren, well motioned; we will to the friar
Before we revel it within the town.
Ralph, see you keep your countenance like a prince.

Ralph. Wherefore have I such a company of cutting
knaves to wait upon me, but to keep and defend my
countenance against all mine enemies: have you not
good swords and bucklers?   22

Enter Bacon *and* Miles.

Erms. Stay, who comes here?

War. Some scholar; and we'll ask him where Friar
Bacon is.

Bacon. Why, thou arrant dunce, shall I never make
thee good scholar? doth not all the town cry out and
say, Friar Bacon's subsizar is the greatest blockhead in
all Oxford? why, thou canst not speak one word of
true Latin.   30

Miles. No, sir? yes! what is this else? *Ego sum tuus
homo,* 'I am your man;' I warrant you, sir, as good
Tully's phrase as any is in Oxford.

Bacon. Come on, sirrah; what part of speech is *Ego?*

Miles. *Ego,* that is 'I'; marry, *nomen substantivo.*

Bacon. How prove you that?

Miles. Why, sir, let him prove himself an 'a will; I
can be heard, felt and understood.

Bacon. O gross dunce!   [*Here beats him.*

19 cutting] swaggering.   28 subsizar] poor scholar
performing menial tasks to support himself (a Cambridge
term).   33 Tully] Cicero.

Edw. Come, let us break off this dispute between these two.—Sirrah, where is Brazen-nose College? 41

Miles. Not far from Coppersmith's Hall.

Edw. What, dost thou mock me?

Miles. Not I, sir, but what would you at Brazen-nose?

Erms. Marry, we would speak with Friar Bacon.

Miles. Whose men be you?

Erms. Marry, scholar, here's our master.

Ralph. Sirrah, I am the master of these good fellows; mayst thou not know me to be a lord by my reparrel? 51

Miles. Then here's good game for the hawk, for here's the master-fool, and a covey of coxcombs: one wise man, I think, would spring you all.

Edw. Gog's wounds, Warren, kill him.

War. Why, Ned, I think the devil be in my sheath, I cannot get out my dagger.

Erms. Nor I mine: swones, Ned, I think I am bewitched.

Miles. A company of scabs! the proudest of you all draw your weapon, if he can.—[*Aside*]. See how boldly I speak, now my master is by. 62

Edw. I strive in vain; but if my sword be shut
And conjur'd fast by magic in my sheath,
Villain, here is my fist.   [*Strikes him a box on the ear.*

Miles. O, I beseech you conjure his hands too, that he may not lift his arms to his head, for he is light-fingered!

Ralph. Ned, strike him; I'll warrant thee by mine honour. 70

Bacon. What! means the English prince to wrong my man?—

Edw. To whom speakest thou?

Bacon. To thee.

Edw. Who art thou?

51 reparrel] a common vulgarism for 'apparel'.   58
swones] 'swounds, *sc.* God's wounds.

Bacon. Could you not judge, when all your swords
      grew fast,
That Friar Bacon was not far from hence!
Edward, King Henry's son and Prince of Wales,
Thy fool disguis'd cannot conceal thyself:
I know both Ermsby and the Sussex Earl,
Else Friar Bacon had but little skill.   80
Thou comest in post from merry Fressingfield,
Fast-fancied to the Keeper's bonny lass,
To crave some succour of the jolly friar,
And Lacy, Earl of Lincoln, hast thou left,
To treat fair Margaret to allow thy loves:
But friends are men, and love can baffle lords.
The earl both woos and courts her for himself.

  War. Ned, this is strange, the friar knoweth all.

  Erms. Apollo could not utter more than this.

  Edw. I stand amazed to hear this jolly friar   90
Tell even the very secrets of my thoughts:—
But learned Bacon, since thou knowest the cause
Why I did post so fast from Fressingfield,
Help, friar, at a pinch, that I may have
The love of lovely Margaret to myself,
And, as I am true Prince of Wales, I'll give
Living and lands to strength thy college state.

  War. Good friar, help the prince in this.

  Ralph. Why, servant Ned, will not the friar do it?—
Were not my sword glued to my scabbard by conjuration, I would cut off his head, and make him do it by
force.   102

  Miles. In faith, my lord, your manhood and your
sword is all alike, they are so fast conjured that we
shall never see them.

  Erms. What, doctor, in a dump! tush, help the
      prince,
And thou shalt see how liberal he will prove.—

---

82 Fast-fancied] tied by love (Dickinson).   86 baffle]
make fools of.   100–1 conjuration] incantation.

Bacon. Crave not such actions greater dumps than
    these?
I will, my lord, strain out my magic spells;
For this day comes the earl to Fressingfield,   110
And 'fore that night shuts in the day with dark,
They'll be betrothed each to other fast.
But come with me; we'll to my study straight,
And in a glass prospective I will show
What's done this day in merry Fressingfield.

Edw. Gramercies, Bacon; I will quite thy pain.

Bacon. But send your train, my lord, into the town:
My scholar shall go bring them to their inn;
Meanwhile we'll see the knavery of the earl.

Edw. Warren, leave me, and Ermsby; take the fool,
Let him be master and go revel it,   121
Till I and Friar Bacon talk awhile.

War. We will, my lord.

Ralph. Faith, Ned, and I'll lord it out till thou
comest; I'll be Prince of Wales over all the black-pots
in Oxford.   [*Exeunt.*

Scene III.

Bacon and Edward goes into the study.

Bacon. Now, frolic Edward, welcome to my cell;
Here tempers Friar Bacon many toys,
And holds this place his consistory court,
Wherein the devils plead homage to his words.
Within this glass prospective thou shalt see
This day what's done in merry Fressingfield
'Twixt lovely Peggy and the Lincoln Earl.

Edw. Friar, thou glad'st me: now shall Edward try
How Lacy meaneth to his sovereign lord.

Bacon. Stand there and look directly in the glass. 10

114 prospective] looking forward (*sc.* into the future).
116 quite] requite.   125 black-pots] wine-jugs.
Heading. *study*] inner stage; thence they watch the outer
stage where Margaret and Friar Bungay enter at line 10.

Enter Margaret *and* Friar Bungay.

What sees my lord?

Edw. I see the Keeper's lovely lass appear,
As brightsome as the paramour of Mars,
Only attended by a jolly friar.

Bacon. Sit still, and keep the crystal in your eye.

Mar. But tell me, Friar Bungay, is it true,
That this fair, courteous, country swain,
Who says his father is a farmer nigh,
Can be Lord Lacy, Earl of Lincolnshire?

Bun. Peggy, 'tis true, 'tis Lacy for my life,   20
Or else mine art and cunning both doth fail—
Left by Prince Edward to procure his loves;
For he in green, that holp you run your cheese,
Is son to Henry, and the Prince of Wales.

Mar. Be what he will, his lure is but for lust.
But did Lord Lacy like poor Margaret,
Or would he deign to wed a country lass,
Friar, I would his humble handmaid be,
And for great wealth, quite him with courtesy.

Bun. Why, Margaret, dost thou love him?   30

Mar. His personage, like the pride of vaunting Troy,
Might well avouch to shadow Helen's scape:
His wit is quick and ready in conceit,
As Greece afforded in her chiefest prime:
Courteous, ah friar, full of pleasing smiles!
Trust me, I love too much to tell thee more;
Suffice to me he is England's paramour.

Bun. Hath not each eye that view'd thy pleasing face
Surnamed thee Fair Maid of Fressingfield?

Mar. Yes, Bungay, and would God the lovely earl
Had that *in esse*, that so many sought.   41

Bun. Fear not, the friar will not be behind
To show his cunning to entangle love.

32 shadow Helen's scape] portray Helen's escapade.

Edw. I think the friar courts the bonny wench;
Bacon, methinks he is a lusty churl.

Bacon. Now look, my lord.

Enter Lacy.

Edw. Gog's wounds, Bacon, here comes Lacy!

Bacon. Sit still, my lord, and mark the comedy.

Bun. Here's Lacy, Margaret, step aside awhile.

[*Retires with* Margaret.

Lacy. Daphne, the damsel that caught Phoebus
    fast,   50
And lock'd him in the brightness of her looks,
Was not so beauteous in Apollo's eyes,
As is fair Margaret to the Lincoln Earl.—
Recant thee, Lacy, thou art put in trust:
Edward, thy sovereign's son, hath chosen thee,
A secret friend, to court her for himself,
And dar'st thou wrong thy prince with treachery!—
Lacy, love makes no exception of a friend,
Nor deems it of a prince but as a man:
Honour bids thee control him in his lust;   60
His wooing is not for to wed the girl,
But to entrap her and beguile the lass:
Lacy, thou lovest; then brook not such abuse,
But wed her, and abide thy prince's frown:
For better die, than see her live disgrac'd.

Mar. Come, friar, I will shake him from his
    dumps.—   [*Comes forward.*
How cheer you, sir? a penny for your thought:
You're early up, pray God it be the near.
What, come from Beccles in a morn so soon!

Lacy. Thus watchful are such men as live in love,
Whose eyes brook broken slumbers for their sleep. 71
I tell thee, Peggy, since last Harleston Fair
My mind hath felt a heap of passions.

Mar. A trusty man, that court it for your friend:

68 near] nearer; alluding to the proverb 'early up and
never the nearer' (Dickinson).

Woo you still for the courtier all in green?—
[*Aside.*] I marvel that he sues not for himself.

Lacy. Peggy, I pleaded first to get your grace for
him,
But when mine eyes survey'd your beauteous looks,
Love, like a wag, straight dived into my heart,
And there did shrine the Idea of yourself: 80
Pity me, though I be a farmer's son,
And measure not my riches but my love.

Mar. You are very hasty; for to garden well,
Seeds must have time to sprout before they spring:
Love ought to creep as doth the dial's shade,
For timely ripe is rotten too too soon.

Bun. [*coming forward.*] *Deus hic*; room for a merry
friar!
What, youth of Beccles, with the Keeper's lass?
'Tis well; but tell me, hear you any news?

Mar. No, friar, what news?   90

Bun. Hear you not how the pursuivants do post
With proclamations through each country-town?

Lacy. For what, gentle friar? tell the news.

Bun. Dwell'st thou in Beccles, and hear'st not of
these news?
Lacy, the Earl of Lincoln, is late fled
From Windsor court, disguised like a swain,
And lurks about the country here unknown.
Henry suspects him of some treachery,
And therefore doth proclaim in every way,
That who can take the Lincoln Earl shall have,   100
Paid in the Exchequer, twenty thousand crowns.

Lacy. The Earl of Lincoln! friar, thou art mad:
It was some other; thou mistakest the man:
The Earl of Lincoln! why, it cannot be.

Mar. Yes, very well, my lord, for you are he,
The Keeper's daughter took you prisoner,
Lord Lacy, yield, I'll be your gaoler once.

85 dial] sundial.   91 pursuivants] messengers.

Edw. How familiar they be, Bacon!

Bacon. Sit still, and mark the sequel of their loves.

Lacy. Then am I double prisoner to thyself: 110
Peggy, I yield; but are these news in jest?

Mar. In jest with you, but earnest unto me;
For why, these wrongs do wring me at the heart!
Ah, how these earls and noblemen of birth
Flatter and feign to forge poor women's ill.

Lacy. Believe me, lass, I am the Lincoln Earl,
I not deny; but 'tired thus in rags
I lived disguis'd to win fair Peggy's love.

Mar. What love is there where wedding ends not
        love?   119

Lacy. I meant, fair girl, to make thee Lacy's wife.

Mar. I little think that earls will stoop so low—

Lacy. Say, shall I make thee countess ere I sleep?

Mar. Handmaid unto the earl, so please himself:
A wife in name, but servant in obedience.

Lacy. The Lincoln Countess, for it shall be so:
I'll plight the bands and seal it with a kiss.

Edw. Gog's wounds, Bacon, they kiss! I'll stab
        them—

Bacon. O, hold your hands, my lord, it is the glass.

Edw. Choler to see the traitors gree so well
Made me think the shadows substances.   130

Bacon. 'Twere a long poniard, my lord, to reach
between Oxford and Fressingfield; but sit still and see
more.

Bun. Well, Lord of Lincoln, if your loves be knit,
And that your tongues and thoughts do both agree,
To avoid ensuing jars, I'll hamper up the match.
I'll take my portas forth, and wed you here:
Then go to bed and seal up your desires.

Lacy. Friar, content.—Peggy, how like you this?

Mar. What likes my lord is pleasing unto me.   140

Bun. Then hand-fast hand, and I will to my book.—

129 gree] agree.   137 portas] portable breviary
(prayer-book).

Bacon.   What sees my lord now?

Edw.   Bacon, I see the lovers hand in hand,
The friar ready with his portas there
To wed them both: then am I quite undone.
Bacon, help now, if e'er thy magic serv'd;
Help, Bacon; stop the marriage now,
If devils or necromancy may suffice,
And I will give thee forty thousand crowns.

Bacon.   Fear not, my lord, I'll stop the jolly friar   151
For mumbling up his orisons this day.

Lacy.   Why speak'st not, Bungay? Friar to thy book.
                    [*Bungay is mute, crying* 'Hud, hud.'

Mar.   How lookest thou, friar, as a man distraught!
Reft of thy senses, Bungay? show by signs
If thou be dumb, what passions holdeth thee.

Lacy.   He's dumb indeed. Bacon hath with his devils
Enchanted him, or else some strange disease
Or apoplexy hath possess'd his lungs:
But, Peggy, what he cannot with his book
We'll 'twixt us both unite it up in heart.   160

Mar.   Else let me die, my lord, a miscreant.

Edw.   Why stands Friar Bungay so amaz'd?

Bacon.   I have struck him dumb, my lord; and if
        your honour please,
I'll fetch this Bungay straightway from Fressingfield,
And he shall dine with us in Oxford here.

Edw.   Bacon, do that, and thou contentest me.

Lacy.   Of courtesy, Margaret, let us lead the friar
Unto thy father's lodge, to comfort him
With broths, to bring him from this hapless trance.

Mar.   Or else, my lord, we were passing unkind
To leave the friar so in his distress.   171

    Enter a Devil, *and carry off* Bungay *on his back.*

O, help, my lord! a devil, a devil, my lord!
Look how he carries Bungay on his back!
Let's hence, for Bacon's spirits be abroad.
                            [*Exit with* Lacy.

Edw. Bacon, I laugh to see the jolly friar
Mounted upon the devil, and how the earl
Flees with his bonny lass for fear.
As soon as Bungay is at Brazen-nose,
And I have chatted with the merry friar,
I will in post hie me to Fressingfield,   180
And quite these wrongs on Lacy ere it be long.

Bacon. So be it, my lord: but let us to our dinner;
For ere we have taken our repast awhile,
We shall have Bungay brought to Brazen-nose.

[*Exeunt.*

Scene IV.

Enter three doctors, Burden, Mason, Clement.

Mason. Now that we are gathered in the Regent
House,
It fits us talk about the king's repair;
For he, troop'd with all the western kings,
That lie along'st the Dantzic seas by east,
North by the clime of frosty Germany,
The Almain monarch and the Saxon duke,
Castile and lovely Elinor with him,
Have in their jests resolved for Oxford town.

Burd. We must lay plots of stately tragedies,
Strange comic shows, such as proud Roscius   10
Vaunted before the Roman Emperors,
To welcome all the western potentates.

Clem. But more; the king by letters hath foretold
That Frederick, the Almain emperor,
Hath brought with him a German of esteem,
Whose surname is Don Jaques Vandermast,
Skilful in magic and those secret arts.

Mason. Then must we all make suit unto the friar,
To Friar Bacon, that he vouch this task,
And undertake to countervail in skill   20
The German; else there's none in Oxford can

181 quite] requite (*sc.* punish).   2 repair] visit.

Match and dispute with learned Vandermast.

Burd. Bacon, if he will hold the German play,
Will teach him what an English friar can do:
The devil, I think, dare not dispute with him.

Clem. Indeed, Mas doctor, he displeasured you,
In that he brought your hostess, with her spit,
From Henley posting unto Brazen-nose.

Burd. A vengeance on the friar for his pains!
But leaving that, let 's hie to Bacon straight,   30
To see if he will take this task in hand.

Clem. Stay, what rumour is this? the town is up in
a mutiny: what hurly-burly is this?

Enter a Constable, *with* Ralph, Warren, Ermsby,
and Miles.

Cons. Nay, masters, if you were ne'er so good, you
shall before the doctors to answer your misdemeanour.

Burd. What 's the matter, fellow?

Cons. Marry, sir, here 's a company of rufflers, that,
drinking in the tavern, have made a great brawl, and
almost kill'd the vintner.

Miles. Salve, Doctor Burden! This lubberly lurden,
Ill-shap'd and ill-faced, disdain'd and disgraced,   41
What he tells unto *vobis, mentitur de nobis.*

Burd. Who is the master and chief of this crew?

Miles. Ecce asinum mundi, figura rotundi,
Neat, sheat, and fine, as brisk as a cup of wine.

Burd. What are you?

Ralph. I am, father doctor, as a man would say, the
bell-wether of this company: these are my lords, and I
the Prince of Wales.

Clem. Are you Edward, the king's son?   50

Ralph. Sirrah Miles, bring hither the tapster that
drew the wine, and, I warrant, when they see how
soundly I have broke his head, they'll say 'twas done
by no less man than a prince.

37 rufflers] rowdies.   45 sheat] trim.

Mason. I cannot believe that this is the Prince of
Wales.

War. And why so, sir?

Mason. For they say the prince is a brave and a
wise gentleman.

War. Why, and thinkest thou, doctor, that he is not
    so?   60
Dar'st thou detract and derogate from him,
Being so lovely and so brave a youth!

Erms. Whose face, shining with many a sugar'd
    smile,
Bewrays that he is bred of princely race.

Miles. And yet, master doctor, to speak like a proctor,
And tell unto you what is veriment and true:
To cease of this quarrel, look but on his apparel;
Then mark but my talis, he is great Prince of Walis,
The chief of our *gregis*, and *filius regis*:   69
Then 'ware what is done, for he is Henry's white son.

Ralph. Doctors, whose doting night-caps are not
capable of my ingenious dignity, know that I am Edward Plantagenet, whom if you displease, will make
a ship that shall hold all your colleges, and so carry
away the niniversity with a fair wind to the Bankside
in Southwark.—How sayest thou, Ned Warren, shall
I not do it?

War. Yes, my good lord; and, if it please your lordship, I will gather up all your old pantofles, and with
the cork make you a pinnace of five hundred ton, that
shall serve the turn marvellous well, my lord.   81

Erms. And I, my lord, will have pioners to under-
mine the town, that the very gardens and orchards be
carried away for your summer walks.

Miles. And I, with *scientia* and great *diligentia*,
Will conjure and charm, to keep you from harm;
That *utrum horum mavis*, your very great *navis*,

68 talis . . . Walis] tales . . . Wales (vulgar forms).   70
white] dear.   75–6 Bankside in Southwark] where most
of the London theatres stood.   79 pantofles] slippers.

Like Barclay's ship, from Oxford do skip
With colleges and schools, full-loaden with fools.
Quid dicis ad hoc, worshipful *Domine* Dawcock?   90
   Clem. Why, hare-brain'd courtiers, are you drunk
     or mad,
To taunt us up with such scurrility?
Deem you us men of base and light esteem,
To bring us such a fop for Henry's son?—
Call out the beadles and convey them hence
Straight to Bocardo: let the roisters lie
Close clapp'd in bolts, until their wits be tame.
   Erms. Why, shall we to prison, my lord?
   Ralph. What say'st, Miles, shall I honour the prison
with my presence?   100
   Miles. No, no: out with your blades, and hamper
     these jades;
Have a flirt and a crash, now play revel-dash,
And teach these sacerdos that the Bocardos,
Like peasants and elves, are meet for themselves.
   Mason. To the prison with them, constable.
   War. Well, doctors, seeing I have sported me
With laughing at these mad and merry wags,
Know that Prince Edward is at Brazen-nose,
And this, attired like the Prince of Wales,
Is Ralph, King Henry's only loved fool;   110
I, Earl of Sussex, and this Ermsby,
One of the privy-chamber to the king,
Who, while the prince with Friar Bacon stays,
Have revell'd it in Oxford as you see.
   Mason. My lord, pardon us, we knew not what you
     were:

88 Barclay's ship] *The Ship of Fools* by Sebastian Brant,
translated into English by Alexander Barclay (1509).
90 *Domine* Dawcock] master fool; expression borrowed
from Skelton.   94 fop] fool (not, as now, a dandy).
96 Bocardo] prison in Oxford.   102 flirt] blow.   revel-
dash] boisterous rush.   103 sacerdos] priests (wrongly
used as a plural).

But courtiers may make greater scapes than these.
Wilt please your honour dine with me to-day?

War. I will, Master doctor, and satisfy the vintner
for his hurt; only I must desire you to imagine him
all this forenoon the Prince of Wales.   120

Mason. I will, sir.

Ralph. And upon that I will lead the way; only I
will have Miles go before me, because I have heard
Henry say that wisdom must go before majesty.

[*Exeunt.*

Act III. Scene I.

Enter Prince Edward *with his poniard in his hand,*
Lacy *and* Margaret.

Edw. Lacy, thou canst not shroud thy traitorous
        thoughts,
Nor cover, as did Cassius all his wiles,
For Edward hath an eye that looks as far
As Lynceus from the shores of Graecia.
Did I not sit in Oxford by the friar,
And see thee court the maid of Fressingfield,
Sealing thy flattering fancies with a kiss?
Did not proud Bungay draw his portas forth,
And joining hand in hand had married you,
If Friar Bacon had not struck him dumb,   10
And mounted him upon a spirit's back,
That we might chat at Oxford with the friar?
Traitor, what answer'st? is not all this true?

Lacy. Truth all, my lord; and thus I make reply.
At Harleston Fair, there courting for your grace,
Whenas mine eye survey'd her curious shape,
And drew the beauteous glory of her looks
To dive into the centre of my heart,
Love taught me that your honour did but jest,
That princes were in fancy but as men;   20
How that the lovely maid of Fressingfield

8 portas] see II. iii. 137.   16 curious shape] rare beauty.

Was fitter to be Lacy's wedded wife,
Than concubine unto the Prince of Wales.

Edw.   Injurious Lacy, did I love thee more
Than Alexander his Hephaestion!
Did I unfold the passions of my love
And lock them in the closet of thy thoughts!
Wert thou to Edward second to himself,
Sole friend and partner of his secret loves!
And could a glance of fading beauty break   30
Th' enchained fetters of such private friends!
Base coward, false, and too effeminate
To be co-rival with a prince in thoughts!
From Oxford have I posted since I din'd,
To quite a traitor 'fore that Edward sleep.

Mar.   'Twas I, my lord, not Lacy, stept awry:
For oft he sued and courted for yourself,
And still woo'd for the courtier all in green;
But I, whom fancy made but over-fond,
Pleaded myself with looks as if I lov'd;   40
I fed mine eye with gazing on his face,
And still bewitch'd lov'd Lacy with my looks;
My heart with sighs, mine eyes pleaded with tears,
My face held pity and content at once,
And more I could not cipher out by signs
But that I lov'd Lord Lacy with my heart.
Then, worthy Edward, measure with thy mind
If women's favours will not force men fall,
If beauty, and if darts of piercing love,
Is not of force to bury thoughts of friends.   50

Edw.   I tell thee, Peggy, I will have thy loves:
Edward or none shall conquer Margaret.
In frigates bottom'd with rich Sethin planks,
Topp'd with the lofty firs of Lebanon,
Stemm'd and encas'd with burnish'd ivory,
And overlaid with plates of Persian wealth,
Like Thetis shalt thou wanton on the waves

35 quite] requite, *sc.* punish.

And draw the dolphins to thy lovely eyes,
To dance lavoltas in the purple streams:
Sirens with harps and silver psalteries,   60
Shall wait with music at thy frigate's stem,
And entertain fair Margaret with her lays.
England and England's wealth shall wait on thee;
Britain shall bend unto her prince's love,
And do due homage to thine excellence,
If thou wilt be but Edward's Margaret.

    Mar. Pardon, my lord: if Jove's great royalty
Sent me such presents as to Danaë;
If Phoebus tired in Latona's webs,
Came courting from the beauty of his lodge;   70
The dulcet tunes of frolic Mercury,—
Not all the wealth heaven's treasury affords,—
Should make me leave Lord Lacy or his love.

    Edw. I have learn'd at Oxford, then, this point
of schools,—

Ablata causa, tollitur effectus:

Lacy—the cause that Margaret cannot love,
Nor fix her liking on the English prince—
Take him away, and then the effects will fail.
Villain, prepare thyself: for I will bathe
My poniard in the bosom of an earl.   80

    Lacy. Rather than live, and miss fair Margaret's love,
Prince Edward, stop not at the fatal doom,
But stab it home: end both my loves and life.

    Mar. Brave Prince of Wales, honoured for royal
deeds,
'Twere sin to stain fair Venus' courts with blood;
Love's conquests end, my lord, in courtesy:
Spare Lacy, gentle Edward; let me die,
For so both you and he do cease your loves.

    Edw. Lacy shall die as traitor to his lord.

    Lacy. I have deserved it; Edward, act it well.   90

    Mar. What hopes the prince to gain by Lacy's death?

59 lavoltas] lively dances.   62 her] their.   69
tired] attired.   88 cease] end.

Edw. To end the loves 'twixt him and Margaret.

Mar. Why, thinks King Henry's son that Margaret's love

Hangs in the uncertain balance of proud time?

That death shall make a discord of our thoughts?

No, stab the earl, and 'fore the morning sun

Shall vaunt him thrice over the lofty east,

Margaret will meet her Lacy in the heavens.

Lacy. If aught betides to lovely Margaret

That wrongs or wrings her honour from content,   100

Europe's rich wealth nor England's monarchy

Should not allure Lacy to over-live:

Then, Edward, short my life and end her loves.

Mar. Rid me, and keep a friend worth many loves.

Lacy. Nay, Edward, keep a love worth many friends.

Mar. And if thy mind be such as fame hath blaz'd,

Then, princely Edward, let us both abide

The fatal resolution of thy rage:

Banish thou fancy, and embrace revenge,

And in one tomb knit both our carcases,   110

Whose hearts were linked in one perfect love.

Edw. Edward, art thou that famous Prince of Wales,

Who at Damasco beat the Saracens,

And brought'st home triumph on thy lance's point,

And shall thy plumes be pull'd by Venus down?

Is it princely to dissever lovers' leagues,

To part such friends as glory in their loves?

Leave, Ned, and make a virtue of this fault,

And further Peg and Lacy in their loves:

So, in subduing fancy's passion,   120

Conquering thyself, thou gett'st the richest spoil.—

Lacy, rise up. Fair Peggy, here's my hand:

The Prince of Wales hath conquered all his thoughts,

And all his loves he yields unto the earl.

Lacy, enjoy the maid of Fressingfield;

Make her thy Lincoln Countess at the church,

And Ned, as he is true Plantagenet,
Will give her to thee frankly for thy wife.

   Lacy. Humbly I take her of my sovereign,
As if that Edward gave me England's right,   130
And rich'd me with the Albion diadem.

   Mar. And doth the English prince mean true?
Will he vouchsafe to cease his former loves,
And yield the title of a country maid
Unto Lord Lacy?

   Edw. I will, fair Peggy, as I am true lord.

   Mar. Then, lordly sir, whose conquest is as great,
In conquering love, as Caesar's victories,
Margaret, as mild and humble in her thoughts
As was Aspasia unto Cyrus self,   140
Yields thanks, and, next Lord Lacy, doth enshrine
Edward the second secret in her heart.

   Edw. Gramercy, Peggy:—now that vows are past,
And that your loves are not to be revolt,
Once, Lacy, friends again. Come, we will post
To Oxford; for this day the king is there,
And brings for Edward Castile Elinor.
Peggy, I must go see and view my wife:
I pray God I like her as I loved thee!
Beside, Lord Lincoln, we shall hear dispute   150
'Twixt Friar Bacon and learned Vandermast.
Peggy, we'll leave you for a week or two.

   Mar. As it please Lord Lacy: but love's foolish looks
Think footsteps miles, and minutes to be hours.

   Lacy. I'll hasten, Peggy, to make short return.—
But please your honour go unto the lodge,
We shall have butter, cheese, and venison;
And yesterday I brought for Margaret
A lusty bottle of neat claret wine:
Thus can we feast and entertain your grace.   160

   Edw. 'Tis cheer, Lord Lacy, for an Emperor,

    144 revolt] overturned (Dickinson); or does it mean 'no
longer against your prince's will'?

If he respect the person and the place:
Come, let us in, for I will all this night
Ride post until I come to Bacon's cell.   [*Exeunt.*

Scene II.

Enter Henry, Emperor, Castile, Elinor, Vandermast, Bungay.

Emp.   Trust me, Plantagenet, these Oxford schools
Are richly seated near the river-side:
The mountains full of fat and fallow deer,
The battling pastures lade with kine and flocks,
The town gorgeous with high-built colleges,
And scholars seemly in their grave attire,
Learned in searching principles of art.—
What is thy judgment, Jaques Vandermast?

Van.   That lordly are the buildings of the town,
Spacious the rooms, and full of pleasant walks;   10
But for the doctors, how that they be learned,
It may be meanly, for aught I can hear.

Bun.   I tell thee, German, Hapsburg holds nonesuch,
None read so deep as Oxenford contains:
There are within our academic state
Men that may lecture it in Germany
To all the doctors of your Belgic schools.

Hen.   Stand to him, Bungay, charm this Vandermast,
And I will use thee as a royal king.

Van.   Wherein darest thou dispute with me?   20

Bun.   In what a doctor and a friar can.

Van.   Before rich Europe's worthies put thou forth
The doubtful question unto Vandermast.

Bun.   Let it be this,—Whether the spirits of pyromancy or geomancy, be most predominant in magic?

Van.   I say, of pyromancy.

4 battling] nourishing.   lade] laden.   24–5 pyro-
mancy] divination by fire.   25 geomancy] divination
by earth.

Bun. And I, of geomancy.

Van. The cabalists that write of magic spells,
As Hermes, Melchie, and Pythagoras,
Affirm that, 'mongst the quadruplicity   30
Of elemental essence, *terra* is but thought
To be a *punctum* squared to the rest;
And that the compass of ascending elements
Exceed in bigness as they do in height;
Judging the concave circle of the sun
To hold the rest in his circumference.
If, then, as Hermes says, the fire be great'st,
Purest, and only giveth shape to spirits,
Then must these *daemones* that haunt that place
Be every way superior to the rest.   40

Bun. I reason not of elemental shapes,
Nor tell I of the concave latitudes,
Noting their essence nor their quality,
But of the spirits that pyromancy calls,
And of the vigour of the geomantic fiends.
I tell thee, German, magic haunts the grounds,
And those strange necromantic spells
That work such shows and wondering in the world
Are acted by those geomantic spirits
That Hermes calleth *terrae filii.*   50
The fiery spirits are but transparent shades,
That lightly pass as heralds to bear news;
But earthly fiends, clos'd in the lowest deep,
Dissever mountains, if they be but charg'd,
Being more gross and massy in their power.

29 Hermes, Melchie] Hermes Trismegistus, Porphyrius.
30–1 quadruplicity|Of elemental essence] the four elements
of the Universe, *sc.* Earth, Water, Air, Fire.   32 *punctum*]
point (having position but no dimensions).   squared]
compared.   33 ascending] *sc.* from the centre of the Universe outward, in the order given.   35 concave] the
sun's apparent course during a day, concave as viewed
from Earth.   39 *daemones*] spirits.   47 necromantic]
pertaining to divination by means of the dead.

Van. Rather these earthly geomantic spirits
Are dull and like the place where they remain;
For when proud Lucifer fell from the heavens,
The spirits and angels that did sin with him,
Retain'd their local essence as their faults,   60
All subject under Luna's continent:
They which offended less hung in the fire,
And second faults did rest within the air;
But Lucifer and his proud-hearted fiends
Were thrown into the centre of the earth,
Having less understanding than the rest,
As having greater sin, and lesser grace.
Therefore such gross and earthly spirits do serve
For jugglers, witches, and vild sorcerers,
Whereas the pyromantic genii   70
Are mighty, swift, and of far-reaching power.
But grant that geomancy hath most force,
Bungay, to please these mighty potentates,
Prove by some instance what thy art can do.
    Bun. I will.
    Emp. Now, English Harry, here begins the game;
We shall see sport between these learned men.
    Van. What wilt thou do?
    Bun. Show thee the tree leav'd with refined gold,
Whereon the fearful dragon held his seat,   80
That watch'd the garden call'd Hesperides,
Subdu'd and won by conquering Hercules.

Here Bungay *conjures, and the Tree appears with the
        Dragon shooting fire.*

    Van. Well done!
    Hen. What say you, royal lordings, to my friar?
Hath he not done a point of cunning skill?
    Van. Each scholar in the necromantic spells
Can do as much as Bungay hath perform'd.
But as Alcmena's bastard raz'd this tree,
So will I raise him up as when he lived,

69 vild] vile.

And cause him pull the dragon from his seat,   90
And tear the branches piecemeal from the root.—
Hercules! *Prodi, prodi*, Hercules!

Hercules appears in his lion's skin.

Her. Quis me vult?

Van. Jove's bastard son, thou Libyan Hercules,
Pull off the sprigs from off the Hesperian tree,
As once thou didst to win the golden fruit.

Her. Fiat.   [*Here he begins to break the branches.*

Van. Now, Bungay, if thou canst, by magic, charm
The fiend appearing like great Hercules
From pulling down the branches of the tree,   100
Then art thou worthy to be counted learned.

Bun. I cannot.

Van. Cease, Hercules, until I give thee charge.—
Mighty commander of this English isle,
Henry, come from the stout Plantagenets,
Bungay is learned enough to be a friar;
But to compare with Jaques Vandermast,
Oxford and Cambridge must go seek their cells
To find a man to match him in his art.
I have given non-plus to the Paduans,   110
To them of Sien, Florence, and Bologna,
Rheims, Louvain, and fair Rotterdam,
Frankfort, Lutrech, and Orleans:
And now must Henry, if he do me right,
Crown me with laurel, as they all have done.

Enter Bacon.

Bacon. All hail to this royal company,
That sit to hear and see this strange dispute!—
Bungay, how stand'st thou as a man amaz'd?
What, hath the German acted more than thou?

Van. What art thou that questions thus?   120

Bacon. Men call me Bacon.

120 questions] questionest.

Van. Lordly thou lookest, as if that thou wert
    learn'd;
Thy countenance, as if science held her seat
Between the circled arches of thy brows.

Hen. Now, monarchs, hath the German found his
    match.

Emp. Bestir thee, Jaques, take not now the foil,
Lest thou dost lose what foretime thou didst gain.

Van. Bacon, wilt thou dispute?

Bacon. No, unless he were more learn'd than
    Vandermast;
For yet, tell me, what hast thou done?   **130**

Van. Rais'd Hercules to ruinate that tree,
That Bungay mounted by his magic spells.

Bacon. Set Hercules to work.

Van. Now, Hercules, I charge thee to thy task;
Pull off the golden branches from the root.

Her. I dare not; see'st thou not great Bacon here,
Whose frown doth act more than thy magic can?

Van. By all the thrones, and dominations,
Virtues, powers, and mighty hierarchies,
I charge thee to obey to Vandermast.   **140**

Her. Bacon, that bridles headstrong Belcephon,
And rules Asmenoth, guider of the north,
Binds me from yielding unto Vandermast.

Hen. How now, Vandermast, have you met with
    your match?

Van. Never before was't known to Vandermast
That men held devils in such obedient awe.
Bacon doth more than art, or else I fail.

Emp. Why, Vandermast, art thou overcome?—
Bacon, dispute with him, and try his skill.

Bacon. I come not, monarchs, for to hold dispute
With such a novice as is Vandermast;   **151**
I come to have your royalties to dine
With Friar Bacon here in Brazen-nose:

126 take not ... the foil] do not be overcome.   147 fail] err.

And, for this German troubles but the place,
And holds this audience with a long suspense,
I'll send him to his academy hence.—
Thou, Hercules, whom Vandermast did raise,
Transport the German unto Hapsburg straight,
That he may learn by travail, 'gainst the spring,
More secret dooms and aphorisms of art.   160
Vanish the tree, and, thou, away with him!
          [*Exit the spirit with* Vandermast *and the Tree.*
     Emp. Why, Bacon, whither dost thou send him?
     Bacon. To Hapsburg: there your highness at return
Shall find the German in his study safe.
     Hen. Bacon, thou hast honoured England with thy skill,
And made fair Oxford famous by thine art:
I will be English Henry to thyself;—
But tell me, shall we dine with thee to-day?
     Bacon. With me, my lord; and while I fit my cheer,
See where Prince Edward comes to welcome you,   170
Gracious as the morning-star of heaven—   [*Exit.*

     Enter Edward, Lacy, Warren, Ermsby.

     Emp. Is this Prince Edward, Henry's royal son?
How martial is the figure of his face!
Yet lovely and beset with amorets.
     Hen. Ned, where hast thou been?
     Edw. At Framlingham, my lord, to try your bucks
If they could scape the teisers or the toil.
But hearing of these lordly potentates
Landed, and progress'd up to Oxford town,
I posted to give entertain to them: 180
Chief to the Almain monarch; next to him,
And joint with him, Castile and Saxony
Are welcome as they may be to the English court.
Thus for the men: but see, Venus appears

---

160 dooms] laws.   169 fit my cheer] prepare my
entertainment.   174 amorets] love-kindling looks.
177 teisers] deerhounds.

Or one that overmatcheth Venus in her shape,
Sweet Elinor, beauty's high-swelling pride,
Rich nature's glory, and her wealth at once!
Fair of all fairs, welcome to Albion,
Welcome to me, and welcome to thine own,
If that thou deign'st the welcome from myself.   190

Elin. Martial Plantagenet, Henry's high-minded son,
The mark that Elinor did count her aim,
I lik'd thee 'fore I saw thee: now I love,
And so as in so short a time I may;
Yet so as time shall never break that 'so':
And therefore so accept of Elinor.

Cast. Fear not, my lord, this couple will agree,
If love may creep into their wanton eyes:—
And therefore, Edward, I accept thee here,
Without suspense, as my adopted son.   200

Hen. Let me that joy in these consorting greets
And glory in these honours done to Ned,
Yield thanks for all these favours to my son,
And rest a true Plantagenet to all.

Enter Miles *with a cloth and trenchers and salt.*

Miles. *Salvete, omnes reges,* that govern your *greges*
In Saxony and Spain, in England and in Almain!
For all this frolic rabble must I cover the table
With trenchers, salt, and cloth, and then look for your
    broth.

Emp. What pleasant fellow is this?   209

Hen. 'Tis, my lord, Doctor Bacon's poor scholar.

Miles. [*aside*] My master hath made me sewer of
these great lords; and, God knows, I am as serviceable
at a table as a sow is under an apple-tree: 'tis no
matter; their cheer shall not be great, and therefore
what skills where the salt stand, before or behind?
    [*Exit.*

---

201 consorting greets] fit speeches of welcome.   211
sewer] waiter at table.   215 what skills] what does
it matter.

Cast. These scholars knows more skill in axioms,
How to use quips and sleights of sophistry,
Than for to cover courtly for a king.

Enter Miles *with a mess of pottage and broth,*
and after him Bacon.

Miles. Spill, sir? why, do you think I never carried
twopenny chop before in my life?—   220
By your leave, *nobile decus,* for here comes Doctor
        Bacon's *pecus,*
Being in his full age to carry a mess of pottage.

Bacon. Lordings, admire not if your cheer be this,
For we must keep our academic fare;
No riot where philosophy doth reign:
And therefore, Henry, place these potentates,
And bid them fall into their frugal cates.

Emp. Presumptuous friar! what, scoff'st thou at a
        king?
What, dost thou taunt us with thy peasant's fare,
And give us cates fit for country swains?—   230
Henry, proceeds this jest of thy consent,
To twit us with a pittance of such price?
Tell me, and Frederick will not grieve thee long.

Hen. By Henry's honour, and the royal faith
The English monarch beareth to his friend,
I knew not of the friar's feeble fare,
Nor am I pleas'd he entertains you thus.

Bacon. Content thee, Frederick, for I show'd the
        cates
To let thee see how scholars use to feed;
How little meat refines our English wits.—   240
Miles, take away, and let it be thy dinner.

Miles. Marry, sir, I will.
This day shall be a festival-day with me,
For I shall exceed in the highest degree.   [*Exit.*

Bacon. I tell thee, monarch, all the German peers
Could not afford thy entertainment such,

223 admire] wonder.   244 exceed] have holiday fare.

So royal and so full of majesty,
As Bacon will present to Frederick.
The basest waiter that attends thy cups
Shall be in honours greater than thyself;   250
And for thy cates, rich Alexandria drugs,
Fetch'd by carvels from Egypt's richest straits,
Found in the wealthy strand of Africa,
Shall royalize the table of my king;
Wines richer than the 'gyptian courtesan
Quaff'd to Augustus' kingly countermatch
Shall be carous'd in English Henry's feasts:
Candy shall yield the richest of her canes;
Persia, down her Volga by canoes,
Send down the secrets of her spicery;   260
The Afric dates, myrobalans of Spain,
Conserves, and suckets from Tiberias,
Cates from Judaea, choicer than the lamp
That fired Rome with sparks of gluttony,
Shall beautify the board for Frederick:
And therefore grudge not at a friar's feast.

Scene III.

Enter two gentlemen, Lambert *and* Serlsby, *with the*
Keeper.

    Lam. Come, frolic Keeper of our liege's game,
Whose table spread hath ever venison
And jacks of wines to welcome passengers,
Know I am in love with jolly Margaret,
That overshines our damsels as the moon
Darkeneth the brightest sparkles of the night.
In Laxfield here my land and living lies:
I'll make thy daughter jointure of it all,
So thou consent to give her to my wife;
And I can spend five hundreth marks a year.   10

251 drugs] spices.   261 myrobalans] dried plums.
262 suckets] candied fruits.   3 jacks] bowls.   pas-
sengers] travellers.   9 to] to be.

Serl.   I am the lands-lord, Keeper, of thy holds,
By copy all thy living lies in me;
Laxfield did never see me raise my due:
I will enfeoff fair Margaret in all,
So she will take her to a lusty squire.
  Keep.   Now, courteous gentles, if the Keeper's girl
Hath pleased the liking fancy of you both,
And with her beauty hath subdued your thoughts,
'Tis doubtful to decide the question.
It joys me that such men of great esteem   20
Should lay their liking on this base estate,
And that her state should grow so fortunate
To be a wife to meaner men than you:
But sith such squires will stoop to keeper's fee,
I will, to avoid displeasure of you both,
Call Margaret forth, and she shall make her choice.
                                        [*Exit.*

  Lam.   Content, Keeper; send her unto us.
Why, Serlsby, is thy wife so lately dead,
Are all thy loves so lightly passed over,
As thou canst wed before the year be out?   30
  Serl.   I live not, Lambert, to content the dead,
Nor was I wedded but for life to her:
The grave ends and begins a married state.

Enter Margaret.

  Lam.   Peggy, the lovely flower of all towns,
Suffolk's fair Helen, and rich England's star,
Whose beauty, tempered with her huswifery,
Makes England talk of merry Fressingfield!
  Serl.   I cannot trick up it with poesies,
Nor paint my passions with comparisons,
Nor tell a tale of Phoebus and his loves: 40
But this believe me,—Laxfield here is mine,
Of ancient rent seven hundred pounds a year;
And if thou canst but love a country squire,
I will enfeoff thee, Margaret, in all:
I cannot flatter; try me, if thou please.

Mar. Brave neighbouring squires, the stay of
    Suffolk's clime.
A keeper's daughter is too base in gree
To match with men accounted of such worth:
But might I not displease, I would reply—   49
    Lam. Say, Peggy; naught shall make us discontent.
    Mar. Then, gentles, note that love hath little stay
Nor can the flames that Venus sets on fire
Be kindled but by fancy's motion:
Then pardon, gentles, if a maid's reply
Be doubtful, while I have debated with myself,
Who, or of whom, love shall constrain me like.
    Serl. Let it be me; and trust me, Margaret,
The meads environed with the silver streams,
Whose battling pastures fatteneth all my flocks,
Yielding forth fleeces stapled with such wool   60
As Lemster cannot yield more finer stuff,
And forty kine with fair and burnish'd heads,
With strouting dugs that paggle to the ground,
Shall serve thy dairy, if thou wed with me.
    Lam. Let pass the country wealth, as flocks and
    kine,
And lands that wave with Ceres' golden sheaves,
Filling my barns with plenty of the fields;
But, Peggy, if thou wed thyself to me,
Thou shalt have garments of embroider'd silk,
Lawns, and rich net-works for thy head-attire: 70
Costly shall be thy fair habiliments,
If thou wilt be but Lambert's loving wife.
    Mar. Content you, gentles, you have proffered
    fair,
And more than fits a country maid's degree:
But give me leave to counsel me a time,
For fancy blooms not at the first assault;
Give me but ten days' respite, and I will reply,

47 gree] degree.   59 battling] nourishing.   61
Lemster] Leominster.   63 strouting dugs] swelling
udders.   paggle] bulge.

Which or to whom myself affectionates.

  Serl. Lambert, I tell thee thou art importunate;
Such beauty fits not such a base esquire: 80
It is for Serlsby to have Margaret.

  Lam. Think'st thou with wealth to overreach me?
Serlsby, I scorn to brook thy country braves:
I dare thee, coward, to maintain this wrong,
At dint of rapier, single in the field.

  Serl. I'll answer, Lambert, what I have avouch'd.—
Margaret, farewell; another time shall serve.   [*Exit.*

  Lam. I'll follow.—Peggy, farewell to thyself;
Listen how well I'll answer for thy love.   [*Exit.*

  Mar. How fortune tempers lucky haps with frowns,
And wrongs me with the sweets of my delight!   91
Love is my bliss, and love is now my bale.
Shall I be Helen in my forward fates,
As I am Helen in my matchless hue,
And set rich Suffolk with my face afire?
If lovely Lacy were but with his Peggy,
The cloudy darkness of his bitter frown
Would check the pride of these aspiring squires.
Before the term of ten days be expired,
Whenas they look for answer of their loves,   100
My lord will come to merry Fressingfield,
And end their fancies and their follies both:
Till when, Peggy, be blithe and of good cheer.

    Enter a Post *with a letter and a bag of gold.*

  Post. Fair, lovely damsel, which way leads this
    path?
How might I post me unto Fressingfield?
Which footpath leadeth to the Keeper's lodge?

  Mar. Your way is ready, and this path is right:
Myself do dwell hereby in Fressingfield;
And if the Keeper be the man you seek,
I am his daughter: may I know the cause?   110

  Post. Lovely, and once beloved of my lord,—
No marvel if his eye was lodg'd so low,

When brighter beauty is not in the heavens!—
The Lincoln Earl hath sent you letters here,
And, with them, just an hundred pounds in gold.
Sweet, bonny wench, read them, and make reply.

Mar. The scrolls that Jove sent Danaë,
Wrapt in rich closures of fine burnish'd gold,
Were not more welcome than these lines to me.
Tell me, whilst that I do unrip the seals,   120
Lives Lacy well? how fares my lovely lord?

Post. Well, if that wealth may make men to live well.

The letter, and Margaret *reads it.*

The blooms of the almond-tree grow in a night, and
vanish in a morn; the flies hemerae, fair Peggy, take
life with the sun, and die with the dew; fancy that
slippeth in with a gaze, goeth out with a wink; and
too timely loves, have ever the shortest length. I
write this as thy grief, and my folly, who at Fressingfield lov'd that which time hath taught me to be but
mean dainties: eyes are dissemblers, and fancy is but
queasy; therefore know, Margaret, I have chosen a
Spanish lady to be my wife, chief waiting-woman to
the Princess Elinor; a lady fair, and no less fair than
thyself, honourable and wealthy. In that I forsake
thee, I leave thee to thine own liking; and for thy
dowry I have sent thee an hundred pounds; and ever
assure thee of my favour, which shall avail thee and
thine much. Farewell.

Not thine, nor his own,
Edward Lacy.

Fond Ate, doomer of bad-boding fates,   141
That wraps proud fortune in thy snaky locks,
Did'st thou enchant my birth-day with such stars
As lightned mischief from their infancy?
If heavens had vow'd, if stars had made decree,
To show on me their froward influence,

127 timely] early (or 'sudden'?).

If Lacy had but lov'd, heavens, hell, and all
Could not have wrong'd the patience of my mind.

 Post. It grieves me, damsel, but the earl is forc'd
To love the lady by the king's command.   150

 Mar. The wealth combin'd within the English
  shelves,
Europe's commander, nor the English king,
Should not have mov'd the love of Peggy from her
  lord.

 Post. What answer shall I return to my lord?

 Mar. First, for thou cam'st from Lacy whom I
  lov'd,—
Ah, give me leave to sigh at every thought!—
Take thou, my friend, the hundred pound he sent;
For Margaret's resolution craves no dower:
The world shall be to her as vanity;
Wealth, trash; love, hate; pleasure, despair: 160
For I will straight to stately Framlingham,
And in the abbey there be shorn a nun,
And yield my loves and liberty to God.
Fellow, I give thee this, not for the news,
For those be hateful unto Margaret,
But for th'art Lacy's man, once Margaret's love.

 Post. What I have heard, what passions I have seen,
I'll make report of them unto the earl.   [*Exit Post.*

 Mar. Say that she joys his fancies be at rest,
And prays that his misfortune may be hers.   [*Exit.*

Act IV. Scene I.

Enter Friar Bacon, *drawing the curtains, with a white stick,*
a book in his hand, and a lamp lighted by him, and the
Brazen Head; *and* Miles, *with weapons by him.*

 Bacon. Miles, where are you?

 Miles. Here, sir.

Bacon. How chance you tarry so long?

Miles. Think you that the watching of the Brazen Head craves no furniture? I warrant you, sir, I have so armed myself that if all your devils come, I will not fear them an inch.

Bacon. Miles, thou knowest that I have dived into hell,
And sought the darkest palaces of fiends;
That with my magic spells great Belcephon   10
Hath left his lodge and kneeled at my cell;
The rafters of the earth rent from the poles,
And three-form'd Luna hid her silver looks,
Trembling upon her concave continent,
When Bacon read upon his magic book.
With seven years' tossing necromantic charms,
Poring upon dark Hecat's principles,
I have fram'd out a monstrous head of brass,
That, by the enchanting forces of the devil,
Shall tell out strange and uncouth aphorisms,   20
And girt fair England with a wall of brass.
Bungay and I have watch'd these threescore days,
And now our vital spirits crave some rest:
If Argus liv'd, and had his hundred eyes,
They could not over-watch Phobetor's night.
Now, Miles, in thee rests Friar Bacon's weal:
The honour and renown of all his life
Hangs in the watching of this Brazen Head;
Therefore I charge thee by the immortal God,
That holds the souls of men within his fist,   30
This night thou watch; for ere the morning-star
Sends out his glorious glister on the north,
The head will speak: then, Miles, upon thy life,
Wake me; for then by magic art I'll work
To end my seven years' task with excellence.
If that a wink but shut thy watchful eye,
Then farewell Bacon's glory and his fame!

5 furniture] equipment.   20 uncouth] unknown.

Draw close the curtains, Miles: now, for thy life,
Be watchful, and—   [*Here he falleth asleep.*

Miles. So; I thought you would talk yourself asleep
anon, and 'tis no marvel, for Bungay on the days,
and he on the nights, have watch'd just these ten and
fifty days; now this is the night, and 'tis my task, and
no more. Now, Jesus bless me, what a goodly head it
is! and a nose! you talk of *nos autem glorificare*; but
here's a nose that I warrant may be call'd *nos autem
populare* for the people of the parish. Well, I am furnished with weapons: now, sir, I will set me down by
a post, and make it as good as a watchman to wake
me, if I chance to slumber. I thought, Goodman

*Sit down
and knock
your head.*

Head, I would call you out of your *memento*
. . . Passion o' God, I have almost broke my
pate! Up, Miles, to your task; take your

brown-bill in your hand; here's some of your master's
hobgoblins abroad.   55
                [*With this a great noise.   The* Head *speaks.*

Head. Time is.

Miles. Time is! Why, Master Brazen-head, have
you such a capital nose, and answer you with syllables,
'Time is'! Is this all my master's cunning, to spend
seven years' study about 'Time is'? Well, sir, it may
be we shall have some better orations of it anon: well,
I'll watch you as narrowly as ever you were watch'd,
and I'll play with you as the nightingale with the
slow-worm; I'll set a prick against my breast. Now
rest there, Miles.—Lord have mercy upon me, I have
almost killed myself! [*A great noise*]. Up, Miles; list
how they rumble.

Head. Time was.   68

Miles. Well, Friar Bacon, you have spent your seven
years' study well, that can make your head speak but
two words at once, 'Time was.' Yea, marry, time was
when my master was a wise man, but that was before

54 brown-bill] watchman's pike.

he began to make the Brazen Head. You shall lie
while your arse ache, an your Head speak no better.
Well, I will watch, and walk up and down, and be
a peripatetian and a philosopher of Aristotle's stamp.
[*A great noise.*] What, a fresh noise? Take thy pistols
in hand, Miles.

Here the Head *speaks and a lightning flasheth forth,
and a hand appears that breaketh down the* Head *with
a hammer.*

Head.   Time is past.   79
Miles.   Master, master, up, hell's broken loose!
your Head speaks, and there's such a thunder and
lightning, that I warrant all Oxford is up in arms!
Out of your bed, and take a brown-bill in your hand;
the latter day is come.
Bacon.   Miles, I come. O passing warily watch'd!
Bacon will make thee next himself in love.
When spake the head?
Miles.   When spake the head! did not you say that
he should tell strange principles of philosophy? Why,
sir, it speaks but two words at a time.   90
Bacon.   Why, villain, hath it spoken oft?
Miles.   Oft! ay, marry, hath it, thrice: but in all
those three times it hath uttered but seven words.
Bacon.   As how?
Miles.   Marry, sir, the first time he said, 'Time is,'
as if Fabius Cumentator should have pronounc'd a
sentence; he said 'Time was'; and the third time with
thunder and lightning, as in great choler, he said,
'Time is past.'
Bacon.   'Tis past indeed. Ah, villain! time is past:
My life, my fame, my glory, all are past.—   101
Bacon, the turrets of thy hope are ruin'd down,
Thy seven years' study lieth in the dust:
Thy Brazen Head lies broken through a slave,

74 while] until.   96 Cumentator] *sc.* Cunctator.

G

That watch'd, and would not when the Head did will.—
What said the Head first?

Miles. Even, sir, 'Time is.'

Bacon. Villain, if thou hadst call'd to Bacon then,
If thou hadst watch'd, and wak'd the sleepy friar,
The Brazen Head had uttered aphorisms,   110
And England had been circled round with brass:
But proud Asmenoth, ruler of the north,
And Demogorgon, master of the fates,
Grudge that a mortal man should work so much.
Hell trembled at my deep-commanding spells,
Fiends frown'd to see a man their over-match;
Bacon might boast more than a man might boast:
But now the braves of Bacon have an end,
Europe's conceit of Bacon hath an end,
His seven years' practice sorteth to ill end: 120
And, villain, sith my glory hath an end,
I will appoint thee to some fatal end.
Villain, avoid! get thee from Bacon's sight!
Vagrant, go roam and range about the world,
And perish as a vagabond on earth.

Miles. Why, then, sir, you forbid me your service?

Bacon. My service, villain! with a fatal curse,
That direful plagues and mischief fall on thee.   128

Miles. 'Tis no matter, I am against you with the old
proverb—'The more the fox is curst the better he
fares.' God be with you, sir; I'll take but a book in my
hand, a wide-sleeved gown on my back, and a crowned
cap on my head, and see if I can want promotion.

           [*Exit.*

Bacon. Some fiend or ghost haunt on thy weary
     steps,   134
Until they do transport thee quick to hell,
For Bacon shall have never merry day,
To lose the fame and honour of his Head.   [*Exit.*

---

119 conceit] esteem.   130 curst] pun on (*a*) cursed
and (*b*) coursed.

Scene II.

Enter Emperor, Castile, Henry, Elinor, Edward, Lacy,
Ralph.

Emp. Now, lovely prince, the prime of Albion's
  wealth,
How fares the Lady Elinor and you?
What, have you courted and found Castile fit
To answer England in equivalence?
Will 't be a match 'twixt bonny Nell and thee?

Edw. Should Paris enter in the courts of Greece,
And not lie fettered in fair Helen's looks,
Or Phoebus scape those piercing amorets,
That Daphne glanced at his deity!
Can Edward, then, sit by a flame and freeze,   10
Whose heat puts Helen and fair Daphne down?
Now, monarchs, ask the lady if we gree.

Hen. What, madam, hath my son found grace or
  no?

Elin. Seeing, my lord, his lovely counterfeit,
And hearing how his mind and shape agreed,
I came not, troop'd with all this warlike train,
Doubting of love, but so affectionate,
As Edward hath in England what he won in Spain.

Cast. A match, my lord; these wantons needs must
  love:
Men must have wives, and women will be wed: 20
Let 's haste the day to honour up the rites.

Ralph. Sirrah Harry, shall Ned marry Nell?

Hen. Ay, Ralph; how then?

Ralph. Marry, Harry, follow my counsel: send for
Friar Bacon to marry them, for he'll so conjure him and
her with his necromancy, that they shall love together
like pig and lamb whilst they live.

Cast. But hearest thou, Ralph, art thou content to
have Elinor to thy lady?

4 equivalence] equal value.   8 amorets] love-kindling
looks.   12 gree] agree.   29 to thy lady] for, &c.

Ralph. Ay, so she will promise me two things.   30

Cast. What's that, Ralph?

Ralph. That she will never scold with Ned, nor
fight with me.—Sirrah Harry, I have put her down
with a thing unpossible.

Hen. What's that, Ralph?

Ralph. Why, Harry, didst thou ever see that a
woman could both hold her tongue and her hands?
No! but when egg-pies grows on apple-trees, then will
thy grey mare prove a bag-piper.

Emp. What say the Lord of Castile and the Earl of
Lincoln, that they are in such earnest and secret talk?

Cast. I stand, my lord, amazed at his talk,   42
How he discourseth of the constancy
Of one surnam'd, for beauty's excellence,
The Fair Maid of merry Fressingfield.

Hen. 'Tis true, my lord, 'tis wondrous for to hear;
Her beauty passing Mars's paramour,
Her virgin's right as rich as Vesta's was:
Lacy and Ned hath told me miracles.

Cast. What says Lord Lacy? shall she be his wife?

Lacy. Or else Lord Lacy is unfit to live.—   51
May it please your highness give me leave to post
To Fressingfield, I'll fetch the bonny girl,
And prove in true appearance at the court,
What I have vouched often with my tongue.

Hen. Lacy, go to the querry of my stable,
And take such coursers as shall fit thy turn:
Hie thee to Fressingfield, and bring home the lass:
And, for her fame flies through the English coast,
If it may please the Lady Elinor,   60
One day shall match your excellence and her.

Elin. We Castile ladies are not very coy;
Your highness may command a greater boon:
And glad were I to grace the Lincoln Earl
With being partner of his marriage-day.

33 put her down] overcome her.   56 querry] equerry.

Edw. Gramercy, Nell, for I do love the lord,
As he that's second to myself in love.

Ralph. You love her?—Madam Nell, never believe
him you, though he swears he loves you.

Elin. Why, Ralph?   70

Ralph. Why, his love is like unto a tapster's glass
that is broken with every touch; for he loved the fair
maid of Fressingfield once out of all ho.—Nay, Ned,
never wink upon me: I care not, I.

Hen. Ralph tells all; you shall have a good secre-
tary of him.—

But, Lacy, haste thee post to Fressingfield;
For ere thou hast fitted all things for her state,
The solemn marriage-day will be at hand.

Lacy. I go, my lord.   [*Exit* Lacy.

Emp. How shall we pass this day, my lord?   80

Hen. To horse, my lord; the day is passing fair:
We'll fly the partridge, or go rouse the deer.
Follow, my lords; you shall not want for sport.

                                              [*Exeunt.*

Scene III.

Enter Friar Bacon, *with* Friar Bungay, *in his cell.*

Bun. What means the friar that frolick'd it of late,
To sit as melancholy in his cell,
As if he had neither lost nor won to-day?

Bacon. Ah, Bungay, my Brazen Head is spoil'd,
My glory gone, my seven years' study lost!
The fame of Bacon, bruited through the world,
Shall end and perish with this deep disgrace.

Bun. Bacon hath built foundation of his fame
So surely on the wings of true report,
With acting strange and uncouth miracles,   10
As this cannot infringe what he deserves.

Bacon. Bungay, sit down, for by prospective skill
I find this day shall fall out ominous:

      73 all ho] all bounds.

Some deadly act shall tide me ere I sleep:
But what and wherein little can I guess.
My mind is heavy, whatso'er shall hap.

Enter two Scholars, *sons to* Lambert *and* Serlsby.
Knock.

Who's that knocks?

Bun. Two scholars that desires to speak with you.

Bacon. Bid them come in.—Now, my youths, what
would you have?   20

1st Schol. Sir, we are Suffolkmen and neighbouring
    friends:
Our fathers in their countries lusty squires;
Their lands adjoin: in Cratfield mine doth dwell,
And his in Laxfield. We are college-mates,
Sworn brothers, as our fathers lives as friends.

Bacon. To what end is all this?

2nd Schol. Hearing your worship kept within your
    cell
A glass prospective, wherein men might see
Whatso their thoughts or hearts' desire could wish,
We come to know how that our fathers fare.   30

Bacon. My glass is free for every honest man.
Sit down, and you shall see ere long,
How or in what state your friendly fathers lives.
Meanwhile, tell me your names.

1st Schol. Mine Lambert.

2nd Schol. And mine Serlsby.

Bacon. Bungay, I smell there will be a tragedy.

Enter Lambert *and* Serlsby, *with rapiers and daggers.*

Lam. Serlsby, thou hast kept thine hour like a man:
Th'art worthy of the title of a squire,
That durst, for proof of thy affection   40
And for thy mistress' favour, prize thy blood.
Thou know'st what words did pass at Fressingfield,

14. tide] betide.   37 s.d. *Enter* Lambert *&c.*] as before
(II. iii. 10) on the outer stage.   41 prize] venture.

Such shameless braves as manhood cannot brook:
Ay, for I scorn to bear such piercing taunts,
Prepare thee, Serlsby; one of us will die.

Serl.   Thou seest I single thee the field,
And what I spake, I'll maintain with my sword:
Stand on thy guard, I cannot scold it out.
And if thou kill me, think I have a son,
That lives in Oxford in the Broadgates Hall,   50
Who will revenge his father's blood with blood.

Lam.   And, Serlsby, I have there a lusty boy,
That dares at weapon buckle with thy son,
And lives in Broadgates too, as well as thine:
But draw thy rapier, for we'll have a bout.

Bacon.   Now, lusty younkers, look within the glass,
And tell me if you can discern your sires.

1st Schol.   Serlsby, 'tis hard; thy father offers wrong.
To combat with my father in the field.

2nd Schol.   Lambert, thou liest, my father's is the
    abuse,   60
And thou shalt find it, if my father harm.

Bun.   How goes it, sirs?

1st Schol.   Our fathers are in combat hard by Fres-
    singfield.

Bacon.   Sit still, my friends, and see the event.

Lam.   Why stand'st thou, Serlsby? doubt'st thou of
    thy life?
A veney, man! fair Margaret craves so much.

Serl.   Then this for her.

1st Schol.   Ah, well thrust!

2nd Schol.   But mark the ward.

> [*They fight and kill each other.*

Lam.   O, I am slain!   70

Serl.   And I,—Lord have mercy on me!

46 single thee the field] take thee apart to fight; it has
been proposed to read 'single meet thee in the field', which
improves the sense slightly and the metre greatly but is
rather violent.   50 Broadgates Hall] now part of Pem-
broke College.   66 veney] bout.

1st Schol. My father slain!—Serlsby, ward that!

2nd Schol. And so is mine!—Lambert, I'll quite
thee well.   [*The two* Scholars *stab one other.*

Bun. O strange stratagem!

Bacon. See, friar, where the fathers doth lie dead!—
Bacon, thy magic doth effect this massacre:
This glass prospective worketh many woes;
And therefore seeing these brave lusty Brutes,
These friendly youths, did perish by thine art,
End all thy magic and thine art at once.   80
The poniard that did end their fatal lives,
Shall break the cause efficient of their woes.
So fade the glass, and end with it the shows
That necromancy did infuse the crystal with.

            [*He breaks the glass.*

Bun. What means learned Bacon thus to break his
glass?

Bacon. I tell thee, Bungay, it repents me sore
That ever Bacon meddled in this art.
The hours I have spent in pyromantic spells,
The fearful tossing in the latest night
Of papers full of necromantic charms,   90
Conjuring and adjuring devils and fiends,
With stole and alb and strange pentageron;
The wresting of the holy name of God,
As Soter, Eloim, and Adonai,
Alpha, Manoth, and Tetragrammaton,
With praying to the five-fold powers of heaven,
Are instances that Bacon must be damn'd,
For using devils to countervail his God.—
Yet, Bacon, cheer thee, drown not in despair:
Sins have their salves, repentance can do much: 100
Think Mercy sits where Justice holds her seat,
And from those wounds those bloody Jews did pierce,
Which by thy magic oft did bleed afresh,
From thence for thee the dew of mercy drops,

78 Brutes] Britons.

To wash the wrath of high Jehovah's ire,
And make thee as a new-born babe from sin.—
Bungay, I'll spend the remnant of my life
In pure devotion, praying to my God
That he would save what Bacon vainly lost. [*Exeunt.*

Act V. Scene I.

Enter Margaret *in nun's apparel,* Keeper, *her father, and their* Friend.

Keeper. Margaret, be not so headstrong in these vows:
O, bury not such beauty in a cell,
That England hath held famous for the hue!
Thy father's hair, like to the silver blooms
That beautify the shrubs of Africa,
Shall fall before the dated time of death,
Thus to forgo his lovely Margaret.
Mar. Ah, father, when the harmony of heaven
Soundeth the measures of a lively faith,
The vain illusions of this flattering world   10
Seem odious to the thoughts of Margaret.
I loved once—Lord Lacy was my love—
And now I hate myself for that I lov'd,
And doted more on him than on my God:
For this I scourge myself with sharp repents.
But now the touch of such aspiring sins
Tells me all love is lust but love of heavens;
That beauty us'd for love is vanity:
The world contains naught but alluring baits,
Pride, flattery, and inconstant thoughts.   20
To shun the pricks of death, I leave the world,
And vow to meditate on heavenly bliss,
To live in Framlingham a holy nun,
Holy and pure in conscience and in deed;

13 for that] because.

And for to wish all maids to learn of me
To seek heaven's joy before earth's vanity.

Friend. And will you then, Margaret, be shorn a
nun, and so leave us all?

Mar. Now farewell, world, the engine of all woe!
Farewell to friends and father! welcome Christ!   30
Adieu to dainty robes! this base attire
Better befits an humble mind to God
Than all the show of rich habiliments.
Farewell, O love, and, with fond love, farewell
Sweet Lacy, whom I loved once so dear!
Ever be well, but never in my thoughts,
Lest I offend, to think on Lacy's love:
But even to that, as to the rest, farewell!

Enter Lacy, Warren *and* Ermsby, *booted and spurred.*

Lacy.   Come on, my wags, we're near the Keeper's
lodge.
Here have I oft walk'd in the watery meads,   40
And chatted with my lovely Margaret.

War.   Sirrah Ned, is not this the Keeper?

Lacy.   'Tis the same.

Erms.   The old lecher hath gotten holy mutton to
him! A nun, my lord.

Lacy.   Keeper, how farest thou? holla, man, what
cheer?
How doth Peggy, thy daughter and my love?

Keeper.   Ah, good my lord! O, woe is me for Peg!
See where she stands clad in her nun's attire,
Ready for to be shorn in Framlingham: 50
She leaves the world because she left your love.
O, good my lord, persuade her if you can!

Lacy.   Why, how now, Margaret! what, a mal-
content?
A nun? what holy father taught you this,
To task yourself to such a tedious life

44 mutton] cant term for a prostitute.

As die a maid? 'twere injury to me
To smother up such beauty in a cell.

   Mar. Lord Lacy, thinking of thy former miss,
How fond the prime of wanton years were spent
In love—O, fie upon that fond conceit,   60
Whose hap and essence hangeth in the eye!—
I leave both love and love's content at once,
Betaking me to him that is true love,
And leaving all the world for love of him.

   Lacy. Whence, Peggy, comes this metamorphosis?
What, shorn a nun, and I have from the court
Posted with coursers to convey thee hence
To Windsor, where our marriage shall be kept!
Thy wedding robes are in the tailor's hands.
Come, Peggy, leave these peremptory vows.   70

   Mar. Did not my lord resign his interest,
And make divorce 'twixt Margaret and him?

   Lacy. 'Twas but to try sweet Peggy's constancy.
But will fair Margaret leave her love and lord?

   Mar. Is not heaven's joy before earth's fading bliss,
And life above sweeter than life in love?

   Lacy. Why then, Margaret will be shorn a nun?

   Mar. Margaret hath made a vow which may not be
   revok'd.

   War. We cannot stay, my lord; an if she be so
   strict,
Our leisure grants us not to woo afresh.   80

   Erms. Choose you, fair damsel,—yet the choice is
   yours,—
Either a solemn nunnery or the court,
God or Lord Lacy: which contents you best,
To be a nun, or else Lord Lacy's wife?

   Lacy. A good motion.—Peggy, your answer must be
short.

   Mar. The flesh is frail; my lord doth know it well,
That when he comes with his enchanting face,

58 miss] offence.

Whatsoe'er betide I cannot say him nay.
Off goes the habit of a maiden's heart,
And, seeing fortune will, fair Framlingham,   90
And all the show of holy nuns, farewell!
Lacy for me, if he will be my lord.

 Lacy. Peggy, thy lord, thy love, thy husband.
Trust me, by truth of knighthood, that the king
Stays for to marry matchless Elinor,
Until I bring thee richly to the court,
That one day may both marry her and thee.—
How say'st thou, Keeper? art thou glad of this?

 Keeper. As if the English king had given
The park and deer of Fressingfield to me.   100

 Erms. I pray thee, my lord of Sussex, why art thou
in a brown study?

 War. To see the nature of women; that be they
never so near God, yet they love to die in a man's
arms.

 Lacy. What have you fit for breakfast? We have
hied
And posted all this night to Fressingfield.

 Mar. Butter and cheese, and umbles of a deer,
Such as poor keepers have within their lodge

 Lacy. And not a bottle of wine?   110

 Mar. We'll find one for my lord.

 Lacy. Come, Sussex, let's in: we shall have more,
for she speaks least, to hold her promise sure.

            [Exeunt.

Scene II.

Enter a Devil *to seek* Miles.

 Dev. How restless are the ghosts of hellish spirits,
When every charmer with his magic spells
Calls us from nine-fold-trenched Phlegethon,
To scud and over-scour the earth in post

---

108 umbles] liver, kidneys, &c., the Keeper's perquisites.

Upon the speedy wings of swiftest winds!
Now Bacon hath rais'd me from the darkest deep,
To search about the world for Miles his man,
For Miles, and to torment his lazy bones
For careless watching of his Brazen Head.
See where he comes: O, he is mine!   10

Enter Miles *with a gown and a corner-cap.*

Miles. A scholar, quoth you! marry, sir, I would I
had been made a bottle-maker when I was made a
scholar, for I can get neither to be a deacon, reader,
nor schoolmaster, no, not the clerk of a parish. Some
call me dunce; another saith, my head is full of Latin
as an egg's full of oatmeal: thus I am tormented, that
the devil and Friar Bacon haunts me.—Good Lord,
here's one of my master's devils! I'll go speak to him.
—What, Master Plutus, how cheer you?

Dev. Dost thou know me?   20

Miles. Know you, sir! why, are not you one of my
master's devils, that were wont to come to my master,
Doctor Bacon, at Brazen-nose?

Dev. Yes, marry, am I.

Miles. Good Lord, Master Plutus, I have seen you
a thousand times at my master's, and yet I had never
the manners to make you drink. But, sir, I am glad to
see how conformable you are to the statute.—I warrant you, he's as yeomanly a man as you shall see:
mark you, masters, here's a plain, honest man, without welt or guard.—But I pray you, sir, do you come
lately from hell?   32

Dev. Ay, marry: how then?

Miles. Faith, 'tis a place I have desired long to see:
have you not good tippling-houses there? may not a
man have a lusty fire there, a pot of good ale, a pair of

31 welt or guard] ornament or facing; a reference to
one of the many sumptuary laws regulating the dress of
different ranks of society.   36 pair] pack.

cards, a swinging piece of chalk, and a brown toast
that will clap a white waistcoat on a cup of good
drink?

Dev. All this you may have there.   40

Miles. You are for me, friend, and I am for you.
But I pray you, may I not have an office there?

Dev. Yes, a thousand: what would'st thou be?

Miles. By my troth, sir, in a place where I may
profit myself. I know hell is a hot place, and men are
marvellous dry, and much drink is spent there; I
would be a tapster.

Dev. Thou shalt.

Miles. There's nothing lets me from going with
you, but that 'tis a long journey, and I have never
a horse.   51

Dev. Thou shalt ride on my back.

Miles. Now surely here's a courteous devil, that,
for to pleasure his friend, will not stick to make a jade
of himself.—But I pray you, goodman friend, let me
move a question to you.

Dev. What's that?

Miles. I pray you, whether is your pace a trot or an
amble?

Dev. An amble.   60

Miles. 'Tis well; but take heed it be not a trot: but
'tis no matter, I'll prevent it.

Dev. What dost?

Miles. Marry, friend, I put on my spurs; for if
I find your pace either a trot or else uneasy, I'll put
you to a false gallop; I'll make you feel the benefit of
my spurs.

Dev. Get up upon my back.

Miles. O Lord, here's even a goodly marvel, when
a man rides to hell on the devil's back!   70

[*Exeunt roaring.*

49 lets] deters.   55 friend] perhaps the word should
be 'fiend'.

Scene III.

Enter the Emperor *with a pointless sword; next the* King of Castile *carrying a sword with a point;* Lacy *carrying the globe;* Edward; Warren *carrying a rod of gold with a dove on it;* Ermsby *with a crown and sceptre; the* Queen *with the fair maid of Fressingfield on her left hand;* Henry; Bacon *with other Lords attending.*

Edw. Great potentates, earth's miracles for state,
Think that Prince Edward humbles at your feet,
And, for these favours, on his martial sword
He vows perpetual homage to yourselves,
Yielding these honours unto Elinor.

Hen. Gramercies, lordings; old Plantagenet,
That rules and sways the Albion diadem,
With tears discovers these conceived joys,
And vows requital, if his men-at-arms,
The wealth of England, or due honours done   10
To Elinor, may quite his favourites.
But all this while what say you to the dames
That shine like to the crystal lamps of heaven?

Emp. If but a third were added to these two,
They did surpass those gorgeous images
That gloried Ida with rich beauty's wealth.

Mar. 'Tis I, my lords, who humbly on my knee
Must yield her orisons to mighty Jove
For lifting up his handmaid to this state,
Brought from her homely cottage to the court,   20
And grac'd with kings, princes, and emperors,
To whom (next to the noble Lincoln Earl)
I vow obedience, and such humble love
As may a handmaid to such mighty men.

Elin. Thou martial man that wears the Almain
   crown,

Heading. pointless sword] emblem of Mercy.   sword
with a point] emblem of Justice.   globe] emblem of
Sovereignty.   rod of gold] emblem of Equity.   11
quite] requite.

And you the western potentates of might,
The Albion princess, English Edward's wife,
Proud that the lovely star of Fressingfield,
Fair Margaret, Countess to the Lincoln Earl,
Attends on Elinor,—gramercies, lord, for her,—   30
'Tis I give thanks for Margaret to you all,
And rest for her due-bounden to yourselves.

Hen.   Seeing the marriage is solemnized,
Let's march in triumph to the royal feast.—
But why stands Friar Bacon here so mute?

Bacon.   Repentant for the follies of my youth,
That magic's secret mysteries misled,
And joyful that this royal marriage
Portends such bliss unto this matchless realm.

Hen.   Why, Bacon, what strange event shall happen
  to this land?   40
Or what shall grow from Edward and his Queen?

Bacon.   I find by deep prescience of mine art,
Which once I temper'd in my secret cell,
That here where Brute did build his Troynovant,
From forth the royal garden of a king
Shall flourish out so rich and fair a bud,
Whose brightness shall deface proud Phoebus' flower,
And overshadow Albion with her leaves.
Till then Mars shall be master of the field,
But then the stormy threats of wars shall cease: 50
The horse shall stamp as careless of the pike,
Drums shall be turn'd to timbrels of delight;
With wealthy favours plenty shall enrich
The strand that gladded wandering Brute to see;
And peace from heaven shall harbour in these leaves,
That, gorgeous, beautifies this matchless flower:
Apollo's Hellitropian then shall stoop,
And Venus' hyacinth shall vail her top;
Juno shall shut her gilliflowers up,

44 Brute] the mythical Trojan founder of Britain.
Troynovant] New Troy, *sc.* London.   46 bud] *sc.* Queen
Elizabeth.   57 Hellitropian] heliotrope.

And Pallas' bay shall bash her brightest green; 60
Ceres' carnation, in consort with those,
Shall stoop and wonder at Diana's rose.
    Hen.   This prophecy is mystical.—
But, glorious commanders of Europa's love,
That make fair England like that wealthy isle
Circled with Gihon and swift Euphrates,
In royalizing Henry's Albion
With presence of your princely mightiness,
Let's march: the tables all are spread,
And viands such as England's wealth affords 70
Are ready set to furnish out the boards.
You shall have welcome, mighty potentates:
It rests to furnish up this royal feast,
Only your hearts be frolic; for the time
Craves that we taste of naught but jouissance.
Thus glories England over all the west.

[Exeunt Omnes.

Finis Friar Bacon, made by Robert Greene,
Master of Arts.

Omne tulit punctum qui miscuit utile dulci.

60 bash] be ashamed of.   *Omne tulit punctum &c.*]
Horace, *Ars Poetica*, line 343, adopted by Greene as his
motto: 'He gains the applause of all who combines what is
useful with what is pleasing.'

THE SHOEMAKER'S HOLIDAY

BY

THOMAS DEKKER

THOMAS DEKKER (1572–1632)

The Shoemaker's Holiday

Acted perhaps not long before 1600; printed in 1600.

[*Dramatic Works*, ed. R. H. Shepherd (Pearson's Reprints), 4 vols., 1873, and *Non-Dramatic Works*, ed. A. B. Grosart, 5 vols., 1884–6 (including a play omitted by Shepherd), are scarce, costly, and unreliable. Some of the non-dramatic works are collected in *The Plague Pamphlets of Thomas Dekker*, ed. F. P. Wilson, Oxford, 1925, and the Cambridge University Press has announced that it has in preparation the *Dramatic Works*, ed. W. P. Barrett (to whom the present editor is indebted for the loan of rotographs).]

THE
SHOMAKERS
Holiday.
OR
The Gentle Craft.

With the humorous life of Simon
Eyre, shoomaker, and Lord Maior
of London.

As it was acted before the Queenes most excellent Ma-
iestie on New-yeares day at night last, by the right
honourable the Earle of Notingham, Lord high Ad-
mirall of England, his seruants.

Printed by Valentine Sims dwelling at the foote of Adling
hill, neere Bainards Castle, at the signe of the White
Swanne, and are there to be sold.
1600.

To all good Fellows, Professors of *the Gentle Craft, of what degree* soever.

Kɪɴᴅ Gentlemen, and honest boon companions, I present you here with a merry conceited comedy called *The Shoemaker's Holiday*, acted by my Lord Admiral's Players this present Christmas before the Queen's Most Excellent Majesty, for the mirth and pleasant matter by her Highness graciously accepted, being indeed no way offensive. The Argument of the play I will set down in this Epistle: Sir Hugh Lacy, Earl of Lincoln, had a young gentleman of his own name, his near kinsman, that loved the Lord Mayor's daughter of London, to prevent and cross which love the Earl caused his kinsman to be sent Colonel of a Company into France, who resigned his place to another gentleman his friend, and came disguised like a Dutch shoemaker to the house of Simon Eyre in Tower Street, who served the Mayor and his household with shoes. The merriments that passed in Eyre's house, his coming to be Mayor of London, Lacy's getting his love, and other accidents, with two merry Three-men's songs—take all in good worth that is well intended, for nothing is purposed but mirth; mirth lengtheneth long life, which, with all other blessings, I heartily wish you.   23

Farewell.

Heading. *Gentle Craft*] shoemakers.   2 conceited] spirited.   11 cross] thwart.   19 accidents] incidents. 20 good worth] good part.

The first Three-man's
Song.

O the month of May, the merry month of May,
So frolic, so gay, and so green, so green, so green!
O, and then did I unto my true love say:
'Sweet Peg, thou shalt be my Summer's Queen!

'Now the Nightingale, the pretty Nightingale,
The sweetest singer in all the forest's choir,
Entreats thee, sweet Peggy, to hear thy true love's
       tale;
Lo, yonder she sitteth, her breast against a brier.

'But O, I spy the Cuckoo, the Cuckoo, the Cuckoo;
See where she sitteth: come away, my joy;   10
Come away, I prithee, I do not like the Cuckoo
Should sing where my Peggy and I kiss and toy.'

O the month of May, the merry month of May,
So frolic, so gay, and so green, so green, so green!
And then did I unto my true love say:
'Sweet Peg, thou shalt be my summer's queen!'

The second Three-man's
Song.

This is to be sung at the latter end.

Cold's the wind, and wet's the rain,
    Saint Hugh be our good speed:
Ill is the weather that bringeth no gain,
    Nor helps good hearts in need.

Trowl the bowl, the jolly nut-brown bowl,
    And here, kind mate, to thee:
Let's sing a dirge for Saint Hugh's soul,
    And down it merrily.

2nd Song. 2 Saint Hugh] patron saint of shoemakers.
5 Trowl] pass round.

Down a down, hey down a down,
          [Close with the tenor boy.
  Hey derry derry, down a down!   10
Ho, well done; to me let come!
  Ring compass, gentle joy.

Trowl the bowl, the nut-brown bowl,
  And here, kind, *&c. as often as there be men
  to drink.*

    At last when all have drunk, this verse:

Cold's the wind, and wet's the rain,
  Saint Hugh be our good speed:
Ill is the weather that bringeth no gain,
  Nor helps good hearts in need.

12 Ring compass] produce the full range of notes.

The Prologue as it was pronounced
before the Queen's
Majesty.

As wretches in a storm (expecting day),
With trembling hands and eyes cast up to heaven,
Make prayers the anchor of their conquer'd hopes,
So we, dear goddess, wonder of all eyes,
Your meanest vassals (through mistrust and fear
To sink into the bottom of disgrace
By our imperfect pastimes) prostrate thus
On bended knees, our sails of hope do strike,
Dreading the bitter storms of your dislike.
Since then, unhappy men, our hap is such,   10
That to ourselves ourselves no help can bring,
But needs must perish, if your saint-like ears
(Locking the temple where all mercy sits)
Refuse the tribute of our begging tongues:
Oh grant, bright mirror of true chastity,
From those life-breathing stars, your sun-like eyes,
One gracious smile: for your celestial breath
Must send us life, or sentence us to death.

     1 expecting] awaiting.

Dramatis Personae

THE KING.

THE EARL OF CORNWALL.

SIR HUGH LACY, *Earl of Lincoln.*

ROWLAND LACY, *otherwise* Hans, } *his Nephews.*
ASKEW,

SIR ROGER OTELEY, *Lord Mayor of London.*

MASTER HAMMON,
MASTER WARNER, } *Citizens of London.*
MASTER SCOTT,

SIMON EYRE, *the Shoemaker.*

ROGER, *commonly called* HODGE,
FIRK, } *Eyre's Journeymen.*
RALPH,

LOVELL, *a courtier.*

DODGER, *Servant to the Earl of Lincoln.*

A Dutch Skipper.

A Boy.

Courtiers, Attendants, Officers, Soldiers, Hunters, Shoe-
    makers, Apprentices, Servants.

ROSE, *Daughter of Sir Roger.*

SYBIL, *her maid.*

MARGERY, *Wife of Simon Eyre.*

JANE, *Wife of Ralph.*

A pleasant Comedy of
the Gentle Craft

Act I. Scene I.

Enter Lord Mayor *and* Lincoln.

Lincoln. My lord mayor, you have sundry times
Feasted myself and many courtiers more:
Seldom or never can we be so kind
To make requital of your courtesy.
But leaving this, I hear my cousin **Lacy**
Is much affected to your daughter Rose.

    Lord Mayor. True, my good lord, and she loves him
      so well
That I mislike her boldness in the chase.

    Lincoln. Why, my lord mayor, think you it then a
      shame,
To join a Lacy with an Oteley's name?   10

    Lord Mayor. Too mean is my poor girl for his high
      birth;
Poor citizens must not with courtiers wed,
Who will in silks and gay apparel spend
More in one year than I am worth, by far:
Therefore your honour need not doubt my girl.

    Lincoln. Take heed, my lord, advise you what you
      do!
A verier unthrift lives not in the world,
Than is my cousin; for I'll tell you what:
'Tis now almost a year since he requested
To travel countries for experience;   20
I furnish'd him with coin, bills of exchange,
Letters of credit, men to wait on him,
Solicited my friends in Italy
Well to respect him: but to see the end:

    3 kind] courteous.   6 affected to] attracted by.   15
doubt] fear.   24 respect] treat.

Scant had he journeyed through half Germany,
But all his coin was spent, his men cast off,
His bills embezzl'd, and my jolly coz,
Asham'd to show his bankrupt presence here,
Became a shoemaker in Wittenberg,
A goodly science for a gentleman   30
Of such descent! Now judge the rest by this:
Suppose your daughter have a thousand pound,
He did consume me more in one half year;
And, make him heir to all the wealth you have,
One twelvemonth's rioting will waste it all.
Then seek, my lord, some honest citizen
To wed your daughter to.

    Lord Mayor.   I thank your lordship.—
[*Aside*]. Well, fox, I understand your subtilty.—
As for your nephew, let your lordship's eye
But watch his actions, and you need not fear,   40
For I have sent my daughter far enough.
And yet your cousin Rowland might do well,
Now he hath learn'd an occupation;
And yet I scorn to call him son-in-law.

    Lincoln. Ay, but I have a better trade for him:
I thank his grace, he hath appointed him
Chief colonel of all those companies
Mustered in London and the shires about,
To serve his highness in those wars of France.
See where he comes!—Lovell, what news with you?

          Enter Lovell, Lacy, and Askew.

    Lovell. My Lord of Lincoln, 'tis his highness' will,
That presently your cousin ship for France   52
With all his powers; he would not for a million,
But they should land at Dieppe within four days.

    Lincoln. Go certify his grace it shall be done.

                          [*Exit* Lovell.

26 cast off] dismissed.   27 embezzl'd] misappro-
priated (*sc.* squandered).   53 powers] forces.   55
certify] assure.

Now, Cousin Lacy, in what forwardness
Are all your companies?

    Lacy.   All well prepar'd.
The men of Hertfordshire lie at Mile-end,
Suffolk and Essex train in Tothill-fields,
The Londoners and those of Middlesex,   60
All gallantly prepar'd in Finsbury,
With frolic spirits long for their parting hour.

    Lord Mayor. They have their imprest, coats, and
        furniture,
And, if it please your cousin Lacy come
To the Guildhall, he shall receive his pay;
And twenty pounds besides my brethren
Will freely give him, to approve our loves
We bear unto my lord your uncle here.

    Lacy. I thank your honour.

    Lincoln.   Thanks, my good lord mayor.

    Lord Mayor. At the Guildhall we will expect your
        coming.   [*Exit.*

    Lincoln. To approve your loves to me? No subtilty!
Nephew, that twenty pound he doth bestow   72
For joy to rid you from his daughter Rose.
But, cousins both, now here are none but friends,
I would not have you cast an amorous eye
Upon so mean a project as the love
Of a gay, wanton, painted citizen.
I know, this churl even in the height of scorn
Doth hate the mixture of his blood with thine.
I pray thee, do thou so! Remember, coz,   80
What honourable fortunes wait on thee:
Increase the king's love, which so brightly shines,
And gilds thy hopes. I have no heir but thee,—
And yet not thee, if with a wayward spirit
Thou start from the true bias of my love.

63 imprest] advance pay (the 'Queen's Shilling').
furniture] equipment.   67 approve] prove, show.
70 expect] await.   80 coz] cousin.   85 start] break
away.   bias of my love] course my love for you dictates.

Lacy. My lord, I will (for honour, not desire
Of land or livings, or to be your heir)
So guide my actions in pursuit of France,
As shall add glory to the Lacys' name.

 Lincoln. Cez, for those words here's thirty Portigues,
And, nephew Askew, there's a few for you. 91
Fair Honour in her loftiest eminence
Stays in France for you, till you fetch her thence.
Then, nephews, clap swift wings on your designs:
Begone, begone, make haste to the Guildhall;
There presently I'll meet you. Do not stay:
Where honour beckons, shame attends delay. [*Exit.*

 Askew. How gladly would your uncle have you gone!

 Lacy. True, coz, but I'll o'erreach his policies.
I have some serious business for three days, 100
Which nothing but my presence can dispatch.
You, therefore, cousin, with the companies,
Shall haste to Dover; there I'll meet with you:
Or, if I stay past my prefixed time,
Away for France; we'll meet in Normandy.
The twenty pounds my lord mayor gives to me
You shall receive, and these ten Portigues,
Part of mine uncle's thirty. Gentle coz,
Have care to our great charge; I know your wisdom
Hath tried itself in higher consequence. 110

 Askew. Coz, all myself am yours: yet have this care,
To lodge in London with all secrecy;
Our uncle Lincoln hath, besides his own,
Many a jealous eye, that in your face
Stares only to watch means for your disgrace.

 Lacy. Stay, cousin, who be these?

Enter Simon Eyre, Margery *his wife,* Hodge, Firk,
   Jane, *and* Ralph *with a piece.*

 Eyre. Leave whining, leave whining! Away with

88 France] perhaps read 'fame'. 90 Portigues] gold
coins worth from £3 5 0 to £4 10 0. 116 s.d. *piece*] *sc.*
of work, here a pair of shoes (see 1. i. 246).

this whimpering, this puling, these blubbering tears, and these wet eyes! I'll get thy husband discharg'd, I warrant thee, sweet Jane; go to! 120

Hodge. Master, here be the captains.

Eyre. Peace, Hodge; husht, ye knave, husht!

Firk. Here be the cavaliers and the colonels, master.

Eyre. Peace, Firk; peace, my fine Firk! Stand by with your pishery-pashery, away! I am a man of the best presence; I'll speak to them, an they were Popes. —Gentlemen, captains, colonels, commanders! Brave men, brave leaders, may it please you to give me audience. I am Simon Eyre, the mad shoemaker of Tower Street; this wench with the mealy mouth that will never tire is my wife, I can tell you; here's Hodge, my man and my foreman; here's Firk, my fine firking journeyman, and this is blubbered Jane. All we come to be suitors for this honest Ralph. Keep him at home, and as I am a true shoemaker and a gentleman of the Gentle Craft, buy spurs yourself, and I'll find ye boots these seven years.

Margery. Seven years, husband?

Eyre. Peace, midriff, peace! I know what I do. Peace! 140

Firk. Truly, master cormorant, you shall do God good service to let Ralph and his wife stay together. She's a young new-married woman; if you take her husband away from her a night, you undo her; she may beg in the daytime; for he's as good a workman at a prick and an awl, as any is in our trade.

Jane. O let him stay, else I shall be undone.

Firk. Ay, truly, she shall be laid at one side like a pair of old shoes else, and be occupied for no use.

Lacy. Truly, my friends, it lies not in my power: The Londoners are press'd, paid, and set forth 151 By the lord mayor; I cannot change a man.

120 go to] come, come!   132 firking] frisking.   149 occupied] claimed, possessed (*sc.* by Ralph as his wife). 151 set forth] equipped.

Hodge. Why, then you were as good be a corporal as a colonel, if you cannot discharge one good fellow; and I tell you true, I think you do more than you can answer, to press a man within a year and a day of his marriage.

Eyre. Well said, melancholy Hodge; gramercy, my fine foreman.   159

Margery. Truly, gentlemen, it were ill done for such as you, to stand so stiffly against a poor young wife; considering her case, she is new-married, but let that pass: I pray, deal not roughly with her; her husband is a young man, and but newly entered, but let that pass.

Eyre. Away with your pishery-pashery, your pols and your edipols! Peace, midriff; silence, Cicely Bumtrinket! Let your head speak.

Firk. Yea, and the horns too, master.   169

Eyre. Too soon, my fine Firk, too soon! Peace, scoundrels!—See you this man? Captains, you will not release him? Well, let him go; he's a proper shot; let him vanish! Peace, Jane, dry up thy tears, they'll make his powder dankish. Take him, brave men; Hector of Troy was an hackney to him, Hercules and Termagant scoundrels, Prince Arthur's Round table —by the Lord of Ludgate—ne'er fed such a tall, such a dapper swordman; by the life of Pharaoh, a brave, resolute swordman! Peace, Jane! I say no more, mad knaves.   180

Firk. See, see, Hodge, how my master raves in commendation of Ralph!

Hodge. Ralph, th'art a gull, by this hand, an thou goest not.

Askew. I am glad, good Master Eyre, it is my hap
To meet so resolute a soldier.
Trust me, for your report and love to him,
A common slight regard shall not respect him.

175 hackney] common drudge.   177 tall] brave.

Lacy. Is thy name Ralph?
Ralph.   Yes, sir.
Lacy.   Give me thy hand;
Thou shalt not want, as I am a gentleman.   190
Woman, be patient; God, no doubt, will send
Thy husband safe again; but he must go,
His country's quarrel says it shall be so.
Hodge. Th'art a gull, by my stirrup, if thou dost not
go. I will not have thee strike thy gimlet into these
weak vessels; prick thine enemies, Ralph.

Enter Dodger.

Dodger. My lord, your uncle on the Tower-hill
Stays with the lord mayor and the aldermen,
And doth request you with all speed you may,
To hasten thither.
Askew.   Cousin, let's go.   200
Lacy. Dodger, run you before, tell them we come.—
                              [*Exit* Dodger.
This Dodger is mine uncle's parasite,
The arrant'st varlet that e'er breath'd on earth;
He sets more discord in a noble house
By one day's broaching of his pickthank tales,
Than can be salv'd again in twenty years,
And he, I fear, shall go with us to France,
To pry into our actions.
Askew.   Therefore, coz,
It shall behoove you to be circumspect.
Lacy. Fear not, good cousin.—Ralph, hie to your
    colours.   210
Ralph. I must, because there's no remedy;
But, gentle master and my loving dame,
As you have always been a friend to me,
So in my absence think upon my wife.
Jane. Alas, my Ralph.
Margery.   She cannot speak for weeping.

205 pickthank] told to curry favour.

Eyre. Peace, you crack'd groats, you mustard tokens, disquiet not the brave soldier. Go thy ways, Ralph!

Jane. Ay, ay, you bid him go; what shall I do when he is gone?   220

Firk. Why, be doing with me or my fellow Hodge; be not idle.

Eyre. Let me see thy hand, Jane. This fine hand, this white hand, these pretty fingers must spin, must card, must work; work, you bombast-cotton-candle-quean; work for your living, with a pox to you.— Hold thee, Ralph, here's five sixpences for thee; fight for the honour of the Gentle Craft, for the gentlemen shoemakers, the courageous cordwainers, the flower of St. Martin's, the mad knaves of Bedlam, Fleet Street, Tower Street and Whitechapel; crack me the crowns of the French knaves, a pox on them, crack them; fight, by the Lord of Ludgate, fight, my fine boy!

Firk. Here, Ralph, here's three twopences: two carry into France, the third shall wash our souls at parting, for sorrow is dry. For my sake, firk the *Basa mon cues.*   237

Hodge. Ralph, I am heavy at parting, but here's a shilling for thee. God send thee to cram thy slops with French crowns, and thy enemies' bellies with bullets.

Ralph. I thank you, master, and I thank you all.
Now, gentle wife, my loving lovely Jane,
Rich men, at parting, give their wives rich gifts,
Jewels and rings, to grace their lily hands.
Thou know'st our trade makes rings for women's
    heels:
Here take this pair of shoes, cut out by Hodge,
Stitch'd by my fellow Firk, seam'd by myself,
Made up and pink'd with letters for thy name.

216–17 mustard tokens] contemptuous expression; apparently coupons given to buyers of mustard.   236 firk] trounce.   *Basa mon cues*] kiss-my-tails (*sc.* the French). 239 slops] trouser (-pockets).   248 pink'd] punched

Wear them, my dear Jane, for thy husband's sake,
And every morning, when thou pull'st them on,   250
Remember me, and pray for my return.
Make much of them; for I have made them so,
That I can know them from a thousand mo.

Sound drum. Enter Lord Mayor, Lincoln, Lacy, Askew,
Dodger, *and Soldiers. They pass over the stage;* Ralph *falls
in amongst them;* Firk *and the rest cry 'Farewell', &c., and
so exeunt.*

Act II. Scene I.

Enter Rose, *alone, making a garland.*

Rose. Here sit thou down upon this flow'ry bank,
And make a garland for thy Lacy's head.
These pinks, these roses, and these violets,
These blushing gilliflowers, these marigolds,
The fair embroidery of his coronet,
Carry not half such beauty in their cheeks,
As the sweet countenance of my Lacy doth.
O my most unkind father! O my stars,
Why lower'd you so at my nativity,
To make me love, yet live robb'd of my love?   10
Here as a thief am I imprisoned
(For my dear Lacy's sake) within those walls,
Which by my father's cost were builded up
For better purposes; here must I languish

Enter Sybil.

For him that doth as much lament, I know,
Mine absence, as for him I pine in woe.

Sybil. Good morrow, young mistress, I am sure
you make that garland for me, against I shall be Lady
of the Harvest.

3–4] in the language of flowers pinks = boldness, roses
= love, violets = faithfulness, gilliflowers = bonds of affection, marigolds = grief.

Rose. Sybil, what news at London? 20

Sybil. None but good; my lord mayor your father, and master Philpot your uncle, and Master Scot your cousin, and Mistress Frigbottom by Doctors' Commons, do all, by my troth, send you most hearty commendations.

Rose. Did Lacy send kind greetings to his love?

Sybil. O yes, out of cry. By my troth, I scant knew him; here 'a wore a scarf, and here a scarf, here a bunch of feathers, and here precious stones and jewels, and a pair of garters,—O, monstrous! like one of our yellow silk curtains at home here in Old Ford house, here in Master Bellymount's chamber. I stood at our door in Cornhill, look'd at him, he at me indeed, spake to him, but he not to me, not a word: marry gup, thought I, with a wanion! He pass'd by me as proud —Marry foh! are you grown humorous, thought I; and so shut the door, and in I came.

Rose. O Sybil, how dost thou my Lacy wrong!
My Rowland is as gentle as a lamb,
No dove was ever half so mild as he. 40

Sybil. Mild? yea, as a bushel of stamp'd crabs. He look'd upon me as sour as verjuice. Go thy ways, thought I; thou may'st be much in my gaskins, but nothing in my nether-stocks. This is your fault, mistress, to love him that loves not you; he thinks scorn to do as he's done to; but if I were as you, I'd cry: Go by, Jeronimo, go by!

27 out of cry] beyond measure. 34 gup] meaningless expression of remonstrance. 35 wanion] vengeance. 36 humorous] cantankerous. 41 stamp'd crabs] crushed crab-apples. 43–4 gaskins . . . nether-stocks] breeches . . . stockings; the purport is obscure. 44 fault] misfortune. 47 Go by, *&c.*] *Cf.* T. Kyd, *The Spanish Tragedy*, III. xii. 31, 'Hieronimo beware; go by, go by'. This most popular of Elizabethan plays was constantly ridiculed by later writers, and the present phrase had become a catchword (much as 'Something is rotten in the state of Denmark' is to-day).

I'd set mine old debts against my new driblets,
And the hare's foot against the goose giblets,
For if ever I sigh, when sleep I should take,   50
Pray God I may lose my maidenhead when I wake.

Rose. Will my love leave me then, and go to France?

Sybil. I know not that, but I am sure I see him stalk
before the soldiers. By my troth, he is a proper man;
but he is proper that proper doth. Let him go snick
up, young mistress.

Rose. Get thee to London, and learn perfectly,
Whether my Lacy go to France, or no:
Do this, and I will give thee for thy pains
My cambric apron and my Romish gloves,   60
My purple stockings and a stomacher.
Say, wilt thou do this, Sybil, for my sake?

Sybil. Will I, quoth a? At whose suit? By my troth
yes, I'll go. A cambric apron, gloves, a pair of purple
stockings, and a stomacher! I'll sweat in purple, mistress, for you; I'll take anything that comes a God's
name. O rich! a cambric apron! Faith, then have at
'up tails all'. I'll go jiggy-joggy to London, and be
here in a trice, young mistress.   [*Exit.*

Rose. Do so, good Sybil. Meantime wretched I
Will sit and sigh for his lost company,   [*Exit.*

Scene II.

Enter Rowland Lacy *like a Dutch Shoemaker.*

Lacy. How many shapes have gods and kings devis'd,

48 driblets] small debts; presumably she speaks in one
case of debts she owes and in the other of debts owed to her.
49 the hare's foot &c.] H. G. Bohn, *A Hand-book of Pro-
verbs* (1855), p. 165, has 'Set the hare's head against the
goose giblets, i.e. Balance things, set one against another.'
54 proper] handsome.   55–6 go snick up] go and be
hanged.   68 up tails all] the name of a lively popular
tune.   Heading. Rowland Lacy ... *Shoemaker*] called
Hans, which name the Quartos intermittently use in stage
directions and speech prefixes instead of his own.

Thereby to compass their desired loves!
It is no shame for Rowland Lacy, then,
To clothe his cunning with the Gentle Craft,
That, thus disguis'd, I may unknown possess
The only happy presence of my Rose.
For her have I forsook my charge in France,
Incurr'd the king's displeasure, and stirr'd up
Rough hatred in mine uncle Lincoln's breast.
O love, how powerful art thou, that canst change   10
High birth to baseness, and a nobler mind
To the mean semblance of a shoemaker!
But thus it must be, for her cruel father,
Hating the single union of our souls,
Hath secretly convey'd my Rose from London,
To bar me of her presence; but I trust,
Fortune and this disguise will further me
Once more to view her beauty, gain her sight.
Here in Tower Street with Eyre the shoemaker
Mean I a while to work; I know the trade,   20
I learnt it when I was in Wittenberg.
Then cheer thy hoping spirits, be not dismay'd,
Thou canst not want, do Fortune what she can,
The Gentle Craft is living for a man.   [*Exit.*

Scene III.

Enter Eyre, *making himself ready.*

Eyre. Where be these boys, these girls, these drabs,
these scoundrels? They wallow in the fat brewis of
my bounty, and lick up the crumbs of my table, yet
will not rise to see my walks cleansed. Come out, you
powder-beef-queans! What, Nan! what, Madge
Mumble-crust! Come out, you fat midriff-swag-belly-
whores, and sweep me these kennels, that the noisome
stench offend not the nose of my neighbours. What,
Firk, I say; what, Hodge! Open my shop-windows!
What, Firk, I say!   10

2 brewis] broth.   7 kennels] gutters.

Enter Firk.

Firk. O master, is't you that speak bandog and Bedlam this morning? I was in a dream, and mused what madman was got into the street so early; have you drunk this morning that your throat is so clear?

Eyre. Ah, well said, Firk, well said, Firk. To work, my fine knave, to work! Wash thy face, and thou'lt be more blest.

Firk. Let them wash my face that will eat it. Good master, send for a souse-wife, if you'll have my face cleaner.   20

Enter Hodge.

Eyre. Away, sloven! avaunt, scoundrel!—Good-morrow, Hodge; good-morrow, my fine foreman.

Hodge. O master, good-morrow; y' are an early stirrer. Here's a fair morning.—Good-morrow, Firk, I could have slept this hour. Here's a brave day towards.

Eyre. Oh, haste to work, my fine foreman, haste to work.

Firk. Master, I am dry as dust to hear my fellow Roger talk of fair weather; let us pray for good leather, and let clowns and ploughboys and those that work in the fields pray for brave days. We work in a dry shop; what care I if it rain?   33

Enter Margery.

Eyre. How now, Dame Margery, can you see to rise? Trip and go, call up the drabs your maids.

Margery. See to rise? I hope 'tis time enough, 'tis early enough for any woman to be seen abroad. I marvel how many wives in Tower Street are up so soon! Gods me, 'tis not noon,—here's a yawling!

Eyre. Peace, Margery, peace! Where's Cicely

11 bandog] fierce dog (the phrase meaning 'who growl and rave').   19 souse-wife] woman who pickled pigs' faces.   38 marvel] wonder.

Bumtrinket, your maid? She has a privy fault, she farts in her sleep. Call the quean up; if my men want shoe-thread, I'll swinge her in a stirrup.   43

Firk. Yet, that's but a dry beating; here's still a sign of drought.

Enter Lacy *singing.*

Lacy.   Der was een bore van Gelderland,
          Frolick sie byen;
        He was als dronck he cold nyet stand,
          Upsolce sie byen.
        Tap eens de canneken,   50
        Drincke, schone mannekin.

Firk. Master, for my life, yonder's a brother of the Gentle Craft; if he bear not Saint Hugh's bones, I'll forfeit my bones; he's some uplandish workman; hire him, good master, that I may learn some gibble-gabble; 'twill make us work the faster.

Eyre. Peace, Firk! A hard world! Let him pass, let him vanish; we have journeymen enow. Peace, my fine Firk!

Margery. Nay, nay, y'are best follow your man's counsel; you shall see what will come on't: we have not men enow, but we must entertain every butter-box; but let that pass.   63

Hodge. Dame, 'fore God, if my master follow your counsel, he'll consume little beef. He shall be glad of men, and he can catch them.

Firk. Ay, that he shall.

43 in] with.
46–51] There was a peasant from Gelderland.
          Frolic they be;
        He was so drunk he could not stand,
          Tipsy they be.
        Tap once [*or* Draw us?] a cannikin,
        Drink, pretty mannikin,
53 Saint Hugh's bones] shoemakers' tools.   54
uplandish] foreign.   **62–3** butter-box] Dutchman.   65, 67
shall] should.

Hodge. 'Fore God, a proper man, and, I warrant, a fine workman. Master, farewell; dame, adieu; if such a man as he cannot find work, Hodge is not for you.   [*Offer to go.*

Eyre. Stay, my fine Hodge.   72

Firk. Faith, an your foreman **go**, dame, you must take a journey to seek a new journeyman; if Roger remove, Firk follows. If Saint Hugh's bones shall not be set a-work, I may prick mine awl in the walls, and go play. Fare ye well, master; good-bye, dame.

Eyre. Tarry, my fine Hodge, my brisk foreman! Stay, Firk!—Peace, pudding-broth! By the Lord of Ludgate, I love my men as my life. Peace, you gallimaufry!—Hodge, if he want work, I'll hire him. One of you to him; stay,—he comes to us.   82

Lacy. Goeden dach, meester, ende u vro oak.

Firk. Nails, if I should speak after him without drinking, I should choke. And you, friend Oake, are you of the Gentle Craft?

Lacy. Yaw, yaw, ik bin den skomawker.

Firk. 'Den skomaker', quoth a! And hark you, 'skomaker', have you all your tools, a good rubbing-pin, a good stopper, a good dresser, your four sorts of awls, and your two balls of wax, your paring knife, your hand- and thumb-leathers, and good St. Hugh's bones to smooth up to your work?   93

Lacy. Yaw, yaw; be niet vorveard. Ik hab all de dingen voour mack skooes groot and cleane.

Firk. Ha, ha! Good master, hire him; he'll make me laugh so that I shall work more in mirth than I can in earnest.

Eyre. Hear ye, friend, have ye any skill in the mystery of cordwainers?   100

81 gallimaufry] ridiculous medley (lit. hashed mixed meats).   83] Good day, master, and you mistress too.
87] Yes, yes, I am a shoemaker.   94-5 Yes, yes; be not afraid. I have all the things for making shoes great and small.

Lacy. Ik weet niet wat yow seg; ich verstaw you niet.

Firk. Why, thus, man: [*Makes gesture.*] 'Ich verste u niet,' quoth a!

Lacy. Yaw, yaw, yaw; ick can dat wel doen.

Firk. 'Yaw, yaw!' He speaks yawing like a jackdaw that gapes to be fed with cheese-curds. Oh, he'll give a villainous pull at a can of double-beer; but Hodge and I have the vantage, we must drink first, because we are the eldest journeymen.

Eyre. What is thy name?   110

Lacy. Hans—Hans Meulter.

Eyre. Give me thy hand; th'art welcome.—Hodge, entertain him; Firk, bid him welcome; come, Hans. Run, wife, bid your maids, your trullibubs, make ready my fine men's breakfasts. To him, Hodge!

Hodge. Hans, th'art welcome; use thyself friendly, for we are good fellows; if not, thou shalt be fought with, wert thou bigger than a giant.   118

Firk. Yea, and drunk with, wert thou Gargantua. My master keeps no cowards, I tell thee.—Ho, boy, bring him an heel-block, here's a new journeyman.

Enter Boy.

Lacy. O, ich, wersto you; ich moet een halve dossen cans betaelen; here, boy, nempt dis skilling, tap eens freelicke.   [*Exit boy.*

Eyre. Quick, snipper-snapper, away! Firk, scour thy throat, thou shalt wash it with Castilian liquor.

Enter Boy.

Come, my last of the fives, give me a can. Have to thee, Hans; here, Hodge; here Firk; drink, you mad

101 I know not what you say; I understand you not. 104 Yes, yes, yes; I can do that well.   121 heel-block] block used in fastening a blank heel to a shoe; but there is evidently some elusive pun on drinking.   122–4] O, I understand you; I must pay for a half-dozen cans; here, boy, take this shilling, tap once [*or* draw for us] freely. 127 last of the fives] small last.

Greeks, and work like true Trojans, and pray for
Simon Eyre, the shoemaker.—Here, Hans, and th'art
welcome.   131

Firk. Lo, dame, you would have lost a good fellow
that will teach us to laugh. This beer came hopping
in well.

Margery. Simon, it is almost seven.

Eyre. Is't so, Dame Clapper-dudgeon, is't seven
a clock, and my men's breakfast not ready! Trip and
go, you sous'd conger, away! Come, you mad Hyper-
boreans; follow me, Hodge; follow me, Hans; come
after, my fine Firk; to work, to work a while, and then
to breakfast!   [*Exit.*

Firk. Soft! Yaw, yaw, good Hans, though my
master have no more wit but to call you afore me,
I am not so foolish to go behind you, I being the elder
journeyman.   [*Exeunt.*

Scene IV.

Holloaing within. Enter Warner *and* Hammon, *like
Hunters.*

Hammon. Cousin, beat every brake, the game's not
    far,
This way with winged feet he fled from death,
Whilst the pursuing hounds, scenting his steps,
Find out his highway to destruction.
Besides, the miller's boy told me even now,
He saw him take soil, and he holloaed him,
Affirming him to have been so emboss'd
That long he could not hold.

Warner.   If it be so,
'Tis best we trace these meadows by Old Ford.

A noise of Hunters within. Enter a Boy.

Hammon. How now, boy! Where's the deer? speak,
    saw'st thou him?   10

6 take soil] take to the water.   7 emboss'd] driven
to extremity.

Boy. O yea; I saw him leap through a hedge, and then over a ditch, then at my lord mayor's pale. Over he skipp'd me, and in he went me, and 'holla' the hunters cried, and 'there, boy; there, boy!' But there he is, 'a mine honesty.

Hammon. Boy, God amercy. Cousin, let's away;
I hope we shall find better sport to-day.   [*Exeunt.*

Scene V.

Hunting within. Enter Rose *and* Sybil.

Rose. Why, Sybil, wilt thou prove a forester?

Sybil. Upon some, no; forester, go by; no, faith, mistress. The deer came running into the barn through the orchard and over the pale; I wot well, I look'd as pale as a new cheese to see him. But whip, says goodman Pin-close, up with his flail, and our Nick with a prong, and down he fell, and they upon him, and I upon them. By my troth, we had such sport; and in the end we ended him; his throat we cut, flay'd him, unhorn'd him, and my lord mayor shall eat of him anon, when he comes.   11

                    [*Horns sound within.*

Rose. Hark, hark, the hunters come; y' are best take heed,
They'll have a saying to you for this deed.

Enter Hammon, Warner, *Huntsmen, and Boy.*

Hammon. God save you, fair ladies.

Sybil.   Ladies! O gross!

Warner. Came not a buck this way?

Rose.   No, but two does.

Hammon. And which way went they? Faith, we'll hunt at those.

Sybil. At those? upon some, no: when, can you tell?

       2 Upon some] indeed.

Warner. Upon some, ay.

Sybil.   Good Lord!

Warner.   Wounds! Then farewell!

Hammon. Boy, which way went he?

Boy.   This way, sir, he ran.

Hammon. This way he ran indeed, fair Mistress
  Rose;   20

Our game was lately in your orchard seen.

Warner. Can you advise, which way he took his
  flight?

Sybil. Follow your nose; his horns will guide you
  right.

Warner. Th' art a mad wench.

Sybil.   O, rich!

Rose.   Trust me, not I.

It is not like that the wild forest-deer

Would come so near to places of resort;

You are deceiv'd, he fled some other way.

Warner. Which way, my sugar-candy, can you
  show?

Sybil. Come up, good honeysops, upon some, no.

Rose. Why do you stay, and not pursue your game?

Sybil. I'll hold my life, their hunting-nags be lame.

Hammon. A deer more dear is found within this
  place.   32

Rose. But not the deer, sir, which you had in chase.

Hammon. I chas'd the deer, but this dear chaseth
  me.

Rose. The strangest hunting that ever I see.

But where's your park?   [*She offers to go away.*

Hammon.   'Tis here: O stay!

Rose. Impale me in't, and then I will not stray.

Warner. They wrangle, wench; we are more kind
  than they.

Sybil. What kind of hart is that dear heart you seek?

Warner. A hart, dear heart.

Sybil.   Who ever saw the like?

Rose. To lose your heart, is't possible you can?   41

Hammon. My heart is lost.

Rose.   Alack, good gentleman!

Hammon. This poor lost heart would I wish you
    might find.

Rose. You, by such luck, might prove your hart a
    hind.

Hammon. Why, Luck had horns, so have I heard
    some say.

Rose. Now, God, an't be his will, send Luck into
    your way.

Enter the Lord Mayor *and Servants.*

Lord Mayor. What, Master Hammon! Welcome to
    Old Ford!

Sybil. God's pittikins, hands off, sir! Here's my
    lord.

Lord Mayor. I hear you had ill luck, and lost your
    game.

Hammon. 'Tis true, my lord.

Lord Mayor.   I am sorry for the same. 50
    What gentleman is this?

Hammon.   My brother-in-law.

Lord Mayor. Y'are welcome both; sith Fortune
    offers you

Into my hands, you shall not part from hence,
Until you have refresh'd your wearied limbs.—
Go, Sybil, cover the board!—You shall be guest
To no good cheer, but even a hunter's feast.

Hammon. I thank your lordship.—Cousin, on my
    life,

For our lost venison I shall find a wife.   [*Exeunt.*

Lord Mayor. In, gentlemen; I'll not be absent long.—
This Hammon is a proper gentleman,   60
A citizen by birth, fairly alli'd;
How fit an husband were he for my girl!
Well, I will in, and do the best I can,
To match my daughter to this gentleman.   [*Exit.*

Act III. Scene I.

Enter Lacy, Skipper, Hodge, *and* Firk.

Skipper. Ick sal yow wat seggen, Hans; dis skip, dat comen from Candy, is al wol, by Got's sacrament, van sugar, civet, almonds, cambrick, end alle dingen, towsand towsand ding. Nempt it, Hans, nempt it vor u meester. Daer be de bils van laden. Your meester Simon Eyre sal hae good copen. Wat seggen yow, Hans?

Firk. Wat seggen de reggen, de copen slopen— laugh, Hodge, laugh!   9

Lacy. Mine liever broder Firk, bringt Meester Eyre tot det signe un Swannekin; daer sal yow finde dis skipper end me. Wat seggen yow, broder Firk? Doot it, Hodge. Come, skipper.

[*Exeunt* Lacy *and* Skipper.

Firk. Bring him, quoth you? Here's no knavery, to bring my master to buy a ship worth the lading of two or three hundred thousand pounds. Alas, that's nothing; a trifle, a bauble, Hodge.   17

Hodge. The truth is, Firk, that the merchant owner of the ship dares not show his head, and therefore this skipper that deals for him, for the love he bears to Hans, offers my master Eyre a bargain in the commodities. He shall have a reasonable day of payment; he may sell the wares by that time, and be an huge gainer himself.   24

1–7] I'll tell you what, Hans; this ship, that comes from Candy, is all full, by God's Sacrament, of sugar, civet, almonds, cambric, and all things, a thousand thousand things. Take it, Hans, take it for your master. There be the bills of lading. Your master Simon Eyre will have a good bargain. What say you, Hans?   10–13] My dear brother Firk, bring Master Eyre to the sign of the Swan; there shall you find this skipper and me. What say you, brother Firk? Do it, Hodge.

Firk. Yea, but can my fellow Hans lend my master twenty porpentines as an earnest penny?

Hodge. Portigues, thou wouldst say; here they be, Firk; hark, they jingle in my pocket like St. Mary Overy's bells.

Enter Eyre *and* Margery.

Firk. Mum, here comes my dame and my master. She'll scold, on my life, for loitering this Monday; but all's one, let them all say what they can, Monday's our holiday. 33

Margery. You sing, Sir Sauce, but I beshrew your heart,

I fear, for this your singing we shall smart.

Firk. Smart for me, dame? why, dame, why?

Hodge. Master, I hope you'll not suffer my dame to take down your journeymen.

Firk. If she take me down, I'll take her up; yea, and take her down too, a button-hole lower. 40

Eyre. Peace, Firk; not I, Hodge; by the life of Pharaoh, by the Lord of Ludgate, by this beard every hair whereof I value at a king's ransom, she shall not meddle with you.—Peace, you bombast-cotton-candle-quean; away, queen of clubs; quarrel not with me and my men, with me and my fine Firk; I'll firk you, if you do.

Margery. Yea, yea, man, you may use me as you please; but let that pass. 49

Eyre. Let it pass, let it vanish away; peace! Am I not Simon Eyre! Are not these my brave men, brave shoemakers, all gentlemen of the Gentle Craft? Prince am I none, yet am I nobly born, as being the sole son of a shoemaker. Away, rubbish! vanish, melt, melt like kitchen-stuff!

Margery. Yea, yea, 'tis well, I must be call'd rubbish, kitchen-stuff, for a sort of knaves.

27 Portigues] gold coins (see note on I. i. 90).   57
sort] pack.

Firk. Nay, dame, you shall not weep and wail in woe for me. Master, I'll stay no longer; here's a vennentory of my shop-tools. Adieu, master; Hodge, farewell.   61

Hodge. Nay, stay, Firk; thou shalt not go alone.

Margery. I pray, let them go; there be more maids than Mawkin, more men than Hodge, and more fools than Firk.

Firk. Fools? Nails! if I tarry now, I would my guts might be turn'd to shoe-thread.

Hodge. And if I stay, I pray God I may be turn'd to a Turk, and set in Finsbury for boys to shoot at.— Come, Firk.   70

Eyre. Stay, my fine knaves, you arms of my trade, you pillars of my profession. What, shall a tittle-tattle's words make you forsake Simon Eyre?—Avaunt, kitchen-stuff! Rip, you brown-bread Tannikin! Out of my sight! Move me not! Have not I ta'en you from selling tripes in Eastcheap, and set you in my shop, and made you hail-fellow with Simon Eyre, the shoemaker? And now do you deal thus with my journeymen? Look, you powder-beef-quean, on the face of Hodge, here's a face for a lord!   80

Firk. And here's a face for any lady in Christendom.

Eyre. Rip, you chitterling, avaunt! Boy, bid the tapster of the Boar's Head fill me a dozen cans of beer for my journeymen.

Firk. A dozen cans? O brave! Hodge, now I'll stay.

Eyre. [*Aside to the Boy.*] An the knave fills any more than two, he pays for them. [*Exit Boy. Aloud.*] A dozen cans of beer for my journeymen. [*Re-enter Boy*]. Hear you, mad Mesopotamians! wash your livers with this liquor. Where be the odd ten? [*Aside.*] No more, Madge, no more.—Well said. Drink and to work!—What work dost thou, Hodge? what work? 93

---

60 vennentory] *sc.* inventory.

Hodge. I am a-making a pair of shoes for my lord mayor's daughter, Mistress Rose.

Firk. And I a pair of shoes for Sybil, my lord's maid. I deal with her.

Eyre. Sybil? Fie, defile not thy fine workmanly fingers with the feet of kitchen-stuff and basting-ladles. Ladies of the court, fine ladies, my lads, commit their feet to our apparelling; put gross work to Hans. Yark and seam, yark and seam!   102

Firk. For yarking and seaming let me alone, an I come to't.

Hodge. Well, master, all this is from the bias. Do you remember the ship my fellow Hans told you of? The skipper and he are both drinking at the Swan. Here be the Portigues to give earnest. If you go through with it, you cannot choose but be a lord at least.   110

Firk. Nay, dame, if my master prove not a lord, and you a lady, hang me.

Margery. Yea, like enough, if you may loiter and tipple thus.

Firk. Tipple, dame? No, we have been bargaining with Skellum Skanderbag: can you Dutch spreaken for a ship of silk Cyprus, laden with sugar-candy?

*Enter the Boy with a velvet coat and an Alderman's gown.
Eyre puts it on.*

Eyre. Peace, Firk; silence, Tittle-tattle! Hodge, I'll go through with it. Here's a seal-ring, and I have sent for a guarded gown and a damask cassock. See where it comes; look here, Maggy; help me, Firk; apparel me, Hodge; silk and satin, you mad Philistines, silk and satin.   123

Firk. Ha, ha, my master will be as proud as a dog in a doublet, all in beaten damask and velvet.

102 Yark] stitch.   105 from the bias] beside the mark.
108 Portigues] see note on I. i. 90.   120 guarded]
with facings.   125 beaten] embroidered.

Eyre. Softly, Firk, for rearing of the nap, and wearing threadbare my garments. How dost thou like me, Firk? How do I look, my fine Hodge?

Hodge. Why, now you look like yourself, master. I warrant you, there's few in the city, but will give you the wall, and come upon you with the 'right worshipful'.   132

Firk. Nails, my master looks like a threadbare cloak new turn'd and dress'd. Lord, Lord, to see what good raiment doth! Dame, dame, are you not enamoured?

Eyre. How say'st thou, Maggy, am I not brisk? Am I not fine?

Margery. Fine! By my troth, sweetheart, very fine! By my troth, I never lik'd thee so well in my life, sweetheart. But let that pass; I warrant, there be many women in the city have not such handsome husbands, but only for their apparel; but let that pass too.   143

Enter Lacy *and* Skipper.

Lacy. Godden day, mester. Dis be de skipper dat heb de skip van marchandice; de commodity ben good; nempt it, master, nempt it.

Eyre. Godamercy, Hans; welcome, skipper. Where lies this ship of merchandise?

Skipper. De ship ben in revere; dor be van Sugar, cyvet, almonds, cambrick, and a towsand towsand tings; gotz sacrament, nempt it, mester, ye sal heb good copen.   152

Firk. To him, master! O sweet master! O sweet wares! Prunes, almonds, sugar-candy, carrot-roots, turnips! O brave fatting meat! Let not a man buy a nutmeg but yourself.

144–6] Good day, master. This is the skipper that has the ship of merchandise; the commodity is good; take it, master, take it.   149–52] The ship is in the river; there are sugar, civet, almonds, cambric, and a thousand thousand things; God's Sacrament, take it, master! you will have a good bargain.

Eyre. Peace, Firk! Come, skipper, I'll go abroad with you.—Hans, have you made him drink?

Skipper. Yaw, yaw, ic heb veale gedrunck.   159

Eyre. Come, Hans, follow me. Skipper, thou shalt have my countenance in the city.   [*Exeunt.*

Firk. 'Yaw, heb veale gedrunck', quoth a! They may well be called butter-boxes, when they drink fat veal, and thick beer too! But come, dame, I hope you'll chide us no more.

Margery. No, faith, Firk; no, perdy, Hodge. I do feel honour creep upon me, and which is more, a certain rising in my flesh; but let that pass.

Firk. Rising in your flesh do you feel, say you? Ay, you may be with child, but why should not my master feel a rising in his flesh, having a gown and a gold ring on? But you are such a shrew, you'll soon pull him down.   173

Margery. Ha, ha! prithee, peace! Thou mak'st my worship laugh; but let that pass. Come, I'll go in; Hodge, prithee, go before me; Firk, follow me.

[*Exeunt.*

Scene II.

Enter Lincoln *and* Dodger.

Lincoln. How now, good Dodger, what's the news in France?

Dodger. My lord, upon the eighteen day of May
The French and English were prepar'd to fight;
Each side with eager fury gave the sign
Of a most hot encounter. Five long hours
Both armies fought together; at the length
The lot of victory fell on our sides.
Twelve thousand of the Frenchmen that day died,
Four thousand English, and no man of name

157 abroad] out of doors.   159 Yes, yes, I have drunk plenty.

But Captain Hyam and young Ardington,   10
Two gallant gentlemen, I knew them well.

Lincoln. But Dodger, prithee, tell me, in this fight
How did my cousin Lacy bear himself?

Dodger. My lord, your cousin Lacy was not there.

Lincoln. Not there?

Dodger.   No, my good lord.

Lincoln.   Sure, thou mistakest.
I saw him shipp'd, and a thousand eyes beside
Were witnesses of the farewells which he gave,
When I, with weeping eyes, bid him adieu.
Dodger, take heed.

Dodger.   My lord, I am advis'd,
That what I spake is true: to prove it so,   20
His cousin Askew, that supplied his place,
Sent me for him from France, that secretly
He might convey himself thither.

Lincoln.   Is't even so?
Dares he so carelessly venture his life
Upon the indignation of a king?
Has he despis'd my love, and spurn'd those favours
Which I with prodigal hand pour'd on his head?
He shall repent his rashness with his soul;
Since of my love he makes no estimate,
I'll make him wish he had not known my hate.   30
Thou hast no other news?

Dodger.   None else, my lord.

Lincoln. None worse I know thou hast.—Procure
   the king
To crown his giddy brows with ample honours,
Send him chief colonel, and all my hope
Thus to be dash'd! But 'tis in vain to grieve,
One evil cannot a worse relieve.
Upon my life, I have found out his plot;
That old dog, Love, that fawn'd upon him so,
Love to that puling girl, his fair-cheek'd Rose,
The lord mayor's daughter, hath distracted him,   40
And in the fire of that love's lunacy

Hath he burnt up himself, consum'd his credit.
Lost the king's love, yea, and I fear, his life,
Only to get a wanton to his wife:
Dodger, it is so.

   Dodger.   I fear so, my good lord.

   Lincoln. It is so—nay, sure it cannot be!
I am at my wits' end. Dodger!

   Dodger.   Yea, my lord.

   Lincoln. Thou art acquainted with my nephew's
     haunts;
Spend this gold for thy pains; go seek him out;
Watch at my lord mayor's—there if he live,   50
Dodger, thou shalt be sure to meet with him.
Prithee, be diligent.—Lacy, thy name
Liv'd once in honour, now 'tis dead in shame.—
Be circumspect.   [*Exit.*

   Dodger.   I warrant you, my lord.   [*Exit.*

Scene III.

Enter Lord Mayor *and Master* Scott.

   Lord Mayor. Good Master Scott, I have been bold
     with you,
To be a witness to a wedding-knot
Betwixt young Master Hammon and my daughter.
O, stand aside; see where the lovers come.

Enter Hammon *and* Rose.

   Rose. Can it be possible you love me so?
No, no, within those eyeballs I espy
Apparent likelihoods of flattery.
Pray now, let go my hand.

   Hammon.   Sweet Mistress Rose,
Misconstrue not my words, nor misconceive
Of my affection, whose devoted soul   10
Swears that I love thee dearer than my heart.

   Rose. As dear as your own heart? I judge it right;
Men love their hearts best when th' are out of sight.

Hammon. I love you, by this hand.

Rose.   Yet hands off now!

If flesh be frail, how weak and frail's your vow!

Hammon. Then by my life I swear.

Rose.   Then do not brawl;

One quarrel loseth wife and life and all.

Is not your meaning thus?

Hammon.   In faith, you jest.

Rose. Love loves to sport; therefore leave love,

y' are best.   19

Lord Mayor. What? square they, Master Scott?

Scott.   Sir, never doubt,

Lovers are quickly in, and quickly out.

Hammon. Sweet Rose, be not so strange in fancying

me.

Nay, never turn aside, shun not my sight:

I am not grown so fond, to fond my love

On any that shall quite it with disdain;

If you will love me, so—if not, farewell.

Lord Mayor. Why, how now, lovers, are you both

agreed?

Hammon. Yes, faith, my lord.

Lord Mayor.   'Tis well, give me your hand.

Give me yours, daughter.—How now, both pull

back?

What means this, girl?

Rose.   I mean to live a maid.   30

Hammon. [*Aside.*] But not to die one; pause, ere that

be said.

Lord Mayor. Will you still cross me, still be obsti-

nate?

Hammon. Nay, chide her not, my lord, for doing

well;

If she can live an happy virgin's life,

'Tis far more blessed than to be a wife.

20 square] agree.   22 strange] over-fastidious.   24
fond my love] found &c. (the old spelling must be kept
for the pun).   25 quite] requite.

Rose. Say, sir, I cannot: I have made a vow,
Whoever be my husband, 'tis not you.

Lord Mayor. Your tongue is quick; but Master
 Hammon, know,
I bade you welcome to another end.

Hammon. What, would you have me pule and pine
 and pray,   40
With 'lovely lady, mistress of my heart,
Pardon your servant', and the rhymer play,
Railing on 'Cupid and his tyrant's dart';
Or shall I undertake some martial spoil,
Wearing your glove at tourney and at tilt,
And tell how many gallants I unhors'd—
Sweet, will this pleasure you?

Rose.   Yea, when wilt begin?
What, love-rhymes, man? Fie on that deadly sin!

Lord Mayor. If you will have her, I'll make her
 agree.

Hammon. Enforced love is worse than hate to me.—
[*Aside.*] There is a wench keeps shop in the Old
 Change,   51
To her will I; it is not wealth I seek,
I have enough, and will prefer her love
Before the world.—[*Aloud.*] My good lord mayor,
 adieu.

Old love for me, I have no luck with new.   [*Exit.*

Lord Mayor. Now, mammet, you have well behav'd
 yourself,
But you shall curse your coyness if I live.—
Who's within there? See you convey your mistress
Straight to th' Old Ford! I'll keep you straight enough,
Fore God, I would have sworn the puling girl   60
Would willingly accepted Hammon's love;
But banish him, my thoughts!—Go, minion, in!
                           [*Exit* Rose.

56 mammet] doll, puppet (hence, perhaps, 'silly child').
61 accepted] have accepted (?); Fritsche suggested
'accept of', but perhaps 'Would' should be 'Had'.

Now tell me, Master Scott, would you have thought
That Master Simon Eyre, the shoemaker,
Had been of wealth to buy such merchandise?
   Scott. 'Twas well, my lord, your honour and
     myself
Grew partners with him; for your bills of lading
Show that Eyre's gains in one commodity
Rise at the least to full three thousand pound,
Besides like gain in other merchandise.   70
   Lord Mayor. Well, he shall spend some of his thou-
     sands now,
For I have sent for him to the Guildhall.

Enter Eyre.

See, where he comes.—Good morrow, Master Eyre.
   Eyre. Poor Simon Eyre, my lord, your shoemaker.
   Lord Mayor. Well, well, it likes yourself to term
     you so.

Enter Dodger.

Now, Master Dodger, what's the news with you?
   Dodger. I'd gladly speak in private to your honour.
   Lord Mayor. You shall, you shall.—Master Eyre and
     Master Scott,
I have some business with this gentleman;
I pray, let me entreat you to walk before   80
To the Guildhall; I'll follow presently.
Master Eyre, I hope ere noon to call you sheriff.
   Eyre. I would not care, my lord, if you might call
me King of Spain.—Come, Master Scott.
                         [*Exeunt* Eyre *and* Scott.
   Lord Mayor. Now, Master Dodger, what's the news
     you bring?
   Dodger. The Earl of Lincoln by me greets your
     lordship,
And earnestly requests you, if you can,
Inform him where his nephew Lacy keeps.
   Lord Mayor. Is not his nephew Lacy now in France?
   Dodger. No, I assure your lordship, but disguis'd   90

Lurks here in London.

Lord Mayor.   London? is't even so?
It may be; but upon my faith and soul,
I know not where he lives, or whether he lives:
So tell my Lord of Lincoln.—Lurks in London?
Well, Master Dodger, you perhaps may start him;
Be but the means to rid him into France,
I'll give you a dozen angels for your pains,
So much I love his honour, hate his nephew.
And, prithee, so inform thy lord from me.

Dodger. I take my leave.   [*Exit* Dodger.

Lord Mayor.   Farewell, good Master Dodger.
Lacy in London? I dare pawn my life,   101
My daughter knows thereof, and for that cause
Denied young Master Hammon in his love.
Well, I am glad I sent her to Old Ford.
God's Lord, 'tis late; to Guildhall I must hie;
I know my brethren stay my company.   [*Exit.*

Scene IV.

Enter Firk, Margery, Lacy, *and* Hodge.

Margery. Thou goest too fast for me, Roger. O, Firk!

Firk. Ay, forsooth.

Margery. I pray thee, run—do you hear?—run to Guildhall, and learn if my husband, Master Eyre, will take that worshipful vocation of Master Sheriff upon him. Hie thee, good Firk.

Firk. Take it? Well, I go; an he should not take it, Firk swears to forswear him. Yes, forsooth, I go to Guildhall.   10

Margery. Nay, when? thou art too compendious and tedious.

Firk. O rare, your excellence is full of eloquence. [*Aside.*] How like a new cart-wheel my dame speaks,

95 start] discover.

and she looks like an old musty ale-bottle going to scalding.

Margery. Nay, when? thou wilt make me melancholy.   18

Firk. God forbid your worship should fall into that humour;—I run.   [*Exit.*

Margery. Let me see now, Roger and Hans.

Hodge. Ay, forsooth, dame—mistress I should say, but the old term so sticks to the roof of my mouth, I can hardly lick it off.

Margery. Even what thou wilt, good Roger; dame is a fair name for any honest Christian; but let that pass. How dost thou, Hans?

Lacy. Mee tanck you, vro.   28

Margery. Well, Hans and Roger, you see, God hath blest your master, and, perdy, if ever he comes to be Master Sheriff of London—as we are all mortal—you shall see, I will have some odd thing or other in a corner for you: I will not be your back-friend; but let that pass. Hans, pray thee, tie my shoe.

Lacy. Yaw, ic sal, vro.

Margery. Roger, thou know'st the length of my foot; as it is none of the biggest, so I thank God, it is handsome enough; prithee, let me have a pair of shoes made, cork, good Roger, wooden heel too.

Hodge. You shall.   40

Margery. Art thou acquainted with never a farthin-gale-maker, nor a French hood-maker? I must enlarge my bum, ha, ha! How shall I look in a hood, I wonder! Perdy, oddly, I think.

Hodge. [*Aside.*] As a cat out of a pillory.—Very well, I warrant you, mistress.

Margery. Indeed, all flesh is grass; and, Roger, canst thou tell where I may buy a good hair?

Hodge. Yes, forsooth, at the poulterer's in Gracious Street.   50

28] I thank you, mistress.   33 back-friend] false-friend.   35] Yes, I will, mistress.

Margery. Thou art an ungracious wag, perdy, I mean a false hair for my periwig.

Hodge. Why mistress, the next time I cut my beard, you shall have the shavings of it; but they are all true hairs.

Margery. It is very hot, I must get me a fan or else a mask.

Hodge. [*Aside.*] So you had need, to hide your wicked face.   59

Margery. Fie upon it, how costly this world's calling is; perdy, but that it is one of the wonderful works of God, I would not deal with it. Is not Firk come yet? Hans, be not so sad, let it pass and vanish, as my husband's worship says.

Lacy. Ick bin vrolicke, lot see yow soo.

Hodge. Mistress, will you drink a pipe of tobacco?

Margery. Oh, fie upon it, Roger, perdy! These filthy tobacco-pipes are the most idle slavering baubles that ever I felt. Out upon it! God bless us, men look not like men that use them.   70

Enter Ralph, *being lame.*

Hodge. What, fellow Ralph! Mistress, look here, Jane's husband! Why, how now, lame? Hans, make much of him, he's a brother of our trade, a good workman, and a tall soldier.

Lacy. You be welcome, broder.

Margery. Perdy, I knew him not. How dost thou, good Ralph? I am glad to see thee well.

Ralph. I would God you saw me, dame, as well As when I went from London into France.

Margery. Trust me, I am sorry, Ralph, to see thee impotent. Lord, how the wars have made him sunburnt! The left leg is not well; 'twas a fair gift of God the infirmity took not hold a little higher, considering thou camest from France; but let that pass.   84

65] I am frolic, let's see you so.   66 drink] smoke (the usual term).   74 tall] brave.

Ralph. I am glad to see you well, and I rejoice
To hear that God hath blest my master so
Since my departure.

Margery. Yea, truly, Ralph, I thank my Maker;
but let that pass.

    Hodge. And, sirrah Ralph, what news, what news
    in France? 90

Ralph. Tell me, good Roger, first, what news in
England?
How does my Jane? When didst thou see my
    wife?
Where lives my poor heart? She'll be poor indeed,
Now I want limbs to get whereon to feed.

    Hodge. Limbs? Hast thou not hands, man? Thou
shalt never see a shoemaker want bread, though he
have but three fingers on a hand.

    Ralph. Yet all this while I hear not of my Jane.

    Margery. O Ralph, your wife,—perdy, we know
not what's become of her. She was here a while, and
because she was married, grew more stately than
became her; I check'd her, and so forth; away she
flung, never returned, nor said bye nor bah; and,
Ralph, you know, 'ka me, ka thee.' And so, as I tell
ye—— Roger, is not Firk come yet? 105

    Hodge. No, forsooth.

    Margery. And so, indeed, we heard not of her, but
I hear she lives in London; but let that pass. If she
had wanted, she might have opened her case to me
or my husband, or to any of my men; I am sure there's
not any of them, perdy, but would have done her good
to his power. Hans, look if Firk be come. 112

    Lacy. Yaw, ik sal, vro. [*Exit Lacy.*

    Margery. And so, as I said—but, Ralph, why dost
thou weep? Thou knowest that naked we came out

---

102 check'd] rebuked.   103 bye nor bah] a farewell
courteous or insulting (Wheeler).   104 ka me, ka thee] un-
explained common phrase implying reciprocity in service,
flattery, &c.   113] Yes, I will, mistress.

of our mother's womb, and naked we must return; and, therefore, thank God for all things.

Hodge. No, faith, Jane is a stranger here; but, Ralph, pull up a good heart, I know thou hast one. Thy wife, man, is in London; one told me, he saw her awhile ago very brave and neat; we'll ferret her out, an London hold her. 122

Margery. Alas, poor soul, he's overcome with sorrow; he does but as I do, weep for the loss of any good thing. But, Ralph, get thee in, call for some meat and drink, thou shalt find me worshipful towards thee.

Ralph. I thank you, dame; since I want limbs and lands, 128
I'll trust to God, my good friends, and to my hands.
[*Exit.*

Enter Lacy *and* Firk *running.*

Firk. Run, good Hans! O Hodge, O mistress! Hodge, heave up thine ears; mistress, smug up your looks; on with your best apparel; my master is chosen, my master is called, nay, condemn'd by the cry of the country to be sheriff of the city for this famous year now to come. And time now being, a great many men in black gowns were ask'd for their voices and their hands, and my master had all their fists about his ears presently, and they cried 'Ay, ay, ay, ay',— and so I came away—

Wherefore without all other grieve 140
I do salute you, Mistress Shrieve.

Lacy. Yaw, my mester is de groot man, de shrieve.

Hodge. Did not I tell you, mistress? Now I may boldly say: Good-morrow to your worship.

Margery. Good-morrow, good Roger. I thank you, my good people all.—Firk, hold up thy hand: here's a threepenny piece for thy tidings.

---

131 smug] smarten.   142] Yes, my master is a great man, a sheriff.

Firk. 'Tis but three-half-pence, I think. Yes, 'tis three-pence, I smell the rose.

Hodge. But, mistress, be rul'd by me, and do not speak so pulingly.   151

Firk. 'Tis her worship speaks so, and not she. No, faith, mistress, speak me in the old key: 'To it, Firk', 'there, good Firk', 'ply your business, Hodge', 'Hodge, with a full mouth', 'I'll fill your bellies with good cheer, till they cry twang'.

Enter Simon Eyre *wearing a gold chain.*

Lacy. See, myn liever broder, heer compt my meester.

Margery. Welcome home, Master Shrieve; I pray God continue you in health and wealth.   160

Eyre. See here, my Maggy, a chain, a gold chain for Simon Eyre. I shall make thee a lady; here's a French hood for thee; on with it, on with it! dress thy brows with this flap of a shoulder of mutton, to make thee look lovely. Where be my fine men? Roger, I'll make over my shop and tools to thee; Firk, thou shalt be the foreman; Hans, thou shalt have an hundred for twenty. Be as mad knaves as your master Sim Eyre hath been, and you shall live to be Sheriffs of London. —How dost thou like me, Margery? Prince am I none, yet am I princely born. Firk, Hodge, and Hans!

All three. Ay, forsooth, what says your worship, Master Sheriff?   173

Eyre. Worship and honour, you Babylonian knaves, for the Gentle Craft. But I forgot myself; I am bidden by my lord mayor to dinner to Old Ford; he's gone before, I must after. Come, Madge, on with your trinkets! Now, my true Trojans, my fine Firk, my dapper Hodge, my honest Hans, some device, some odd crotchets, some morris, or such like, for the

149 rose] on the reverse of the coin.   157–8 See, my dear brother, here comes my master.   167–8 an hundred for twenty] referring to his loan of Portigues.

honour of the gentlemen shoemakers. Meet me at
Old Ford, you know my mind. Come, Madge, away.
Shut up the shop, knaves, and make holiday. [*Exeunt.*

    Firk. O rare! O brave! Come, Hodge; follow me,
        Hans;   184
We'll be with them for a morris-dance.   [*Exeunt.*

Scene V.

Enter Lord Mayor, Rose, Eyre, Margery *in a French
hood,* Sybil, *and other Servants.*

    Lord Mayor. Trust me, you are as welcome to Old
      Ford
As I myself.

    Margery. Truly, I thank your lordship.

    Lord Mayor. Would our bad cheer were worth the
      thanks you give.

    Eyre. Good cheer, my lord mayor, fine cheer!
A fine house, fine walls, all fine and neat.

    Lord Mayor. Now, by my troth, I'll tell thee,
      Master Eyre,
It does me good, and all my brethren,
That such a madcap fellow as thyself
Is entered into our society.   9

    Margery. Ay, but, my lord, he must learn now to
put on gravity.

    Eyre. Peace, Maggy, a fig for gravity! When I go
to Guildhall in my scarlet gown, I'll look as demurely
as a saint, and speak as gravely as a justice of peace,
but now I am here at Old Ford, at my good lord
mayor's house, let it go by, vanish, Maggy, I'll be
merry; away with flip-flap, these fooleries, these
gulleries. What, honey? Prince am I none, yet am
I princely born. What says my lord mayor?

    Lord Mayor. Ha, ha, ha! I had rather than a
      thousand pound,   20
had an heart but half so light as yours.

    Eyre. Why, what should I do, my lord? A pound

of care pays not a dram of debt. Hum, let's be merry
whiles we are young; old age, sack and sugar will steal
upon us, ere we be aware.

Lord Mayor. It's well done; Mistress Eyre, pray,
give good counsel
To my daughter.

Margery. I hope Mistress Rose will have the grace
to take nothing that's bad.

Lord Mayor. Pray God she do; for i' faith, Mistress
Eyre,   30
I would bestow upon that peevish girl
A thousand marks more than I mean to give her
Upon condition she'd be rul'd by me.
The ape still crosseth me. There came of late
A proper gentleman of fair revenues,
Whom gladly I would call son-in-law:
But my fine cockney would have none of him.—
You'll prove a coxcomb for it, ere you die:
A courtier, or no man must please your eye.   39

Eyre. Be rul'd, sweet Rose: th'art ripe for a man.
Marry not with a boy that has no more hair on his
face than thou hast on thy cheeks. A courtier? wash,
go by! stand not upon pishery-pashery: those silken
fellows are but painted images, outsides, outsides,
Rose; their inner linings are torn. No, my fine mouse,
marry me with a gentleman grocer like my lord
mayor, your father; a grocer is a sweet trade: plums,
plums. Had I a son or daughter should marry out
of the generation and blood of the shoemakers, he
should pack; what, the Gentle Trade is a living for
a man through Europe, through the world.   51

A noise within of a tabor and a pipe.

Lord Mayor. What noise is this?

Eyre. O my lord mayor, a crew of good fellows that
for love to your honour are come hither with a morris-
dance. Come in, my Mesopotamians, cheerily.

42 wash] rubbish.

I

Enter Hodge, Lacy, Ralph, Firk, *and other Shoemakers,*
in a morris; after a little dancing the Lord Mayor *speaks.*

    Lord Mayor. Master Eyre, are all these shoemakers?

    Eyre. All cordwainers, my good lord mayor.

    Rose. [*Aside.*] How like my Lacy looks yond shoe-
maker!

    Lacy. [*Aside.*] O that I durst but speak unto my
love!

    Lord Mayor. Sybil, go fetch some wine to make these
      drink.   60

You are all welcome.

    All.   We thank your lordship.

        Rose *takes a cup of wine and goes to* Lacy.

    Rose. For his sake whose fair shape thou repre-
      sent'st,

Good friend, I drink to thee.

    Lacy. Ic bedancke, good frister.

    Margery. I see, Mistress Rose, you do not want
judgment; you have drunk to the properest man I
keep.

    Firk. Here be some have done their parts to be as
proper as he.

    Lord Mayor. Well, urgent business calls me back to
      London: 70

Good fellows, first go in and taste our cheer,

And to make merry as you homeward go,

Spend these two angels in beer at Stratford-Bow.

    Eyre. To these two, my mad lads, Sim Eyre adds
another; then cheerily, Firk; tickle it, Hans, and all
for the honour of shoemakers.   [*All go dancing out.*

    Lord Mayor. Come, Master Eyre, let's have your
      company.   [*Exeunt.*

    Rose. Sybil, what shall I do?

    Sybil.   Why, what's the matter?

    Rose. That Hans the shoemaker is my love Lacy,

64] I thank you, good maid.   66 properest] most
handsome.

Disguis'd in that attire to find me out. 80
How should I find the means to speak with him?

Sybil. What, mistress, never fear; I dare venture
my maidenhead to nothing, and that's great odds,
that Hans the Dutchman, when we come to London,
shall not only see and speak with you, but in spite of
all your father's policies steal you away and marry you.
Will not this please you?

Rose. Do this, and ever be assured of my love.

Sybil. Away, then, and follow your father to
London, lest your absence cause him to suspect
something: 91

> To-morrow, if my counsel be obey'd,
> I'll bind you prentice to the Gentle Trade.

[Exeunt.

Act IV. Scene I.

Enter Jane *in a Seamster's shop, working, and* Hammon,
muffled, at another door; he stands aloof.

Hammon. Yonder's the shop, and there my fair
love sits.
She's fair and lovely, but she is not mine.
O, would she were! Thrice have I courted her,
Thrice hath my hand been moistened with her hand,
Whilst my poor famish'd eyes do feed on that
Which made them famish. I am infortunate:
I still love one, yet nobody loves me.
I muse, in other men what women see,
That I so want! Fine Mistress Rose was coy,
And this too curious! Oh, no, she is chaste, 10
And for she thinks me wanton, she denies
To cheer my cold heart with her sunny eyes.
How prettily she works, oh pretty hand!
Oh happy work! It doth me good to stand
Unseen to see her. Thus I oft have stood

86 policies] schemes.   10 curious] fastidious.

In frosty evenings, a light burning by her,
Enduring biting cold, only to eye her.
One only look hath seem'd as rich to me
As a king's crown; such is love's lunacy.
Muffled I'll pass along, and by that try   20
Whether she know me.

    Jane.   Sir, what is't you buy?
What is't you lack, sir, calico, or lawn,
Fine cambric shirts, or bands, what will you buy?

    Hammon. [*Aside.*] That which thou wilt not sell.
    Faith, yet I'll try:
How do you sell this handkercher?

    Jane.   Good cheap.

    Hammon. And how these ruffs?

    Jane.   Cheap too.

    Hammon.   And how this band?

    Jane. Cheap too.

    Hammon.   All cheap; how sell you then this
    hand?

    Jane. My hands are not to be sold.

    Hammon.   To be given then!
Nay, faith, I come to buy.

    Jane.   But none knows when.

    Hammon. Good sweet, leave work a little while;
    let's play.   30

    Jane. I cannot live by keeping holiday.

    Hammon. I'll pay you for the time which shall be
    lost.

    Jane. With me you shall not be at so much cost.

    Hammon. Look, how you wound this cloth, so you
    wound me.

    Jane. It may be so.

    Hammon.   'Tis so.

    Jane.   What remedy?

    Hammon. Nay, faith, you are too coy.

    Jane.   Let go my hand.

    Hammon. I will do any task at your command:
I would let go this beauty, were I not

In mind to disobey you by a power
That controls kings: I love you!
   Jane.   So, now part.   40
   Hammon. With hands I may, but never with my
     heart.
In faith, I love you.
   Jane.   I believe you do.
   Hammon. Shall a true love in me breed hate in you?
   Jane. I hate you not.
   Hammon.   Then you must love?
   Jane.   I do.
What are you better now? I love not you.
   Hammon. All this, I hope, is but a woman's fray,
That means: come to me, when she cries: away!
In earnest, mistress,—I do not jest—
A true chaste love hath entered in my breast.
I love you dearly, as I love my life,   50
I love you as a husband loves a wife;
That, and no other love, my love requires.
Thy wealth, I know, is little; my desires
Thirst not for gold. Sweet, beauteous Jane, what's
   mine
Shall, if thou make myself thine, all be thine.
Say, judge, what is thy sentence, life or death?
Mercy or cruelty lies in thy breath.
   Jane. Good sir, I do believe you love me well;
For 'tis a silly conquest, silly pride
For one like you—I mean a gentleman—   60
To boast that by his love-tricks he hath brought
Such and such women to his amorous lure;
I think you do not so, yet many do,
And make it even a very trade to woo.
I would be coy, as many women be,
Feed you with sunshine smiles and wanton looks,
But I detest witchcraft; say that I
Do constantly believe you, constant have——

   38 In mind] minded (?); or read 'Enjoin'd' (which
Dekker would spell 'inioind').   59 silly] trivial.

Hammon. Why dost thou not believe me?

Jane.   I believe you;
But yet, good sir, because I will not grieve you   70
With hopes to taste fruit which will never fall,
In simple truth this is the sum of all:
My husband lives, at least, I hope he lives.
Press'd was he to these bitter wars in France;
Bitter they are to me by wanting him.
I have but one heart, and that heart's his due.
How can I then bestow the same on you?
Whilst he lives, his I live, be it ne'er so poor,
And rather be his wife than a king's whore.

Hammon. Chaste and dear woman, I will not abuse
   thee,   80
Although it cost my life, if thou refuse me.
Thy husband, press'd for France, what was his
   name?

Jane. Ralph Damport.

Hammon.   Damport?—Here's a letter sent
From France to me, from a dear friend of mine,
A gentleman of place; here he doth write
Their names that have been slain in every fight.

Jane. I hope death's scroll contains not my love's
   name.

Hammon. Cannot you read?

Jane.   I can.

Hammon.   Peruse the same.
To my remembrance such a name I read
Amongst the rest. See here.

Jane.   Ay me, he's dead!   90
He's dead! if this be true, my dear heart's slain!

Hammon. Have patience, dear love.

Jane.   Hence, hence!

Hammon.   Nay, sweet Jane,
Make not poor sorrow proud with these rich tears.
I mourn thy husband's death, because thou mourn'st.

Jane. That bill is forg'd; 'tis sign'd by forgery.

Hammon. I'll bring thee letters sent besides to many,

Carrying the like report: Jane, 'tis too true.
Come, weep not: mourning, though it rise from love,
Helps not the mourned, yet hurts them that mourn.
   Jane. For God's sake, leave me.
   Hammon.   Whither dost thou turn?
Forget the dead, love them that are alive;   101
His love is faded, try how mine will thrive.
   Jane. 'Tis now no time for me to think on love—
   Hammon. 'Tis now best time for you to think on
     love,
Because your love lives not.
   Jane.   Though he be dead,
My love to him shall not be buried;
For God's sake, leave me to myself alone.
   Hammon. 'Twould kill my soul, to leave thee
     drown'd in moan.
Answer me to my suit, and I am gone;
Say to me yea or no.
   Jane.   No.
   Hammon.   Then farewell!   110
One farewell will not serve, I come again;
Come, dry these wet cheeks; tell me, faith, sweet
     Jane,
Yea or no, once more.
   Jane.   Once more I say, no;
Once more be gone, I pray; else will I go.
   Hammon. Nay, then I will grow rude; by this white
     hand,
Until you change that cold 'no', here I'll stand
Till by your hard heart——
   Jane.   Nay, for God's love, peace!
My sorrows by your presence more increase.
Not that you thus are present, but all grief
Desires to be alone: therefore in brief   120
Thus much I say, and saying bid adieu:
If ever I wed man, it shall be you.
   Hammon. O blessed voice! Dear Jane, I'll urge no
     more,

Thy breath hath made me rich.

   Jane.   Death makes me poor.

                                         [Exeunt.

Scene II.

Enter Hodge, *at his shop-board,* Ralph, Firk, Lacy, *and
a Boy at work.*

   All. Hey, down a down, down, derry.

   Hodge. Well said, my hearts; ply your work to-day,
we loitered yesterday; to it pell-mell, that we may
live to be lord mayors, or aldermen at least.

   Firk. Hey, down a down, derry.

   Hodge. Well said, i' faith! How say'st thou, Hans,
doth not Firk tickle it?

   Lacy. Yaw, mester.

   Firk. Not so neither, my organ-pipe squeaks this
morning for want of liquoring. Hey, down a down,
derry!   11

   Lacy. Forward, Firk, tow best un jolly yongster.
Hort, ay, mester, ic bid yo, cut me un pair vampres
vor Mester Jeffre's boots.

   Hodge. Thou shalt, Hans.

   Firk. Master!

   Hodge. How now, boy?

   Firk. Pray, now you are in the cutting vein, cut
me out a pair of counterfeits, or else my work will not
pass current; hey, down a down!   20

   Hodge. Tell me, sirs, are my cousin Mistress
Priscilla's shoes done?

   Firk. Your cousin? No, master; one of your aunts,
hang her; let them alone.

   Ralph. I am in hand with them; she gave charge
that none but I should do them for her.

   Firk. Thou do for her? then 'twill be a lame doing,

12–14] Forward, Firk, thou art a jolly youngster. Hark
ye, master, I ask you to cut me a pair of vamps for Master
Jeffrey's boots.   **23** aunts] bawds.

and that she loves not. Ralph, thou might'st have
sent her to me, in faith, I would have yerk'd and
firk'd your Priscilla. Hey, down a down, derry. This
gear will not hold.   31

Hodge. How say'st thou, Firk, were we not merry
at Old Ford?

Firk. How, merry? why, our buttocks went jiggy-
joggy like a quagmire. Well, Sir Roger Oatmeal, if
I thought all meal of that nature, I would eat nothing
but bagpuddings.

Ralph. Of all good fortunes my fellow Hans had
the best.

Firk. 'Tis true, because Mistress Rose drank to
him.   41

Hodge. Well, well, work apace. They say, seven of
the aldermen be dead, or very sick.

Firk. I care not, I'll be none.

Ralph. No, nor I; but then my Master Eyre will
come quickly to be lord mayor.

Enter Sybil.

Firk. Whoop, yonder comes Sybil.

Hodge. Sybil, welcome, i' faith; and how dost thou,
mad wench?

Firk. Syb-whore, welcome to London.   50

Sybil. Godamercy, sweet Firk; good lord, Hodge,
what a delicious shop you have got! You tickle it,
i' faith.

Ralph. Godamercy, Sybil, for our good cheer at
Old Ford.

Sybil. That you shall have, Ralph.

Firk. Nay, by the mass, we had tickling cheer,
Sybil; and how the plague dost thou and Mistress
Rose and my lord mayor? I put the women in first.

---

35 Oatmeal] the Lord Mayor's name, variously spelt in
the Quartos, was evidently pronounced *Oat*ley.   52 tickle
it] work briskly.

Sybil. Well, Godamercy; but God's me, I forget
myself, where's Hans the Fleming?   61

Firk. Hark, butter-box, now you must yelp out
some spreken.

Lacy. Wat begaie you? Vat vod you, Frister?

Sybil. Marry, you must come to my young mistress,
to pull on her shoes you made last.

Lacy. Vare ben your egle fro, vare ben your mistris?

Sybil. Marry, here at our London house in Cornhill.

Firk. Will nobody serve her turn but Hans?   70

Sybil. No, sir. Come, Hans, I stand upon needles.

Hodge. Why then, Sybil, take heed of pricking.

Sybil. For that let me alone. I have a trick in my
budget. Come, Hans.

Lacy. Yaw, yaw, ic sall meete yo gane.

[Exit Lacy and Sybil.

Hodge. Go, Hans, make haste again. Come, who
lacks work?

Firk. I, master, for I lack my breakfast; 'tis munch-
ing-time and past.   79

Hodge. Is't so? why, then leave work, Ralph. To
breakfast! Boy, look to the tools. Come, Ralph;
come, Firk.   [*Exeunt.*

Enter a Serving-man.

Serving-man. Let me see now, the sign of the Last
in Tower Street. Mass, yonder's the house. What,
haw! Who's within?

Enter Ralph.

Ralph. Who calls there? What want you, sir?

Serving-man. Marry, I would have a pair of shoes
made for a gentlewoman against to-morrow morning.
What, can you do them?   89

64] What want you? What would you, maid?   67]
Where is your noble mistress, where is your mistress?   75]
Yes, yes, I will go with you.

Ralph. Yes, sir, you shall have them. But what length's her foot?

Serving-man. Why, you must make them in all parts like this shoe; but, at any hand, fail not to do them, for the gentlewoman is to be married very early in the morning.   95

Ralph. How? by this shoe must it be made? by this? Are you sure, sir, by this?

Serving-man. How, by this? Am I sure, by this? Art thou in thy wits? I tell thee, I must have a pair of shoes, dost thou mark me? a pair of shoes, two shoes, made by this very shoe, this same shoe, against to-morrow morning by four a clock. Dost understand me? Canst thou do't?   103

Ralph. Yes, sir, yes—ay, ay!—I can do't. By this shoe, you say? I should know this shoe. Yes, sir, yes, by this shoe, I can do't. Four a clock, well. Whither shall I bring them?

Serving-man. To the sign of the Golden Ball in Watling Street; inquire for one Master Hammon, a gentleman, my master.   110

Ralph. Yea, sir; by this shoe, you say?

Serving-man. I say, Master Hammon at the Golden Ball; he's the bridegroom, and those shoes are for his bride.

Ralph. They shall be done by this shoe; well, well, Master Hammon at the Golden Shoe—I would say, the Golden Ball; very well, very well. But I pray you, sir, where must Master Hammon be married?   118

Serving-man. At Saint Faith's Church, under Paul's. But what's that to thee? Prithee, dispatch those shoes, and so farewell.   [*Exit.*

Ralph. By this shoe, said he. How am I amaz'd
At this strange accident! Upon my life,
This was the very shoe I gave my wife
When I was press'd for France; since when, alas!

93 at any hand] in any case.

I never could hear of her: it is the same,
And Hammon's bride no other but my Jane.

Enter Firk.

Firk. 'Snails, Ralph, thou hast lost thy part of three
pots, a countryman of mine gave me to breakfast.

Ralph. I care not; I have found a better thing.

Firk. A thing? away! Is it a man's thing, or a
woman's thing? 132

Ralph. Firk, dost thou know this shoe?

Firk. No, by my troth; neither doth that know me!
I have no acquaintance with it, 'tis a mere stranger
to me.

Ralph. Why, then I do; this shoe, I durst be sworn,
Once covered the instep of my Jane.
This is her size, her breadth, thus trod my love;
These true-love knots I prick'd; I hold my life, 140
By this old shoe I shall find out my wife.

Firk. Ha, ha! Old shoe, that wert new! How a
murrain came this ague-fit of foolishness upon thee?

Ralph. Thus, Firk: even now here came a serving-
man;
By this shoe would he have a new pair made
Against to-morrow morning for his mistress,
That's to be married to a gentleman,
And why may not this be my sweet Jane?

Firk. And why may'st not thou be my sweet ass?
Ha, ha! 150

Ralph. Well, laugh and spare not! But the truth
is this:
Against to-morrow morning I'll provide
A lusty crew of honest shoemakers,
To watch the going of the bride to church.
If she prove Jane, I'll take her in despite
From Hammon and the devil, were he by.
If it be not my Jane, what remedy?

140 hold] wager.

Hereof I am sure, I shall live till I die,   158
Although I never with a woman lie.   [*Exit.*

Firk. Thou lie with a woman, to build nothing but
Cripple-gates! Well, God sends fools fortune, and it
may be he may light upon his matrimony by such a
device; for wedding and hanging goes by destiny.

[*Exit.*

Scene III.

Enter Lacy *and* Rose, *arm in arm.*

Lacy. How happy am I by embracing thee!
Oh, I did fear such cross mishaps did reign,
That I should never see my Rose again.

Rose. Sweet Lacy, since fair opportunity
Offers herself to further our escape,
Let not too over-fond esteem of me
Hinder that happy hour. Invent the means,
And Rose will follow thee through all the world.

Lacy. Oh, how I surfeit with excess of joy,
Made happy by thy rich perfection!   10
But since thou pay'st sweet interest to my hopes,
Redoubling love on love, let me once more
Like to a bold-fac'd debtor crave of thee,
This night to steal abroad, and at Eyre's house,
Who now by death of certain aldermen
Is mayor of London, and my master once,
Meet thou thy Lacy, where in spite of change,
Your father's anger, and mine uncle's hate,
Our happy nuptials will we consummate.   19

Enter Sybil.

Sybil. Oh God, what will you do, mistress? Shift
for yourself, your father is at hand! He's coming,
he's coming! Master Lacy, hide yourself! In, my
mistress! For God's sake, shift for yourselves!

Lacy. Your father come, sweet Rose—what shall
I do?

2 cross] adverse.

Where shall I hide me? How shall I escape?

Rose. A man, and want wit in extremity!
Come, come, be Hans still, play the shoemaker,
Pull on my shoe.

Enter the Lord Mayor.

Lacy.   Mass, and that's well remembered.

Sybil. Here comes your father.

Lacy. Forware, metresse, 'tis un good skow, it sal
vel dute, or ye sal neit betallen.   31

Rose. Oh God, it pincheth me; what will you do?

Lacy. [*Aside.*] You father's presence pincheth, not
    the shoe.

Lord Mayor. Well done; fit my daughter well, and
she shall please thee well.

Lacy. Yaw, yaw, ick weit dat well; forware, 'tis
un good skoo, 'tis gimait van neits leither; se euer,
mine here.

Enter a Prentice.

Lord Mayor. I do believe it.—What's the news with
    you?

Prentice. Please you, the Earl of Lincoln at the gate
Is newly lighted, and would speak with you.   41

Lord Mayor. The Earl of Lincoln come to speak
    with me?
Well, well, I know his errand. Daughter Rose,
Send hence your shoemaker, dispatch, have done!
Syb, make things handsome! Sir boy, follow me.
                                                      [*Exit.*

Lacy. Mine uncle come! Oh, what may this
    portend?
Sweet Rose, this of our love threatens an end.

28 s.d. Lord Mayor] *sc.* the ex-Lord Mayor, Sir Roger
Oteley; the Quarto stage directions sensibly continue his
old style to the end to avoid confusion.   30–1] Truly,
mistress, it is a good shoe, it will fit well, or you shall not pay.
36–8] Yes, yes, I know that well; truly, it is a good shoe, it
is made of neat's leather; only look, sir.

Rose. Be not dismay'd at this; whate'er befall,
Rose is thine own. To witness I speak truth,
Where thou appoints the place, I'll meet with thee.
I will not fix a day to follow thee,   51
But presently steal hence. Do not reply:
Love which gave strength to bear my father's hate,
Shall now add wings to further our escape.

                                                    [*Exeunt.*

Scene IV.

Enter Lord Mayor *and* Lincoln.

Lord Mayor. Believe me, on my credit, I speak truth:
Since first your nephew Lacy went to France,
I have not seen him. It seem'd strange to me,
When Dodger told me that he stay'd behind,
Neglecting the high charge the king imposed.
Lincoln. Trust me, Sir Roger Oteley, I did think
Your counsel had given head to this attempt,
Drawn to it by the love he bears your child.
Here I did hope to find him in your house;
But now I see mine error, and confess,   10
My judgement wrong'd you by conceiving so.
Lord Mayor. Lodge in my house, say you? Trust
        me, my lord,
I love your nephew Lacy too too dearly,
So much to wrong his honour; and he hath done so,
That first gave him advice to stay from France.
To witness I speak truth, I let you know,
How careful I have been to keep my daughter
Free from all conference or speech of him;
Not that I scorn your nephew, but in love
I bear your honour, lest your noble blood   20
Should by my mean worth be dishonoured.
Lincoln. [*Aside.*] How far the churl's tongue wan-
        ders from his heart!
—Well, well, Sir Roger Oteley, I believe you,
With more than many thanks for the kind love

    50 appoints] appointest.   52 presently] at once.

So much you seem to bear me. But, my lord,
Let me request your help to seek my nephew,
Whom if I find, I'll straight embark for France.
So shall your Rose be free, my thoughts at rest,
And much care die which now lies in my breast.

Enter Sybil.

Sybil. O Lord! Help, for God's sake! my mistress!
oh, my young mistress!   31

Lord Mayor. Where is thy mistress? What's become of her?

Sybil. She's gone, she's fled!

Lord Mayor.   Gone! Whither is she fled?

Sybil. I know not, forsooth; she's fled out of doors
with Hans the shoemaker; I saw them scud, scud,
scud, apace, apace!

Lord Mayor. Which way? What, John! Where be
my men? Which way?

Sybil. I know not, an it please your worship.

Lord Mayor. Fled with a shoemaker? Can this be
true?

Sybil. Oh Lord, sir, as true as God's in Heaven.   40

Lincoln. [*Aside*]. Her love turn'd shoemaker? I am
glad of this.

Lord Mayor. A Fleming butter-box, a shoemaker!
Will she forget her birth, requite my care
With such ingratitude? Scorn'd she young Hammon
To love a honnikin, a needy knave?
Well, let her fly, I'll not fly after her,
Let her starve, if she will; she's none of mine.

Lincoln. Be not so cruel, sir.

Enter Firk *with shoes.*

Sybil. [*Aside*.]   I am glad, she's 'scap'd.

Lord Mayor. I'll not account of her as of my child.
Was there no better object for her eyes   50
But a foul drunken lubber, swill-belly,
A shoemaker? That's brave!

45 honnikin] spoiled darling (?).

Firk. Yea, forsooth; 'tis a very brave shoe, and as fit as a pudding.

Lord Mayor. How now, what knave is this? From whence comest thou?

Firk. No knave, sir. I am Firk the shoemaker, lusty Roger's chief lusty journeyman, and I come hither to take up the pretty leg of sweet Mistress Rose, and thus hoping your worship is in as good health, as I was at the making thereof, I bid you farewell, yours, Firk. 60

Lord Mayor. Stay, stay, Sir Knave!

Lincoln.   Come hither, shoemaker!

Firk. 'Tis happy the knave is put before the shoemaker, or else I would not have vouchsafed to come back to you. I am moved, for I stir.

Lord Mayor. My lord, this villain calls us knaves by craft.

Firk. Then 'tis by the Gentle Craft, and to call one knave gently, is no harm. Sit your worship merry! [*Aside to* Sybil].—Syb, your young mistress—I'll so bob them, now my Master Eyre is lord mayor of London. 70

Lord Mayor. Tell me, sirrah, whose man are you?

Firk. I am glad to see your worship so merry. I have no maw to this gear, no stomach as yet to a red petticoat.   [*Pointing to* Sybil.

Lincoln. He means not, sir, to woo you to his maid, But only doth demand whose man you are.

Firk. I sing now to the tune of Rogero. Roger, my fellow, is now my master.

Lincoln. Sirrah, know'st thou one Hans, a shoemaker?   79

Firk. Hans, shoemaker? Oh yes, stay, yes. I have him. I tell you what, I speak it in secret: Mistress Rose and he are by this time—no, not so, but shortly are to come over one another with 'Can you dance the shaking of the sheets?' It is that Hans—[*Aside.*] I'll so gull these diggers!

85 diggers] diggers for information (Wheeler)

Lord Mayor. Know'st thou, then, where he is?

Firk. Yes, forsooth; yea, marry!

Lincoln. Canst thou, in sadness?

Firk. No, forsooth; no marry!

Lord Mayor. Tell me, good honest fellow, where
    he is,   90
And thou shalt see what I'll bestow of thee.

Firk. Honest fellow? No, sir; not so, sir; my profession is the Gentle Craft; I care not for seeing, I love
feeling; let me feel it here; *aurium tenus*, ten pieces of
gold; *genuum tenus*, ten pieces of silver; and then Firk
is your man—[*Aside*] in a new pair of stretchers.

Lord Mayor. Here is an angel, part of thy reward,
Which I will give thee; tell me where he is.   98

Firk. No point! Shall I betray my brother? no!
Shall I prove Judas to Hans? no! Shall I cry treason
to my corporation? no! I shall be firk'd and yerk'd
then. But give me your angel; your angel shall tell
you.

Lincoln. Do so, good fellow; 'tis no hurt to thee.

Firk. Send simpering Syb away.

Lord Mayor. Huswife, get you in.   [*Exit* Sybil.

Firk. Pitchers have ears, and maids have wide
mouths; but for Hauns-prauns, upon my word,
to-morrow morning he and young Mistress Rose go
to this gear, they shall be married together, by this
rush, or else turn Firk to a firkin of butter, to tan
leather withal.   112

Lord Mayor. But art thou sure of this?

Firk. Am I sure that Paul's steeple is a handful
higher than London Stone, or that the Pissing-
Conduit leaks nothing but pure Mother Bunch?
Am I sure I am lusty Firk? God's nails, do you think
I am so base to gull you?

Lincoln. Where are they married? Dost thou know
    the church?   119

88 Canst] knowest.   sadness] earnest.   96
stretchers] lies.   99 No point] not a bit.

Firk. I never go to church, but I know the name of it; it is a swearing church—stay a while, 'tis—Ay, by the mass, no, no,—tis—Ay, by my troth, no, nor that; 'tis—Ay, by my faith, that, that, 'tis, Ay, by my Faith's Church under Paul's Cross. There they shall be knit like a pair of stockings in matrimony; there they'll be inconie.

Lincoln. Upon my life, my nephew Lacy walks In the disguise of this Dutch shoemaker.

Firk. Yes, forsooth.

Lincoln. Doth he not, honest fellow?   130

Firk. No, forsooth; I think Hans is nobody but Hans, no spirit.

Lord Mayor. My mind misgives me now, 'tis so, indeed.

Lincoln. My cousin speaks the language, knows the trade.

Lord Mayor. Let me request your company, my lord;

Your honourable presence may, no doubt,
Refrain their headstrong rashness, when myself
Going alone perchance may be o'erborne.
Shall I request this favour?

Lincoln.   This, or what else.   139

Firk. Then you must rise betimes, for they mean to fall to their 'hey-pass and repass', 'pindy-pandy, which hand will you have', very early.

Lord Mayor. My care shall every way equal their haste.

This night accept your lodging in my house,
The earlier shall we stir, and at Saint Faith's
Prevent this giddy hare-brain'd nuptial.
This traffic of hot love shall yield cold gains:
They ban our loves, and we'll forbid their banns.

                                                    [*Exit.*

Lincoln. At Saint Faith's Church thou say'st?

126 inconie] fine; a (rather vague) cant word of approval.

Firk. Yes, by my troth.   150

Lincoln. Be secret, on thy life.   [*Exit.*

Firk. Yes, when I kiss your wife! Ha, ha, here's
no craft in the Gentle Craft! I came hither of purpose
with shoes to Sir Roger's worship, whilst Rose, his
daughter, be cony-catched by Hans. Soft now; these
two gulls will be at Saint Faith's Church to-morrow
morning, to take Master Bridegroom and Mistress
Bride napping, and they, in the meantime, shall chop
up the matter at the Savoy. But the best sport is, Sir
Roger Oteley will find my fellow lame Ralph's wife
going to marry a gentleman, and then he'll stop her
instead of his daughter. Oh, brave! there will be fine
tickling sport. Soft now, what have I to do? Oh,
I know; now a mess of shoemakers meet at the Wool-
sack in Ivy Lane, to cozen my gentleman of lame
Ralph's wife, that's true.   166

      Alack, alack!
      Girls, hold out tack!
      For now smocks for this jumbling
      Shall go to wrack.   [*Exit.*

Act V. Scene I.

Enter Eyre, Margery, Lacy, *and* Rose.

Eyre. This is the morning, then, say, my bully, my
honest Hans, is it not?

Lacy. This is the morning that must make us two
happy or miserable; therefore, if you——

Eyre. Away with these ifs and ans, Hans, and these
et ceteras! By mine honour, Rowland Lacy, none but
the king shall wrong thee. Come, fear nothing, am
not I Sim Eyre? Is not Sim Eyre lord mayor of
London? Fear nothing, Rose: let them all say what
they can; dainty, come thou to me—laughest thou?

168 hold out tack] hold your own, keep at bay.

Margery. Good my lord, stand her friend in what thing you may. 12

Eyre. Why, my sweet Lady Madgy, think you Simon Eyre can forget his fine Dutch journeyman? No, vah! Fie, I scorn it, it shall never be cast in my teeth, that I was unthankful. Lady Madgy, thou had'st never cover'd thy Saracen's head with this French flap, nor loaden thy bum with this farthingale ('tis trash, trumpery, vanity); Simon Eyre had never walk'd in a red petticoat, nor wore a chain of gold, but for my fine journeyman's Portigues, and shall I leave him? No! Prince am I none, yet bear a princely mind. 23

Lacy. My lord, 'tis time for us to part from hence.

Eyre. Lady Madgy, Lady Madgy, take two or three of my pie-crust-eaters, my buff-jerkin varlets, that do walk in black gowns at Simon Eyre's heels; take them, good Lady Madgy; trip and go, my brown queen of periwigs, with my delicate Rose and my jolly Rowland to the Savoy; see them link'd, countenance the marriage; and when it is done, cling, cling together, you Hamborow turtle-doves. I'll bear you out, come to Simon Eyre; come, dwell with me, Hans, thou shalt eat minc'd-pies and marchpane. Rose, away, cricket; trip and go, my Lady Madgy, to the Savoy; Hans, wed, and to bed; kiss, and away! Go, vanish!

Margery. Farewell, my lord.

Rose. Make haste, sweet love.

Margery.　　　She'd fain the deed were done. 39

Lacy. Come, my sweet Rose; faster than deer we'll run.　　　[*They go out.*

Eyre. Go, vanish, vanish! Avaunt, I say! By the Lord of Ludgate, it's a mad life to be a lord mayor; it's a stirring life, a fine life, a velvet life, a careful life. Well, Simon Eyre, yet set a good face on it, in the

---

34 marchpane] marzipan.

honour of Saint Hugh. Soft, the king this day comes
to dine with me, to see my new buildings; his majesty
is welcome, he shall have good cheer, delicate cheer,
princely cheer. This day, my fellow prentices of
London come to dine with me too; they shall have
fine cheer, gentlemanlike cheer. I promised the mad
Cappadocians, when we all served at the Conduit
together, that if ever I came to be mayor of London,
I would feast them all, and I'll do 't, I'll do 't, by the
life of Pharaoh; by this beard, Sim Eyre will be no
flincher. Besides, I have procur'd that upon every
Shrove Tuesday, at the sound of the pancake bell, my
fine dapper Assyrian lads shall clap up their shop
windows, and away. This is the day, and this day
they shall do 't, they shall do 't.   59

    Boys, that day are you free, let masters care,
    And prentices shall pray for Simon Eyre.

                                 [Exit.

Scene II.

Enter Hodge, Firk, Ralph, *and five or six Shoemakers, all
with cudgels or such weapons.*

Hodge. Come, Ralph; stand to it, Firk. My masters,
as we are the brave bloods of the shoemakers, heirs
apparent to Saint Hugh, and perpetual benefactors
to all good fellows, thou shalt have no wrong; were
Hammon a king of spades, he should not delve in
thy close without thy sufferance. But tell me, Ralph,
art thou sure 'tis thy wife?   7

Ralph. Am I sure this is Firk? This morning, when
I strok'd on her shoes, I look'd upon her, and she upon
me, and sighed, ask'd me if ever I knew one Ralph.
Yes, said I. For his sake, said she—tears standing in

    51 the Conduit] whence it was part of an apprentice's
duty to fetch water.   56 pancake bell] rung on Shrove
Tuesday about 11 a.m.   6 close] enclosure, property
(*sc.* Jane).   9 strok'd] fitted.

her eyes—and for thou art somewhat like him, spend this piece of gold. I took it; my lame leg and my travel beyond sea made me unknown. All is one for that: I know she's mine. 15

Firk. Did she give thee this gold? O glorious glittering gold! She's thine own, 'tis thy wife, and she loves thee; for I'll stand to 't, there's no woman will give gold to any man, but she thinks better of him than she thinks of them she gives silver to. And for Hammon, neither Hammon nor hangman shall wrong thee in London. Is not our old master Eyre, lord mayor? Speak, my hearts. 23

All. Yes, and Hammon shall know it to his cost.

Enter Hammon, *his man,* Jane, *and others.*

Hodge. Peace, my bullies; yonder they come.

Ralph. Stand to 't, my hearts. Firk, let me speak first.

Hodge. No, Ralph, let me.—Hammon, whither away so early?

Hammon. Unmannerly, rude slave, what's that to thee? 30

Firk. To him, sir? Yes, sir, and to me, and others. Good-morrow, Jane, how dost thou? Good Lord, how the world is changed with you! God be thanked!

Hammon. Villains, hands off! How dare you touch my love?

All the shoemakers. Villains? Down with them! Cry clubs for prentices!

Hodge. Hold, my hearts! Touch her, Hammon? Yea, and more than that: we'll carry her away with us. My masters and gentlemen, never draw your bird-spits; shoemakers are steel to the back, men every inch of them, all spirit. 41

All of Hammon's side. Well, and what of all this?

Hodge. I'll show you.—Jane, dost thou know this

35–6 Cry clubs] the usual cry for summoning apprentices to defend or offend the honour of the citizens.

man? 'Tis Ralph, I can tell thee; nay, 'tis he in faith, though he be lam'd by the wars. Yet look not strange, run to him, fold him about the neck and kiss him.

Jane. Lives then my husband? Oh God, let me go, Let me embrace my Ralph.

Hammon. What means my Jane?

Jane. Nay, what meant you, to tell me, he was slain? 50

Hammon. Pardon me, dear love, for being misled. 'Twas rumour'd here in London, thou wert dead.

Firk. Thou seest he lives. Lass, go, pack home with him. Now, Master Hammon, where's your mistress, your wife?

Serving-man. 'Swounds, master, fight for her! Will you thus lose her?

Shoemakers. Down with that creature! Clubs! Down with him!

Hodge. Hold, hold! 60

Hammon. Hold, fool! Sirs, he shall do no wrong. Will my Jane leave me thus, and break her faith?

Firk. Yea, sir! She must, sir! She shall, sir! What then? Mend it!

Hodge. Hark, fellow Ralph, follow my counsel: set the wench in the midst, and let her choose her man, and let her be his woman.

Jane. Whom should I choose? Whom should my thoughts affect
But him whom Heaven hath made to be my love?
Thou art my husband, and these humble weeds 70
Make thee more beautiful than all his wealth.
Therefore, I will but put off his attire,
Returning it into the owner's hand,
And after ever be thy constant wife.

Hodge. Not a rag, Jane! The law's on our side; he that sows in another man's ground, forfeits his harvest. Get thee home, Ralph; follow him, Jane; he shall not have so much as a busk-point from thee.

Firk. Stand to that, Ralph; the appurtenances are
thine own. Hammon, look not at her!   80
Serving-man. O, 'swounds, no!
Firk. Blue coat, be quiet, we'll give you a new livery
else; we'll make Shrove Tuesday Saint George's Day
for you. Look not, Hammon, leer not! I'll firk you!
For thy head now,—one glance, one sheep's eye,
anything, at her! Touch not a rag, lest I and my
brethren beat you to clouts.
    Serving-man. Come, Master Hammon, there's no
    striving here.
    Hammon. Good fellows, hear me speak; and, honest
    Ralph,
Whom I have injured most by loving Jane,   90
Mark what I offer thee: here in fair gold
Is twenty pound, I'll give it for thy Jane;
If this content thee not, thou shalt have more.
    Hodge. Sell not thy wife, Ralph: make her not a
    whore.
    Hammon. Say, wilt thou freely cease thy claim in
    her,
And let her be my wife?
    All the shoemakers.   No, do not, Ralph.
    Ralph. Sirrah Hammon, Hammon, dost thou think
a shoemaker is so base to be a bawd to his own wife
for commodity? Take thy gold, choke with it! Were
I not lame, I would make thee eat thy words.   100
    Firk. A shoemaker sell his flesh and blood? Oh,
indignity!
    Hodge. Sirrah, take up your pelf, and be packing.
    Hammon. I will not touch one penny, but in lieu
Of that great wrong I offered thy Jane,
To Jane and thee I give that twenty pound.
Since I have fail'd of her, during my life,
I vow, no woman else shall be my wife.
Farewell, good fellows of the Gentle Trade:

    82 Blue coat] servingmen's livery.

Your morning mirth my mourning day hath made.

[*Exeunt.*

Firk. Touch the gold, creature, if you dare! Y'are best be trudging. Here, Jane, take thou it. Now let's home, my hearts. 113

Hodge. Stay! Who comes here? Jane, on again with thy mask!

Enter Lincoln, Lord Mayor, *and Servants.*

Lincoln. Yonder's the lying varlet mock'd us so.

Lord Mayor. Come hither, sirrah!

Firk. I, sir? I am sirrah? You mean me, do you not?

Lincoln. Where is my nephew married? 120

Firk. Is he married? God give him joy, I am glad of it. They have a fair day, and the sign is in a good planet, Mars in Venus.

Lord Mayor. Villain, thou toldst me that my
           daughter Rose
This morning should be married at Saint Faith's;
We have watched there these three hours at the least,
Yet see we no such thing.

Firk. Truly, I am sorry for't; a bride's a pretty thing. 129

Hodge. Come to the purpose. Yonder's the bride and bridegroom you look for, I hope. Though you be lords, you are not to bar by your authority men from women, are you?

Lord Mayor. See, see, my daughter's mask'd.

Lincoln.   True, and my nephew,
To hide his guilt, counterfeits him lame.

Firk. Yea, truly; God help the poor couple, they are lame and blind.

Lord Mayor. I'll ease her blindness.

Lincoln.   I'll his lameness cure.

Firk. [*Aside to the Shoemakers.*] Lie down, sirs, and

137 blind] Firk puns on the possible alternative sense of 'blindfold'.

laugh! My fellow Ralph is taken for Rowland Lacy, and Jane for Mistress Damask Rose. This is all my knavery. 142

Lord Mayor. What, have I found you, minion?

Lincoln.   O base wretch!
Nay, hide thy face, the horror of thy guilt
Can hardly be wash'd off. Where are thy powers?
What battles have you made? O yes, I see,
Thou fought'st with Shame, and Shame hath con-
    quer'd thee.
This lameness will not serve.

Lord Mayor.   Unmask yourself.

Lincoln. Lead home your daughter.

Lord Mayor.   Take your nephew hence.

Ralph. Hence! 'Swounds, what mean you? Are you mad? I hope you cannot enforce my wife from me. Where's Hammon? 152

Lord Mayor. Your wife?

Lincoln. What Hammon?

Ralph. Yea, my wife; and, therefore, the proudest of you that lays hands on her first, I'll lay my crutch 'cross his pate.

Firk. To him, lame Ralph! Here's brave sport!

Ralph. Rose call you her? Why, her name is Jane. Look here else; do you know her now?— 160

Lincoln. Is this your daughter?

Lord Mayor.   No, nor this your nephew.
My Lord of Lincoln, we are both abus'd
By this base, crafty varlet.

Firk. Yea, forsooth, no varlet; forsooth, no base; forsooth, I am but mean; no crafty neither, but of the Gentle Craft.

Lord Mayor. Where is my daughter Rose? Where is my child?

Lincoln. Where is my nephew Lacy married?

Firk. Why, here is good laced mutton, as I promis'd you. 170

169 mutton] cant term for a prostitute.

Lincoln. Villain, I'll have thee punish'd for this wrong.

Firk. Punish the journeyman villain, but not the journeyman shoemaker.

Enter Dodger.

Dodger. My lord, I come to bring unwelcome news.
Your nephew Lacy and your daughter Rose
Early this morning wedded at the Savoy,
None being present but the lady mayoress.
Besides, I learnt among the officers,
The lord mayor vows to stand in their defence
'Gainst any that shall seek to cross the match.   180

Lincoln. Dares Eyre the shoemaker uphold the deed?

Firk. Yes, sir, shoemakers dare stand in a woman's quarrel, I warrant you, as deep as another, and deeper too.

Dodger. Besides, his grace to-day dines with the mayor;
Who on his knees humbly intends to fall
And beg a pardon for your nephew's fault.

Lincoln. But I'll prevent him! Come, Sir Roger Oteley;
The king will do us justice in this cause.   189
Howe'er their hands have made them man and wife,
I will disjoin the match, or lose my life.   [*Exeunt.*

Firk. Adieu, Monsieur Dodger! Farewell, fools! Ha, ha!—Oh if they had stay'd, I would have so lamb'd them with flouts! O heart, my codpiece-point is ready to fly in pieces every time I think upon Mistress Rose; but let that pass, as my lady mayoress says.   197

Hodge. This matter is answer'd. Come, Ralph, home with thy wife. Come, my fine shoemakers, let's to our master's, the new lord mayor, and there swagger

194 lamb'd] whipped.   flouts] taunts, jeers.   194–5 codpiece-point] lace joining breeches in front.

this Shrove Tuesday. I'll promise you wine enough, for Madge keeps the cellar. 202

All. O rare! Madge is a good wench.

Firk. And I'll promise you meat enough, for simpering Susan keeps the larder. I'll lead you to victuals, my brave soldiers; follow your captain. O brave! Hark, hark! [*Bell rings.*

All. The pancake-bell rings, the pancake-bell! Trilill, my hearts! 209

Firk. O brave! O sweet bell! O delicate pancakes! Open the doors, my hearts, and shut up the windows! keep in the house, let out the pancakes! Oh, rare, my hearts! Let's march together for the honour of Saint Hugh to the great new hall in Gracious Street corner, which our master, the new lord mayor, hath built.

Ralph. O the crew of good fellows that will dine at my lord mayor's cost to-day!

Hodge. By the Lord, my lord mayor is a most brave man. How shall prentices be bound to pray for him and the honour of the gentlemen shoemakers! Let's feed and be fat with my lord's bounty. 222

Firk. O musical bell, still! O Hodge, O my brethren! There's cheer for the heavens: venison pasties walk up and down piping hot, like sergeants; beef and brewis comes marching in dry-fats, fritters and pancakes comes trowling in in wheel-barrows; hens and oranges hopping in porters' baskets, collops and eggs in scuttles, and tarts and custards comes quavering in in malt-shovels. 230

Enter more prentices.

All. Whoop, look here, look here!

Hodge. How now, mad lads, whither away so fast?

1st prentice. Whither? Why, to the great new hall,

214 great new hall] see v. v. 135–9.   219 brave] fine.
226 brewis] broth.   dry-fats] hogsheads.

know you not why? The lord mayor hath bidden all the prentices in London to breakfast this morning.

All. Oh, brave shoemaker, oh, brave lord of incomprehensible good fellowship! Whoo! Hark you! The pancake-bell rings.   [*Cast up caps.*

Firk. Nay, more, my hearts! Every Shrove Tuesday is our year of jubilee: and when the pancake-bell rings, we are as free as my lord mayor; we may shut up our shops, and make holiday. I'll have it call'd Saint Hugh's Holiday.   243

All. Agreed, agreed! Saint Hugh's Holiday.

Hodge. And this shall continue for ever.

All. Oh, brave! Come, come, my hearts! Away, away!

Firk. O eternal credit to us of the Gentle Craft! March fair, my hearts! Oh, rare!   [*Exeunt.*

Scene III.

Enter King and his Train over the stage.

King. Is our lord mayor of London such a gallant?

Nobleman. One of the merriest madcaps in your land.
Your grace will think, when you behold the man,
He's rather a wild ruffian than a mayor:
Yet thus much I'll ensure your majesty,
In all his actions that concern his state,
He is as serious, provident, and wise,
As full of gravity amongst the grave,
As any mayor hath been these many years.

King. I am with child till I behold this huff-cap, 10
But all my doubt is, when we come in presence,
His madness will be dash'd clean out of countenance.

Nobleman. It may be so, my liege.

King.   Which to prevent
Let some one give him notice, 'tis our pleasure

10 with child] in suspense.   huff-cap] madcap.

That he put on his wonted merriment.
Set forward!

    All.   On afore!   [*Exeunt.*

Scene IV.

Enter Eyre, Hodge, Firk, Ralph, *and other Shoemakers,
all with napkins on their shoulders.*

Eyre. Come, my fine Hodge, my jolly gentlemen
shoemakers; soft, where be these cannibals, these
varlets, my officers? Let them all walk and wait upon
my brethren; for my meaning is, that none but shoemakers, none but the livery of my company shall in
their satin hoods wait upon the trencher of my
sovereign.

Firk. O my lord, it will be rare!   **8**

Eyre. No more, Firk; come, lively! Let your fellow
prentices want no cheer; let wine be plentiful as
beer, and beer as water. Hang these penny-pinching
fathers, that cram wealth in innocent lambskins. Rip,
knaves, avaunt! Look to my guests!

Hodge. My lord, we are at our wits' end for room;
those hundred tables will not feast the fourth part of
them.

Eyre. Then cover me those hundred tables again,
and again, till all my jolly prentices be feasted. Avoid,
Hodge! Run, Ralph! Frisk about, my nimble Firk!
Carouse me fathom-healths to the honour of the shoemakers. Do they drink lively, Hodge? Do they tickle
it, Firk?   **22**

Firk. Tickle it? Some of them have taken their
liquor standing so long that they can stand no longer;
but for meat, they would eat it, an they had it.

Eyre. Want they meat? Where's this swag-belly,
this greasy kitchenstuff cook? Call the varlet to me!
Want meat? Firk, Hodge, lame Ralph, run, my tall

18 Avoid] away with you!

men, beleaguer the shambles, beggar all Eastcheap,
serve me whole oxen in chargers, and let sheep whine
upon the tables like pigs for want of good fellows
to eat them. Want meat? Vanish, Firk! Avaunt,
Hodge!   33

Hodge. Your lordship mistakes my man Firk; he
means, their bellies want meat, not the boards; for
they have drunk so much, they can eat nothing.

Enter Lacy, Rose, *and* Margery.

Margery. Where is my lord?

Eyre. How now, Lady Madgy?

Margery. The king's most excellent majesty is new
come; he sends me for thy honour; one of his most
worshipful peers bade me tell thou must be merry,
and so forth; but let that pass.   42

Eyre. Is my sovereign come? Vanish, my tall shoemakers, my nimble brethren; look to my guests, the
prentices. Yet stay a little! How now, Hans? How
looks my little Rose?

Lacy. Let me request you to remember me.
I know your honour easily may obtain
Free pardon of the king for me and Rose,
And reconcile me to my uncle's grace.   50

Eyre. Have done, my good Hans, my honest
journeyman; look cheerily! I'll fall upon both my
knees, till they be as hard as horn, but I'll get thy
pardon.

Margery. Good my lord, have a care what you speak
to his grace.   56

Eyre. Away, you Islington whitepot! hence, you
hopperarse! you barley-pudding full of maggots!
you broil'd carbonado! avaunt, avaunt, avoid,
Mephistophilus! Shall Sim Eyre learn to speak of
you, Lady Madgy? Vanish, Mother Miniver-cap;

57 whitepot] custard.   59 carbonado] steak.   61
Miniver-cap] fur cap; the prerogative of wealthier citizens'
wives.

vanish, go, trip and go; meddle with your partlets and your pishery-pashery, your flewes and your whirligigs; go, rub, out of mine alley! Sim Eyre knows how to speak to a Pope, to Sultan Soliman, to Tamburlaine, an he were here, and shall I melt, shall I droop before my sovereign? No! Come, my Lady Madgy! Follow me, Hans! About your business, my frolic free-booters! Firk, frisk about, and about, and about, for the honour of mad Simon Eyre, lord mayor of London.   71

Firk. Hey, for the honour of the shoemakers.

Exeunt.

Scene V.

A long flourish or two. Enter King, Nobles, Eyre, Margery, Lacy, Rose.   Lacy *and* Rose *kneel.*

King. Well, Lacy, though the fact was very foul
Of your revolting from our kingly love
And your own duty, yet we pardon you.
Rise both, and, Mistress Lacy, thank my lord mayor
For your young bridegroom here.

Eyre. So, my dear liege, Sim Eyre and my brethren, the gentlemen shoemakers, shall set your sweet majesty's image cheek by jowl by Saint Hugh for this honour you have done poor Simon Eyre. I beseech your grace, pardon my rude behaviour; I am a handicraftsman, yet my heart is without craft; I would be sorry at my soul, that my boldness should offend my king.   13

King. Nay, I pray thee, good lord mayor, be even as merry

62 partlets] collars or ruffs.   63 flewes] properly the chaps of a hound; here perhaps the flaps of a hood (Wheeler).   65 Soliman] *Soliman and Perseda,* probably by Thomas Kyd, was written in or before 1592, probably about 1588.   Tamburlaine] the two parts of Marlowe's *Tamburlaine* are generally dated 1587 and 1588.   1 fact] deed.

As if thou wert among thy shoemakers;
It does me good to see thee in this humour.

Eyre. Say'st thou me so, my sweet Dioclesian?
Then, humph! Prince am I none, yet am I princely
born. By the Lord of Ludgate, my liege, I'll be as
merry as a pie.   20

King. Tell me, in faith, mad Eyre, how old thou
art.

Eyre. My liege, a very boy, a stripling, a younker;
you see not a white hair on my head, not a grey in
this beard. Every hair, I assure thy majesty, that
sticks in this beard, Sim Eyre values at the King of
Babylon's ransom, Tamar Cham's beard was a
rubbing brush to't: yet I'll shave it off, and stuff
tennis-balls with it, to please my bully king.   28

King. But all this while I do not know your age.

Eyre. My liege, I am six and fifty year old, yet
I can cry Humph! with a sound heart for the honour
of Saint Hugh. Mark this old wench, my king: I
danc'd the shaking of the sheets with her six and
thirty years ago, and yet I hope to get two or three
young lord mayors ere I die. I am lusty still, Sim
Eyre still. Care and cold lodging brings white hairs.
My sweet Majesty, let care vanish, cast it upon thy
nobles, it will make thee look always young like
Apollo, and cry Humph! Prince am I none, yet am
I princely born.   40

King. Ha, ha! Say, Cornwall, didst thou ever see
his like?

Nobleman. Not I, my lord.

Enter Lincoln *and* Lord Mayor.

King.   Lincoln, what news with you?

Lincoln. My gracious lord, have care unto yourself,
For there are traitors here.

All.   Traitors! Where? Who?

Eyre. Traitors in my house? God forbid! Where

20 pie] magpie.

be my officers? I'll spend my soul, ere my king feel
harm.

King. Where is the traitor, Lincoln?

Lincoln.   Here he stands.

King. Cornwall, lay hold on Lacy!—Lincoln, speak,
What canst thou lay unto thy nephew's charge?   50

Lincoln. This, my dear liege: your Grace, to do me
     honour,
Heap'd on the head of this degenerous boy
Desertless favours; you made choice of him,
To be commander over powers in France.
But he——

King. Good Lincoln, prithee pause a while!
Even in thine eyes I read what thou wouldst speak.
I know how Lacy did neglect our love,
Ran himself deeply, in the highest degree,
Into vile treason——

Lincoln.   Is he not a traitor?

King. Lincoln, he was; now have we pardoned him.
'Twas not a base want of true valour's fire,   61
That held him out of France, but love's desire.

Lincoln. I will not bear his shame upon my back.

King. Nor shalt thou, Lincoln; I forgive you both.

Lincoln. Then, good my liege, forbid the boy to wed
One whose mean birth will much disgrace his bed.

King. Are they not married?

Lincoln.   No, my liege.

Both.   We are.

King. Shall I divorce them then? O be it far,
That any hand on earth should dare untie
The sacred knot, knit by God's majesty;   70
I would not for my crown disjoin their hands,
That are conjoin'd in holy nuptial bands.
How say'st thou, Lacy, wouldst thou lose thy Rose?

Lacy. Not for all India's wealth, my sovereign.

King. But Rose, I am sure, her Lacy would forgo.

52 degenerous] degenerate, false to birth and breeding.
53 desertless] undeserved.

Rose. If Rose were ask'd that question, she'd say no.

King. You hear them, Lincoln?

Lincoln.   Yea, my liege, I do.

King. Yet canst thou find i' th' heart to part these
    two?

Who seeks, besides you, to divorce these lovers?   79

Lord Mayor. I do, my gracious lord, I am her father.

King. Sir Roger Oteley, our last mayor, I think?

Nobleman. The same, my liege.

King.   Would you offend Love's laws?

Well, you shall have your wills. You sue to me,

To prohibit the match. Soft, let me see—

You are both married, Lacy, art thou not?

Lacy. I am, dread sovereign.

King.   Then, upon thy life,

I charge thee not to call this woman wife.

Lord Mayor. I thank your grace.

Rose.   O my most gracious lord!
                                    [*Kneel.*

King. Nay, Rose, never woo me; I tell you true,

Although as yet I am a bachelor,   90

Yet I believe, I shall not marry you.

Rose. Can you divide the body from the soul,

Yet make the body live?

King.   Yea, so profound?

I cannot, Rose, but you I must divide.

Fair maid, this bridegroom cannot be your bride.

Are you pleas'd, Lincoln? Oteley, are you pleas'd?

Both. Yes, my lord.

King.   Then must my heart be eas'd;

For, credit me, my conscience lives in pain,

Till these whom I divorc'd, be join'd again.

Lacy, give me thy hand; Rose, lend me thine!   100

Be what you would be! Kiss now! So, that's fine.

At night, lovers, to bed!—Now, let me see,

Which of you all mislikes this harmony.

95 bride] used of either sex.

Lord Mayor. Will you then take from me my child
    perforce?

King. Why, tell me, Oteley: shines not Lacy's name
As bright in the world's eye as the gay beams
Of any citizen?

Lincoln.   Yea, but, my gracious lord,
I do mislike the match far more than he;
Her blood is too too base.

King.   Lincoln, no more.
Dost thou not know that love respects no blood,   110
Cares not for difference of birth or state?
The maid is young, well born, fair, virtuous,
A worthy bride for any gentleman.
Besides, your nephew for her sake did stoop
To bare necessity, and, as I hear,
Forgetting honours and all courtly pleasures,
To gain her love, became a shoemaker.
As for the honour which he lost in France,
Thus I redeem it: Lacy, kneel thee down!—
Arise, Sir Rowland Lacy! Tell me now,   120
Tell me in earnest, Oteley, canst thou chide,
Seeing thy Rose a lady and a bride?

Lord Mayor. I am content with what your grace
    hath done.

Lincoln. And I, my liege, since there's no remedy.

King. Come on, then, all shake hands: I'll have
    you friends;
Where there is much love, all discord ends.
What says my mad lord mayor to all this love?

Eyre. O my liege, this honour you have done to my
fine journeyman here, Rowland Lacy, and all these
favours which you have shown to me this day in my
poor house, will make Simon Eyre live longer by one
dozen of warm summers more than he should.   132

King. Nay, my mad lord mayor—that shall be thy
    name,—
If any grace of mine can length thy life,
One honour more I'll do thee: that new building,

Which at thy cost in Cornhill is erected,
Shall take a name from us; we'll have it call'd
The Leadenhall, because in digging it
You found the lead that covereth the same.

Eyre. I thank your majesty.

Margery.   God bless your grace!

King. Lincoln, a word with you!   141

Enter Hodge, Firk, Ralph, *and more Shoemakers.*

Eyre. How now, my mad knaves? Peace, speak
softly, yonder is the king.

King. With the old troop which there we keep in pay,
We will incorporate a new supply.
Before one summer more pass o'er my head,
France shall repent England was injured.
What are all those?

Lacy.   All shoemakers, my liege,
Sometimes my fellows; in their companies
I liv'd as merry as an emperor.   150

King. My mad lord mayor, are all these shoemakers?

Eyre. All shoemakers, my liege; all gentlemen of the
Gentle Craft, true Trojans, courageous cordwainers;
they all kneel to the shrine of holy Saint Hugh.

All the shoemakers. God save your majesty!

King. Mad Simon, would they anything with us?

Eyre. Mum, mad knaves! Not a word! I'll do't;
I warrant you.—They are all beggars, my liege; all
for themselves, and I for them all, on both my knees
do entreat, that for the honour of poor Simon Eyre
and the good of his brethren, these mad knaves, your
grace would vouchsafe some privilege to my new
Leadenhall, that it may be lawful for us to buy and
sell leather there two days a week.   164

King. Mad Sim, I grant your suit, you shall have
patent
To hold two market-days in Leadenhall,
Mondays and Fridays, those shall be the times.

Will this content you?

All.   Jesus bless your grace!

Eyre. In the name of these my poor brethren shoemakers, I most humbly thank your grace. But before
I rise, seeing you are in the giving vein and we in the
begging, grant Sim Eyre one boon more.   172

King. What is it, my lord mayor?

Eyre. Vouchsafe to taste of a poor banquet that
stands sweetly waiting for your sweet presence.

King. I shall undo thee, Eyre, only with feasts;
Already have I been too troublesome;
Say, have I not?

Eyre. O my dear king, Sim Eyre was taken un-
awares upon a day of shroving, which I promis'd long
ago to the prentices of London. For, an't please your
highness, in time past,   182

    I bare the water-tankard, and my coat
    Sits not a whit the worse upon my back;
    And then, upon a morning, some mad boys,
    It was Shrove Tuesday, even as 'tis now,
gave me my breakfast, and I swore then by the
stopple of my tankard, if ever I came to be lord mayor
of London, I would feast all the prentices. This day,
my liege, I did it, and the slaves had an hundred tables
five times covered; they are gone home and vanish'd;
    Yet add more honour to the Gentle Trade,   192
    Taste of Eyre's banquet, Simon's happy made.

King. Eyre, I will taste of thy banquet, and will say,
I have not met more pleasure on a day.
Friends of the Gentle Craft, thanks to you all,
Thanks, my kind lady mayoress, for our cheer.—
Come, lords, a while let's revel it at home!
When all our sports and banquetings are done,
Wars must right wrongs which Frenchmen have
    begun.   [*Exeunt.*

THE MERRY DEVIL OF
EDMONTON

ANONYMOUS

The Merry Devil of Edmonton

Acted between 1601 and 1604; printed in 1608.

[In *The Shakespeare Apocrypha*, ed. C. F. Tucker
Brooke, Oxford, 1908.]

S'è vero che gli uomini si conoscon dalle opere
sappiamo tante cose d'Ignoto! Direi anzi, se
potessi esser creduto, che egli è stato il personag-
gio più importante della storia, il massimo eroe
dell' umanità.

. . . .

Gli uomini, in generale, son troppo inclinati a dar
importanza a tutto ciò che ha un nome ed è legitti-
mato da una firma, da una stampa, o da un foglio
d'archivio.

G. PAPINI, *Ignoto.*

THE
MERRY DEVILL
OF
EDMONTON.

*As it hath beene sundry times Acted,
by his Maiesties Seruants, at the
Globe, on the banke-side.*

LONDON
Printed by *Henry Ballard* for *Arthur Iohnson,* dwelling
at the signe of the white-horse in Paules Church
yard, ouer against the great North
doore of Paules. 1608.

Dramatis Personae

Sir Arthur Clare.
Sir Richard Moun-
    chensey.
Sir Ralph Jerningham.
Harry Clare.
Raymond Mounchensey.
Frank Jerningham.
Peter Fabell, *the Merry
    Devil*.
Coreb, *a Spirit*.
Blague, *the Host*.
Sir John, *a Priest*.
Banks, *the Miller of Waltham*.
Smug, *the Smith of Edmonton*.

Sexton.
Bilbo.
Brian.
Ralph, *Brian's man*.
Friar Hildersham.
Benedick.
Chamberlain.

Lady Dorcas Clare.
Millicent Clare, *her
    Daughter*.
The Prioress of Cheston
    Nunnery.
Nuns and Attendants.

The Prologue

YOUR silence and attention, worthy friends,
That your free spirits may with more pleasing sense
Relish the life of this our active scene!
To which intent, to calm this murmuring breath,
We ring this round with our invoking spells;
If that your listening ears be yet prepar'd
To entertain the subject of our play,
Lend us your patience.
'Tis Peter Fabell, a renowned scholar,
Whose fame hath still been hitherto forgot   10
By all the writers of this latter age.
In Middlesex his birth and his abode,
Not full seven mile from this great famous city;
That, for his fame in sleights and magic won,
Was call'd the merry Fiend of Edmonton.
If any here make doubt of such a name,
In Edmonton yet fresh unto this day,
Fix'd in the wall of that old ancient church,
His monument remaineth to be seen;
His memory yet in the mouths of men,   20
That whilst he liv'd he could deceive the Devil.
Imagine now that whilst he is retir'd
From Cambridge back unto his native home,
Suppose the silent, sable-visag'd night
Casts her black curtain over all the world;
And whilst he sleeps within his silent bed,
Toil'd with the studies of the passed day,
The very time and hour wherein that spirit
That many years attended his command,
And oftentimes 'twixt Cambridge and that town   30
Had in a minute borne him through the air,
By composition 'twixt the fiend and him,

5 ring this round] draw this magic circle.   10 still]
always.   27 Toil'd] wearied.   32 composition]
agreement.

Comes now to claim the scholar for his due.

[Draw the curtains.

Behold him here, laid on his restless couch,
His fatal chime prepared at his head,
His chamber guarded with these sable sleights,
And by him stands that necromantic chair,
In which he makes his direful invocations,
And binds the fiends that shall obey his will.
Sit with a pleased eye, until you know   40
The comic end of our sad tragic show.   *[Exit.*

36 sable sleights] devices of black magic.

THE MERRY DEVIL OF EDMONTON

Induction

The Chime goes, in which time Fabell *is oft seen to stare about him, and hold up his hands.*

Fab. What means the tolling of this fatal chime?
O, what a trembling horror strikes my heart!
My stiffen'd hair stands upright on my head,
As do the bristles of a porcupine.

Enter Coreb, *a Spirit.*

Cor. Fabell, awake! or I will bear thee hence
Headlong to hell.
Fab.   Ha, ha,
Why dost thou wake me? Coreb, is it thou?
Cor. 'Tis I.
Fab. I know thee well: I hear the watchful dogs
With hollow howling tell of thy approach;   11
The lights burn dim, affrighted with thy presence;
And this distemper'd and tempestuous night
Tells me the air is troubled with some devil.
Cor. Come, art thou ready?
Fab.   Whither? or to what?
Cor. Why, Scholar, this the hour my date expires;
I must depart, and come to claim my due.
Fab. Ha, what is thy due?
Cor.   Fabell, thyself!
Fab. O, let not darkness hear thee speak that word,   20
Lest that with force it hurry hence amain,
And leave the world to look upon my woe:
Yet overwhelm me with this globe of earth,

16 this] this is.

And let a little sparrow with her bill
Take but so much as she can bear away,
That, every day thus losing of my load,
I may again in time yet hope to rise.

   Cor. Didst thou not write thy name in thine own
      blood,
And drew'st the formal deed 'twixt thee and me,
And is it not recorded now in hell?

   Fab. Why com'st thou in this stern and horrid
      shape,   30
Not in familiar sort, as thou wast wont?

   Cor. Because the date of thy command is out,
And I am master of thy skill and thee.

   Fab. Coreb, thou angry and impatient spirit,
I have earnest business for a private friend;
Reserve me, spirit, until some further time.

   Cor. I will not for the mines of all the earth.

   Fab. Then let me rise, and ere I leave the world
Dispatch some business that I have to do;
And in mean time repose thee in that chair.   40

   Cor. Fabel, I will.   [*Sit down.*

   Fab. O, that this soul, that cost so great a price
As the dear precious blood of her Redeemer,
Inspir'd with knowledge, should by that alone
Which makes a man so mean unto the powers,
Even lead him down into the depth of hell,
When men in their own pride strive to know more
Than man should know!
For this alone God cast the angels down.
The infinity of arts is like a sea,   50
Into which, when man will take in hand to sail
Further than reason, which should be his pilot,
Hath skill to guide him, losing once his compass,
He falleth to such deep and dangerous whirlpools,
As he doth lose the very sight of heaven:
The more he strives to come to quiet harbour,

    32 date] period, time.   45 Which . . . powers] in
which (*sc.* knowledge) man is so inferior to the spirits.

The further still he finds himself from land.
Man, striving still to find the depth of evil,
Seeking to be a God, becomes a devil.

  Cor. Come, Fabell, hast thou done?

  Fab.   Yes, yes; come hither! **60**

  Cor. Fabell, I cannot.

  Fab. Cannot?—What ails your hollowness?

  Cor. Good Fabell, help me!

  Fab. Alas! where lies your grief? some aqua-vitae!
The Devil's very sick, I fear he'll die,
For he looks very ill.

  Cor. Dar'st thou deride the minister of darkness?
In Lucifer's dread name Coreb conjures thee
To set him free.

  Fab. I will not for the mines of all the earth, **70**
Unless thou give me liberty to see
Seven years more, before thou seize on me.

  Cor. Fabell, I give it thee.

  Fab.   Swear, damned fiend!

  Cor. Unbind me, and by hell I will not touch
    thee,
Till seven years from this hour be full expir'd.

  Fab. Enough, come out.

  Cor.   A vengeance take thy art!
Live and convert all piety to evil;
Never did man thus over-reach the Devil.
No time on earth, like Phaetonic flames,
Can have perpetual being. I'll return **80**
To my infernal mansion; but be sure,
Thy seven years done, no trick shall make me tarry,
But, Coreb, thou to hell shalt Fabell carry. [*Exit.*

  Fab. Then, thus betwixt us two this variance ends,
Thou to thy fellow fiends, I to my friends! [*Exit.*

79–80 No time . . . being] Like Phaeton's flames all
earthly periods must have an end. Phaeton almost destroyed the world by his failure to manage the flaming
chariot of his father the Sun, but Jove destroyed him in
time to prevent the catastrophe.

Act I. Scene I.

Enter Sir Arthur Clare, Dorcas, *his lady,* Millicent, *his
daughter, young* Harry Clare; *the men booted, the Gentle-
women in cloaks and safeguards.* Blague, *the merry Host of
the George, comes in with them.*

Host. Welcome, good knight, to the George at
Waltham, my free-hold, my tenements, goods and
chattels! Madame, here's a room is the very Homer
and Iliads of a lodging, it hath none of the four
elements in it; I built it out of the centre, and I
drink ne'er the less sack. Welcome, my little waste
of maidenheads! What? I serve the good Duke of
Norfolk.

Sir Ar. God-a-mercy, my good host Blague! Thou
has a good seat here.   10

Host. 'Tis correspondent or so: there's not a Tar-
tarian nor a carrier shall breathe upon your geldings;
they have villainous rank feet, the rogues, and they
shall not sweat in my linen. Knights and lords too
have been drunk in my house, I thank the destinies.

Har. Prithee, good sinful innkeeper, will that
corruption, thine ostler, look well to my gelding. Hey,
a pox o' these rushes!

Host. You, Saint Dennis, your gelding shall walk
without doors, and cool his feet for his master's sake.
By the body of St. George, I have an excellent intellect
to go steal some venison: now, when wast thou in the
forest?   23

Har. Away, you stale mess of white broth! Come
hither, sister, let me help you.

Sir Ar. Mine host, is not Sir Richard Mounchensey
come yet, according to our appointment, when we
last din'd here?

11–12 Tartarian] thief.   18 rushes] with which the floor
was strewn for warmth and cleanliness before the days of
carpets.

Host. The knight's not yet apparent.—Marry,
here's a forerunner that summons a parle, and saith,
he'll be here top and top-gallant presently.   31

Sir Ar. 'Tis well. Good sire host, go down, and
see breakfast be provided.

Host. Knight, thy breath hath the force of a woman,
it takes me down; I am for the baser element of the
kitchen: I retire like a valiant soldier, face point-
blank to the foeman, or, like a courtier, that must not
show the Prince his posteriors; I vanish to know my
canvasadoes, and my interrogatories, for I serve the
good Duke of Norfolk.   [*Exit.*

Sir Ar. How doth my Lady? are you not weary,
          Madam?   41
Come hither, I must talk in private with you;
My daughter Millicent must not overhear.

Mil. [*Aside.*] Ay, whispering? pray God it tend my
good! Strange fear assails my heart, usurps my blood.

Sir Ar. You know our meeting with the knight
          Mounchensey
Is to assure our daughter to his heir.

L. Dor. 'Tis, without question.

Sir Ar. Two tedious winters have past o'er, since
          first
These couple lov'd each other, and in passion   50
Glu'd first their naked hands with youthful mois-
          ture—
Just so long, on my knowledge.

L. Dor.   And what of this?

Sir Ar. This morning should my daughter lose her
          name,
And to Mounchensey's house convey our arms,
Quartered within his scutcheon; th' affiance, made
'Twixt him and her, this morning should be seal'd.

31 top and top-gallant] under all sail, at full speed
(Walker).   39 canvasadoes] sudden or night attacks;
or perhaps the Host's expansion of 'canvasses', 'inquiries'.
47 assure] betroth.

L. Dor. I know it should.

Sir Ar. But there are crosses, wife;—here's one in
    Waltham,
Another at the Abbey, and the third
At Cheston; and 'tis ominous to pass   60
Any of these without a pater-noster.
Crosses of love still thwart this marriage,
Whilst that we two, like spirits, walk in night
About those stony and hard-hearted plots.

Mil. [*Aside.*] O God, what means my father?

Sir Ar. For look you, wife, the riotous old knight
Hath overrun his annual revenue
In keeping jolly Christmas all the year:
The nostrils of his chimney are still stuff'd
With smoke, more chargeable than cane-tobacco:
His hawks devour his fattest dogs, whilst simple, 71
His leanest curs eat him hounds' carrion.
Besides, I heard of late, his younger brother,
A Turkey merchant, hath sore suck'd the knight
By means of some great losses on the sea;
That, you conceive me, before God, all's naught,
His seat is weak. Thus, each thing rightly scann'd,
You'll see a flight, wife, shortly of his land.

Mil. [*Aside.*] Treason to my heart's truest sovereign!
How soon is love smothered in foggy gain!

L. Dor. But how shall we prevent this dangerous
    match?   81

Sir Ar. I have a plot, a trick, and this it is—
Under this colour I'll break off the match:
I'll tell the knight that now my mind is chang'd

---

58 crosses] pun on two senses, (*a*) impediments, (*b*) way-
side shrines.   70 cane-tobacco] plug tobacco.   71–2
His hawks . . . carrion] His hawks are given such food as
his best dogs should have and his stray mongrels what
would be fit for his best hounds. (But the passage is probably corrupt.)   74 Turkey merchant] merchant trad-
ing into Turkey.   78 a flight . . . of his land] *sc.* to the
moneylenders.   83 colour] pretence.

For marrying of my daughter: for I intend
To send her unto Cheston Nunnery.

Mil. [*Aside.*] O me accurst!

Sir Ar. There to become a most religious nun.

Mil. [*Aside.*] I'll first be buried quick.

Sir Ar. To spend her beauty in most private prayers.

Mil. [*Aside.*] I'll sooner be a sinner in forsaking   91
Mother and father.

Sir Ar.   How dost like my plot?

L. Dor. Exceeding well; but is it your intent
She shall continue there?

Sir Ar. Continue there? Ha, ha, that were a jest!
You know a virgin may continue there
A twelvemonth and a day only on trial.
There shall my daughter sojourn some three months,
And in meantime I'll compass a fair match
'Twixt youthful Jerningham, the lusty heir   100
Of Sir Ralph Jerningham, dwelling in the forest—
I think they'll both come hither with Mounchensey.

L. Dor. Your care argues the love you bear our
          child;
I will subscribe to anything you'll have me. [*Exeunt.*

Mil. You will subscribe to it! Good, good, 'tis well;
Love hath two chairs of state, heaven and hell.
My dear Mounchensey, thou my death shalt rue,
Ere to thy heart Millicent prove untrue.   [*Exit.*

Scene II.

Enter Blague.

Host. Ostlers, you knaves and commanders, take
the horses of the knights and competitors: your
honourable hulks have put into harbour, they'll take
in fresh water here, and I have provided clean
chamber-pots. *Via*, they come!

104 subscribe] agree.   5 *Via*] quickly.

Enter Sir Richard Mounchensey, Sir Ralph Jerningham, *young* Frank Jerningham, Raymond Mounchensey, Peter Fabell, *and* Bilbo.

Host. The destinies be most neat chamberlains to these swaggering puritans, knights of the subsidy.

Sir Rich. God-a-mercy, good mine host.

Sir Ralph. Thanks, good host Blague.   9

Host. Room for my case of pistols, that have Greek and Latin bullets in them; let me cling to your flanks, my nimble Gibraltars, and blow wind in your calves to make them swell bigger. Ha, I'll caper in mine own fee-simple. Away with punctilios and orthography! I serve the good Duke of Norfolk. Bilbo, *Tityre, tu patulae recubans sub tegmine fagi.*

Bil. Truly, mine host, Bilbo, though he be somewhat out of fashion, will be your only blade still. I have a villainous sharp stomach to slice a breakfast.   20

Host. Thou shalt have it without any more discontinuance, releases, or attournment. What! we know our terms of hunting and the sea-card.

Bil. And do you serve the good Duke of Norfolk still?

Host. Still, and still, and still, my soldier of St. Quentin's! Come, follow me; I have Charles' Wain below in a butt of sack, 'twill glister like your crabfish.   29

7 knights of the subsidy] mere knights of the shire, whose business it is to vote money, not men of the old warlike class (Walker).   12 Gibraltars] Gibraltar apes.   16 *Tityre, . . . fagi*] Vergil, *Ecl.* i. 1: 'Tityrus, happily thou liest tumbling under a beech-tree' (Webbe, 1586).   17–18 Bilbo . . . only blade] pun on (*a*) the speaker's name, (*b*) the Bilboa sword.   23 sea-card] compass.   26–7 soldier of St. Quentin's] veteran; the town was stormed in 1557.   28–9 crab-fish] phosphorescent when decaying; the preceding allusion to *Ursa Major* (Charles's Wain) suggested another to *Cancer* (the Crab).

Bil. You have fine scholar-like terms; your Cooper's Dictionary is your only book to study in a cellar, a man shall find very strange words in it. Come, my host, let's serve the good Duke of Norfolk.   33

Host. And still, and still, and still, my boy, I'll serve the good Duke of Norfolk.   [*Exeunt* Host *and* Bilbo.

Enter Sir Arthur Clare, Harry Clare, *and* Millicent.

Sir Ralph. Good Sir Arthur Clare!

Sir Ar. What gentleman is that? I know him not.

Sir Rich. 'Tis Master Fabell, sir, a Cambridge scholar, My son's dear friend.

Sir Ar.   Sir, I entreat you know me.

Fab. Command me, sir; I am affected to you   40
For your Mounchensey's sake.

Sir Ar.   Alas, for him,
I not respect whether he sink or swim!
A word in private, Sir Ralph Jerningham.

Ray. Methinks your father looketh strangely on me:
Say, love, why are you sad?

Mil.   I am not, sweet;
Passion is strong, when woe with woe doth meet.

Sir Ar. Shall 's in to breakfast? After we'll conclude
The cause of this our coming: in and feed,
And let that usher a more serious deed.

Mil. Whilst you desire his grief, my heart shall bleed.

Frank. Raymond Mounchensey, come, be frolic, friend,   51
This is the day thou hast expected long.

Ray. Pray God, dear Jerningham, it prove so happy.

Frank. There 's nought can alter it! Be merry, lad!

Fab. There 's nought shall alter it! Be lively, Raymond!
Stand any opposition 'gainst thy hope,
Art shall confront it with her largest scope.   [*Exeunt.*

30–1 Cooper's Dictionary] *Thesaurus linguae romanae & britannicae,* a Latin-English dictionary published in 1565. 47 Shall 's] shall us, *sc.* shall we.

Scene III.

Peter Fabell, *solus*.

Fab. Good old Mounchensey, is thy hap so ill,
That for thy bounty and thy royal parts
Thy kind alliance should be held in scorn,
And after all these promises by Clare—
Refuse to give his daughter to thy son,
Only because thy revenues cannot reach
To make her dowage of so rich a jointure
As can the heir of wealthy Jerningham?
And therefore is the false fox now in hand
To strike a match betwixt her and the other;   10
And the old grey-beards now are close together,
Plotting it in the garden. Is't even so?
Raymond Mounchensey, boy, have thou and I
Thus long at Cambridge read the liberal arts,
The metaphysics, magic, and those parts
Of the most secret deep philosophy?
Have I so many melancholy nights
Watch'd on the top of Peterhouse highest tower,
And come we back unto our native home,
For want of skill to lose the wench thou lov'st?   20
We'll first hang Enfield in such rings of mist
As never rose from any dampish fen:
I'll make the brined sea to rise at Ware,
And drown the marshes unto Stratford Bridge;
I'll drive the deer from Waltham in their walks,
And scatter them like sheep in every field.
We may perhaps be cross'd, but, if we be,
He shall cross the Devil, that but crosses me.

Enter Raymond, *young* Frank Jerningham, *and young*
Harry Clare.

But here comes Raymond, disconsolate and sad,
And here's the gallant that must have the wench.   30

2 parts] qualities.

Frank. I prithee, Raymond, leave these solemn
    dumps:
Revive thy spirits, thou that before hast been
More watchful than the day-proclaiming cock,
As sportive as a kid, as frank and merry
As Mirth herself!
If aught in me may thy content procure,
It is thine own, thou may'st thyself assure.

Ray. Ha, Jerningham, if any but thyself
Had spoke that word, it would have come as cold
As the bleak northern winds upon the face   40
Of winter.
From thee they have some power upon my blood;
Yet being from thee, had but that hollow sound
Come from the lips of any living man,
It might have won the credit of mine ear;
From thee it cannot.

Frank. If I understand thee, I am a villain:
What, dost thou speak in parables to thy friends?

Harry. Come, boy, and make me this same groaning
    love,
Troubled with stitches and the cough o' th' lungs, 50
That wept his eyes out when he was a child,
And ever since hath shot at hoodman-blind,
Make her leap, caper, jerk, and laugh, and sing,
And play me horse-tricks;
Make Cupid wanton as his mother's dove:
But in this sort, boy, I would have thee love.

Fab. Why, how now, madcap? What, my lusty Frank,

31 dumps] depression (not at this time an undignified
expression).   38–46 if any but thyself. . . . From thee it
cannot] offers of assistance from any but Jerningham would
seem cold to Mounchensey, because of the inability of any
one else to help him; yet he could believe in the sincerity of
such offers from anybody except Jerningham, who is to
profit by the injustice done him (Tucker Brooke).   52
hoodman-blind] blind man's buff.   53 her] love. jerk]
dance jerkily.

So near a wife, and will not tell your friend?
But you will to this gear in hugger-mugger;
Art thou turn'd miser, rascal, in thy loves?   60

Frank. Who, I? 'Sblood, what should all you see in
me, that I should look like a married man, ha? Am
I bald? are my legs too little for my hose? If I feel
anything in my forehead, I am a villain! Do I wear
a nightcap? do I bend in the hams? What dost thou
see in me, that I should be towards marriage, ha?

Harry. What, thou married? let me look upon thee,
rogue. Who has given out this of thee? how cam'st
thou into this ill name? What company hast thou
been in, rascal?   70

Fab. You are the man, sir, must have Millicent:
The match is making in the garden now;
Her jointure is agreed on, and th' old men,
Your fathers, mean to launch their busy bags;
But in meantime to thrust Mounchensey off,
For colour of this new intended match,
Fair Millicent to Cheston must be sent,
To take the approbation for a nun.
Ne'er look upon me, lad, the match is done.

Frank. Raymond Mounchensey, now I touch thy
grief   80
With the true feeling of a zealous friend.
And as for fair and beauteous Millicent,
With my vain breath I will not seek to slubber
Her angel-like perfections; but thou know'st
That Essex hath the saint that I adore.
Where e'er did we meet thee and wanton springs,
That like a wag thou hast not laugh'd at me,
And with regardless jesting mock'd my love?
How many a sad and weary summer night

---

64 forehead] the perennial Elizabethan joke on horns
as a sign of cuckoldry.   74 bags] *sc.* money-bags.   76
colour] camouflage.   78 approbation] period of pro-
bation.   86 wanton springs] carefree youths.   88
regardless] *sc.* of my feelings.

My sighs have drunk the dew from off the earth,   90
And I have taught the nightingale to wake,
And from the meadows sprung the early lark
An hour before she should have list to sing:
I have loaded the poor minutes with my moans,
That I have made the heavy slow-pac'd hours
To hang like heavy clogs upon the day.
But, dear Mounchensey, had not my affection
Seiz'd on the beauty of another dame,
Before I would wrong the chase, and overgive love
Of one so worthy and so true a friend,   100
I will abjure both beauty and her sight,
And will in love become a counterfeit.

   Ray. Dear Jerningham, thou hast begot my life,
And from the mouth of hell, where now I sate,
I feel my spirit rebound against the stars:
Thou hast conquer'd me, dear friend, in my free soul;
There time or death can by their power control.

   Fab. Frank Jerningham, thou art a gallant boy;
And were he not my pupil, I would say
He were as fine a mettled gentleman,   110
Of as free spirit, and of as fine a temper
As is in England; and he is a man
That very richly may deserve thy love.
But, noble Clare, this while of our discourse,
What may Mounchensey's honour to thyself
Exact upon the measure of thy grace?

   Harry. Raymond Mounchensey? I would have thee
     know,
He does not breathe this air,
Whose love I cherish, and whose soul I love
More than Mounchensey's: 120
Nor ever in my life did see the man
Whom, for his wit and many virtuous parts,
I think more worthy of my sister's love.

   99 overgive] surrender.   115–16 What . . . grace]
how far do your generous feelings reciprocate Mounchensey's high esteem of you?   122 parts] qualities.

But since the matter grows unto this pass,
I must not seem to cross my father's will;
But when thou list to visit her by night,
My horses saddled, and the stable door
Stands ready for thee; use them at thy pleasure.
In honest marriage wed her frankly, boy,
And if thou gett'st her, lad, God give thee joy!   130

   Ray. Then, care, away! Let fates my fall pretend,
Back'd with the favours of so true a friend!

   Fab. Let us alone, to bustle for the set;
For age and craft with wit and art have met.
I'll make my spirits to dance such nightly jigs
Along the way 'twixt this and Tot'nam cross,
The carriers' jades shall cast their heavy packs,
And the strong hedges scarce shall keep them in:
The milkmaids' cuts shall turn the wenches off,
And lay the dossers tumbling in the dust: 140
The frank and merry London prentices,
That come for cream and lusty country cheer,
Shall lose their way; and, scrambling in the ditches,
All night shall whoop and hollow, cry and call,
Yet none to other find the way at all.

   Ray. Pursue the project, scholar: what we can do
To help endeavour, join our lives thereto!   [*Exeunt.*

Act II.   Scene I.

Enter Banks, Sir John, *and* Smug.

   Banks. Take me with you, good Sir John! A plague
on thee, Smug! an thou touchest liquor, thou art

127–8 My horses . . . ready for thee] the singular verb with
a plural subject is common.   131 pretend] intend (*sc.* in
vain, since I am backed &*c*.)   133 bustle for] bestir
ourselves to win.   139 cuts] labouring horses.   turn
. . . off] throw.   140 dossers] baskets.   1 Take me
with you] hear me out.

founder'd straight. What, are your brains always water-mills? must they ever run round?

Smug. Banks, your ale is a Philistine fox; 'sheart, there's fire i' th' tail on 't; you are a rogue to charge us with mugs i' th' rearward. A plague of this wind; O, it tickles our catastrophe.   8

Sir John. Neighbour Banks of Waltham, and Goodman Smug, the honest smith of Edmonton, as I dwell betwixt you both at Enfield, I know the taste of both your ale-houses; they are good both, smart both. Hem, grass and hay! we are all mortal; let's live till we die, and be merry; and there's an end.

Banks. Well said, Sir John, you are of the same humour still; and doth the water run the same way still, boy?   17

Smug. Vulcan was a rogue to him; Sir John, lock, lock, lock fast, Sir John! so, Sir John. I'll one of these years, when it shall please the goddesses and the destinies, be drunk in your company; that's all now, and God send us health. Shall I swear I love you?

Sir John. No oaths, no oaths, good neighbour Smug; We'll wet our lips together and hug; Carouse in private, and elevate the heart, and the liver and the lights—and the lights, mark you me, within us; for, hem, grass and hay! we are all mortal; let's live till we die, and be merry; and there's an end.   29

Banks. But to our former motion about stealing some venison; whither go we?

Sir John. Into the forest, neighbour Banks, into Brian's walk, the mad keeper.

Smug. 'Sblood! I'll tickle your keeper.

3 founder'd] drunk and incapable (literally lame, of a horse); cf. below, II. i. 35-6.   straight] straightway. 5 Philistine fox] the allusion is to the story of Samson tying firebrands to the foxes' tails (Walker).   8 catastrophe] rear end (used humorously of the human anatomy, as below, v. ii. 12).

Banks. I' faith, thou art always drunk when we have need of thee.

Smug. Need of me? 'sheart! you shall have need of me always while there's iron in an anvil.

Banks. Master Parson, may the smith go, think you, being in this taking?   40

Smug. Go? I'll go in spite of all the bells in Waltham.

Sir John. The question is, good neighbour Banks— let me see: the moon shines to-night,—there's not a narrow bridge betwixt this and the forest,—his brain will be settled ere night; he may go, he may go, neighbour Banks. Now we want none but the company of mine host Blague at the George at Waltham; if he were here, our consort were full. Look where comes my good host, the Duke of Norfolk's man! and how? and how? ahem, grass and hay! we are not yet mortal; let's live till we die, and be merry; and there's an end.   53

Enter Host.

Host. Ha, my Castilian dialogues! and art thou in breath still, boy? Miller, doth the match hold? Smith, I see by thy eyes thou hast been reading little Geneva print: but wend we merrily to the forest, to steal some of the king's deer! I'll meet you at the time appointed. Away, I have knights and colonels at my house, and must tend the Hungarians. If we be scar'd in the forest, we'll meet in the church-porch at Enfield; is 't correspondent?   62

Banks. 'Tis well; but how, if any of us should be taken?

Smug. He shall have ransom, by the Lord.

Host. Tush, the knave keepers are my bosonians and

49 consort] company.   54 my Castilian dialogues] my fine friend is making a speech.   56–7 Geneva print] strong drink.   60 Hungarians] pun on 'hungry ones'. 62 correspondent] suitable, a good plan.   66 bosonians] (more commonly besonians), needy ones.

my pensioners. Nine o'clock! be valiant, my little
Gogmagogs; I'll fence with all the Justices in Hertfordshire. I'll have a buck till I die; I'll slay a doe
while I live. Hold your bow straight and steady!
I serve the good Duke of Norfolk.   71

Smug. O rare! who-ho-ho, boy!

Sir John. Peace, neighbour Smug! You see this is
a boor, a boor of the country, an illiterate boor, and
yet the citizen of good fellows. Come, let's provide;
ahem, grass and hay! we are not yet all mortal; we'll
live till we die, and be merry, and there's an end.
Come, Smug!

Smug. Good night, Waltham—who-ho-ho, boy!

                                        [*Exeunt.*

Scene II.

Enter the Knights and Gentlemen from breakfast again.

Sir Rich. Nor I for thee, Clare, not of this.
What? hast thou fed me all this while with shalls,
And com'st to tell me now thou lik'st it not?

Sir Ar. I do not hold thy offer competent;
Nor do I like th' assurance of thy land,
The title is so brangled with thy debts.

Sir Rich. Too good for thee; and, knight, thou
      know'st it well,
I fawn'd not on thee for thy goods, not I;
'Twas thine own motion; that thy wife doth know.

L. Dor. Husband, it was so; he lies not in that.   10

Sir Ar. Hold thy chat, quean.

Sir Rich. To which I heark'ned willingly, and the
      rather,
Because I was persuaded it proceeded
From love thou bor'st to me and to my boy;
And gav'st him free access unto thy house,

---

68 Gogmagogs] giants (Gog and Magog).   75 citizen]
companion on equal terms.   4 competent] adequate.
6 brangled] rendered uncertain.   9 motion] proposal.
11 quean] wench.

Where he hath not behav'd him to thy child
But as befits a gentleman to do:
Nor is my poor distressed state so low,
That I'll shut up my doors, I warrant thee.

   Sir Ar. Let it suffice, Mounchensey, I mislike it;   20
Nor think thy son a match fit for my child.

   Sir Rich. I tell thee, Clare, his blood is good and clear,
As the best drop that panteth in thy veins:
But for this maid, thy fair and virtuous child,
She is no more disparag'd by thy baseness
Than the most orient and the precious jewel,
Which still retains his lustre and his beauty,
Although a slave were owner of the same.

   Sir Ar. She is the last is left me to bestow,
And her I mean to dedicate to God.   30

   Sir Rich. You do, sir?

   Sir Ar.   Sir, sir, I do, she is mine own.

   Sir Rich. And pity she is so!—
[*Aside.*] Damnation dog thee and thy wretched pelf!

   Sir Ar. Not thou, Mounchensey, shalt bestow my child.

   Sir Rich. Neither should'st thou bestow her where thou mean'st.

   Sir Ar. What wilt thou do?

   Sir Rich.   No matter, let that be;
I will do that, perhaps, shall anger thee:
Thou hast wrong'd my love, and, by God's blessed angel,
Thou shalt well know it.

   Sir Ar.   Tut, brave not me!

   Sir Rich. Brave thee, base churl! Were't not for manhood sake—   40
I say no more, but that there be some by
Whose blood is hotter than ours is,
Which, being stirr'd, might make us both repent

26 orient] brilliant.

This foolish meeting. But, Harry Clare,
Although thy father have abused my friendship,
Yet I love thee, I do, my noble boy,
I do, i' faith.

    L. Dor. Ay, do, do, fill all the world with talk of us,
man, man, I never look'd for better at your hands.

    Fab. I hop'd your great experience and your years
Would have prov'd patience rather to your soul,   51
Than with this frantic and untamed passion
To whet their skeins; and, but for that,
I hope their friendships are too well confirm'd,
And their minds temper'd with more kindly heat,
Than for their froward parents' sores,
That they should break forth into public brawls.
Howe'er the rough hand of th' untoward world
Hath moulded your proceedings in this matter,
Yet I am sure the first intent was love: 60
Thence since the first spring was so sweet and warm,
Let it die gently; ne'er kill it with a scorn.

    Ray. O thou base world! How leprous is that soul
That is once lim'd in that polluted mud!
O Sir Arthur, you have startled his free active spirits
With a too sharp spur for his mind to bear.
Have patience, sir; the remedy to woe
Is to leave what of force we must forego.

    Mil. [*Aside.*] And I must take a twelvemonth's
        approbation,
That in meantime this sole and private life   70
At the year's end may fashion me a wife:
But, sweet Mounchensey, ere this year be done,
Thou'st be a friar, if that I be a nun.
And, father, ere young Jerningham's I'll be,
I will turn mad to spite both him and thee.

    Sir Ar. Wife, come, to horse, and, huswife, make you
        ready;
For, if I live, I swear by this good light,

    53 skeins] Irish knives.   56 sores] grievances.   **68 of**
force] perforce.   73 Thou'st] thou shalt.

I'll see you lodg'd in Cheston house to-night. [*Exeunt.*
  Sir Rich. Raymond, away! Thou seest how matters fall.

Churl, hell consume thee, and thy pelf, and all!   80
  Fab. Now, Master Clare, you see how matters fadge;
Your Millicent must needs be made a nun.
Well, sir, we are the men must ply this match:
Hold you your peace, and be a looker on;
And send her unto Cheston, where he will,
I'll send me fellows of a handful high
Into the cloisters where the nuns frequent,
Shall make them skip like does about the dale,
And make the lady prioress of the house
To play at leap-frog, naked in their smocks,   90
Until the merry wenches at their mass
Cry teehee weehee;
And tickling these mad lasses in their flanks,
Shall sprawl, and squeak, and pinch their fellow-nuns.
Be lively, boys, before the wench we lose,
I'll make the abbess wear the canon's hose.   [*Exeunt.*

Scene III.

Enter Harry Clare, Frank Jerningham, Peter Fabell,
    and Millicent.

  Harry. Spite now hath done her worst; sister, be patient!
  Frank. Forewarn'd poor Raymond's company! O heaven!
When the composure of weak frailty meet
Upon this mart of dirt, O then weak love
Must in her own unhappiness be silent,
And wink on all deformities.

81 fadge] proceed.   83 ply] work at.   85 where]
wherever.   2 Forewarn'd] warned off.   3 composure
of weak frailty] those composed of weak frailty (*sc.* Sir
Arthur Clare and Sir Ralph Jerningham).   4 mart of
dirt] money-market.

Mil.   'Tis well:
Where's Raymond, brother? Where's my dear Moun-
                chensey?
Would we might weep together and then part;
Our sighing parle would much ease my heart.
    Fab. Sweet beauty, fold your sorrows in the thought
Of future reconcilement. Let your tears   11
Show you a woman; but be no farther spent
Than from the eyes; for, sweet, experience says
That love is firm that's flattered with delays.
    Mil. Alas, sir, think you I shall e'er be his?
    Fab. As sure as parting smiles on future bliss.
Yond comes my friend: see, he hath doted
So long upon your beauty, that your want
Will with a pale retirement waste his blood;
For in true love music doth sweetly dwell: 20
Sever'd, these less worlds bear within them hell.

            Enter Raymond Mounchensey.

    Ray. Harry and Frank, you are enjoin'd to wean
Your friendship from me; we must part: the breath
Of all advised corruption—pardon me!
Faith, I must say so; you may think I love you,
I breathe not rougher spite!—do sever us;
We'll meet by stealth, sweet friend, by stealth you
                twain;
Kisses are sweetest got with struggling pain.
    Frank. Our friendship dies not, Raymond.
    Ray.   Pardon me:
I am busied; I have lost my faculties,   30
And buried them in Millicent's clear eyes.
    Mil. Alas, sweet love, what shall become of me?

12–13 be no farther . . . the eyes] do not take your grief to
heart.   21 less worlds] the microcosms of the disunited
youth and maid (Walker).   24 all advised corruption]
deliberate dishonesty (*sc.* their fathers).   26 breathe not
rougher spite] use no angrier words (*sc.* than 'advised
corruption').

I must to Cheston to the nunnery,
I shall ne'er see thee more.

Ray.   How, sweet?
I'll be thy votary, we'll often meet:
This kiss divides us, and breathes soft adieu,—
This be a double charm to keep both true.

Fab. Have done: your fathers may chance spy your
      parting.
Refuse not you by any means, good sweetness,
To go unto the nunnery; far from hence   40
Must we beget your love's sweet happiness.
You shall not stay there long; your harder bed
Shall be more soft when nun and maid are dead.

Enter Bilbo.

Ray. Now, sirrah, what's the matter?

Bil. Marry, you must to horse presently; that
villainous old gouty churl, Sir Arthur Clare, longs till
he be at the nunnery.

Harry. How, sir?

Bil. O, I cry you mercy, he is your father, sir,
indeed; but I am sure that there's less affinity betwixt
your two natures than there is between a broker and
a cutpurse.   52

Ray. Bring my gelding, sirrah.

Bil. Well, nothing grieves me, but for the poor
wench; she must now cry *vale* to lobster pies, arti-
chokes, and all such meats of mortality. Poor gentlewoman! the sign must not be in *Virgo* any longer
with her, and that me grieves full well.

              Poor Millicent
              Must pray and repent: 60
              O fatal wonder!
              She'll now be no fatter,

43 when . . dead] when you are no longer either nun or
maiden.   49 cry you mercy] beg your pardon.   51
broker] pawnbroker.   52 cutpurse] thief, pickpocket.
55 *vale*] farewell.

        Love must not come at her,

        Yet she shall be kept under.   [*Exit.*

  Frank. Farewell, dear Raymond.

  Harry.   Friend, adieu.

  Mil.   Dear sweet,

No joy enjoys my heart till we next meet.   [*Exeunt.*

  Fab. Well, Raymond, now the tide of discontent

Beats in thy face; but, ere 't be long, the wind

Shall turn the flood. We must to Waltham Abbey,

And as fair Millicent in Cheston lives,   70

A most unwilling nun, so thou shalt there

Become a beardless novice; to what end,

Let time and future accidents declare:

Taste thou my sleights, thy love I'll only share.

    Ray. Turn friar? Come, my good counsellor, let 's

      go,

Yet that disguise will hardly shroud my woe. [*Exeunt.*

Act III. Scene I.

Enter the Prioress *of Cheston, with a nun or two,* Sir
Arthur Clare, Sir Ralph Jerningham, Henry *and*
Frank, *the* Lady, *and* Bilbo, *with* Millicent.

  L. Dor. Madam,

The love unto this holy sisterhood,

And our confirm'd opinion of your zeal,

Hath truly won us to bestow our child

Rather on this than any neighbouring cell.

  Pri. Jesus' daughter, Mary's child,

      Holy matron, woman mild,

      For thee a mass shall still be said,

      Every Sister drop a bead;

      And those again succeeding them   10

      For you shall sing a requiem.

  Frank. [*Aside.*] The wench is gone, Harry; she is no
more a woman of this world. Mark her well, she
looks like a nun already. What think'st on her?

              74 sleights] tricks.

Harry. [*Aside.*] By my faith, her face comes handsomely to't. But peace, let's hear the rest.

Sir Ar. Madam, for a twelvemonth's approba-
     tion,
We mean to make this trial of our child.
Your care and our dear blessing, in meantime,
We pray, may prosper this intended work.   20

Pri. May your happy soul be blythe,
     That so truly pay your tithe:
     He who many children gave,
     'Tis fit that He one child should have.
     Then, fair virgin, hear my spell,
     For I must your duty tell.

Mil. [*Aside.*] Good men and true, stand together,
and hear your charge!

Pri. First, a-mornings take your book,
     The glass wherein yourself must look;   30
     Your young thoughts, so proud and jolly,
     Must be turn'd to motions holy;
     For your busk, attires, and toys,
     Have your thoughts on heavenly joys;
     And for all your follies past
     You must do penance, pray, and fast.

Bil. [*Aside.*] Let her take heed of fasting; and if
ever she hurt herself with praying, I'll ne'er trust
beast.

Mil. [*Aside.*] This goes hard, by'r Lady!   40

Pri. You shall ring the sacring bell,
     Keep your hours, and tell your knell,
     Rise at midnight to your matins,
     Read your Psalter, sing your Latins,
     And when your blood shall kindle pleasure
     Scourge yourself in plenteous measure.

Mil. [*Aside.*] Worse and worse, by Saint Mary!

Frank. [*Aside.*] Sirrah Hal, how does she hold her

25 spell] discourse.   32 motions] emotions.   33
busk] corset.   41 sacring bell] small bell rung at the
elevation of the host.   44 Latins] Latin psalms.

countenance? Well, go thy ways, if ever thou prove
a nun, I'll build an Abbey.   50

Harry. [*Aside.*] She may be a nun; but if ever
she prove an anchoress, I'll dig her grave with my
nails.

Frank. [*Aside.*] To her again, mother!

Harry. [*Aside.*] Hold thine own, wench!

Pri. You must read the morning's mass,
    You must creep unto the cross,
    Put cold ashes on your head,
    Have a hair-cloth for your bed.

Bil. [*Aside.*] She had rather have a man in her
bed.   61

Pri. Bid your beads, and tell your needs,
    Your holy *aves*, and your creeds;
    Holy maid, this must be done,
    If you mean to live a nun.

Mil. [*Aside.*] The holy maid will be no nun.

Sir Ar. Madam, we have some business of import,
And must be gone.
Will't please you take my wife into your closet,
Who further will acquaint you with my mind;   70
And so, good madam, for this time adieu.

                     [*Exeunt women.*

Sir Ralph. Well now, Frank Jerningham, how sayest
    thou?
To be brief,—
What wilt thou say for all this, if we two,
Her father and myself, can bring about
That we convert this nun to be a wife,
And thou the husband to this pretty nun?
How then, my lad? ha, Frank, it may be done.

Harry. [*Aside.*] Ay, now it works.

Frank. O God, sir, you amaze me at your words;
Think with yourself, sir, what a thing it were   81
To cause a recluse to remove her vow:

  52 anchoress] forbidden to see men.   82 remove]
change, i.e. recall.

A maimed, contrite, and repentant soul,
Ever mortified with fasting and with prayer,
Whose thoughts, even as her eyes, are fix'd on
   heaven,
To draw a virgin, thus devour'd with zeal,
Back to the world: O impious deed!
Nor by the canon law can it be done
Without a dispensation from the Church;
Besides, she is so prone unto this life,   90
As she'll even shriek to hear a husband nam'd.

  Bil. [*Aside.*] Ay, a poor innocent she! Well,
here's no knavery! He flouts the old fools to their
teeth.

  Sir Ralph. Boy, I am glad to hear
Thou mak'st such scruple of that conscience;
And in a man so young as is yourself,
I promise you 'tis very seldom seen.
But Frank, this is a trick, a mere device,
A sleight plotted betwixt her father and myself,   100
To thrust Mounchensey's nose besides the cushion;
That, being thus debarr'd of all access,
Time yet may work him from her thoughts,
And give thee ample scope to thy desires.

  Bil. [*Aside.*] A plague on you both for a couple of
Jews!

  Harry. How now, Frank, what say you to that?

  Frank. Let me alone, I warrant thee.
Sir, assur'd that this motion doth proceed
From your most kind and fatherly affection,   110
I do dispose my liking to your pleasure:
But for it is a matter of such moment
As holy marriage, I must crave thus much,
To have some conference with my ghostly father,
Friar Hildersham, here by, at Waltham Abbey,
To be absolv'd of things that it is fit
None only but my confessor should know.

  101 thrust . . . cushion] disappoint Mounchensey.   108
Let me alone] trust me.

Sir Ralph. With all my heart. He is a reverend
man; and to-morrow morning we will meet all at the
Abbey,   120
Where by th' opinion of that reverend man
We will proceed; I like it passing well.
Till then we part, boy; ay, think of it; farewell!
A parent's care no mortal tongue can tell.   [*Exeunt.*

Scene II.

Enter Sir Arthur Clare, *and* Raymond Mounchensey,
like a Friar.

Sir Ar. Holy young novice, I have told you now
My full intent, and do refer the rest
To your professed secrecy and care:
And see,
Our serious speech hath stol'n upon the way,
That we are come unto the Abbey gate.
Because I know Mounchensey is a fox,
That craftily doth overlook my doings,
I'll not be seen, not I; tush, I have done,
I had a daughter, but she's now a nun.   10
Farewell, dear son, farewell.   [*Exit.*

Ray. Fare you well!—Ay, you have done!
Your daughter, sir, shall not be long a nun.
O my rare tutor, never mortal brain
Plotted out such a mass of policy;
And my dear bosom is so great with laughter,
Begot by his simplicity and error,
My soul is fallen in labour with her joy.
O my true friends, Frank Jerningham and Clare,
Did you now know but how this jest takes fire—   20
That good Sir Arthur, thinking me a novice,
Hath even pour'd himself into my bosom,

5 stol'n upon] *sc.* stolen **so** much of our attention while
we were upon the way.   16 dear] inmost.

O, you would vent your spleens with tickling mirth!
But, Raymond, peace, and have an eye about,
For fear perhaps some of the nuns look out.

> Peace and charity within,
> Never touch'd with deadly sin;
> I cast my holy water pure
> On this wall and on this door,
> That from evil shall defend,   30
> And keep you from the ugly fiend:
> Evil spirit, by night nor day,
> Shall approach or come this way;
> Elf nor fairy, by this grace,
> Day nor night shall haunt this place.

Holy maidens!   [*Knock.*

[*Answer within*]. Who's that which knocks? ha, who's there?

Ray. Gentle nun, here is a friar.

Enter Nun.

Nun. A friar without, now Christ us save!   40
Holy man, what wouldst thou have?
Ray. Holy maid, I hither come
From Friar and Father Hildersham,
By the favour and the grace
Of the Prioress of this place
Amongst you all to visit one
That's come for approbation;
Before she was as now you are,
The daughter of Sir Arthur Clare,
But since she now became a nun,   50
Call'd Millicent of Edmonton.
Nun. Holy man, repose you there;
This news I'll to our Abbess bear,
To tell her what a man is sent,
And your message and intent.

23 tickling] lively.   48 Before she . . . you are]
grammar requires another 'she was'—'Before she was as
now you are, she was the daughter, &c.'

Ray. Benedicite.

Nun. Benedicite.   [*Exit.*

Ray. Do, my good plump wench; if all fall right,
I'll make your sisterhood one less by night.
Now happy fortune speed this merry drift,   60
I like a wench comes roundly to her shrift.

Enter Lady Dorcas, Millicent.

L. Dor. Have friars recourse then to the house of
nuns?

Mil. Madam, it is the order of this place,
When any virgin comes for approbation,—
Lest that for fear or such sinister practice
She should be forc'd to undergo this veil,
Which should proceed from conscience and devo-
tion,—
A visitor is sent from Waltham House,
To take the true confession of the maid.   69

L. Dor. Is that the order? I commend it well:
You to your shrift, I'll back unto the cell.   [*Exit.*

Ray. Life of my soul! bright angel!

Mil. What means the friar?

Ray.   O Millicent, 'tis I.

Mil. My heart misgives me; I should know that
voice.
You? who are you? the Holy Virgin bless me!
Tell me your name: you shall, ere you confess me.

Ray. Mounchensey, thy true friend.

Mil. My Raymond, my dear heart!
Sweet life, give leave to my distracted soul,
To wake a little from this swoon of joy.   80
By what means cam'st thou to assume this shape?

Ray. By means of Peter Fabell, my kind tutor,
Who in the habit of Friar Hildersham,
Frank Jerningham's old friend and confessor,

65 sinister practice] evil design (*sc.* be frightened or deceived into doing it).   82–6 By means ... Clare] by
means of Peter Fabell ... who ... devised a plot for the

Plotted by Frank, by Fabell and myself,
And so delivered to Sir Arthur Clare,
Who brought me here unto the Abbey gate,
To be his nun-made daughter's visitor.

Mil. You are all sweet traitors to my poor old father.
O my dear life! I was a-dream'd to-night   90
That, as I was a-praying in mine Psalter,
There came a spirit unto me as I kneel'd,
And by his strong persuasions tempted me
To leave this nunnery: and methought
He came in the most glorious angel shape
That mortal eye did ever look upon.
Ha, thou art sure that spirit, for there 's no form
Is in mine eye so glorious as thine own.

Ray. O thou idolatress, that dost this worship
To him whose likeness is but praise of thee!   100
Thou bright, unsetting star, which through this veil,
For very envy, mak'st the sun look pale!

Mil. Well, visitor, lest that perhaps my mother
Should think the friar too strict in his decrees,
I this confess to my sweet ghostly father:
If chaste pure love be sin, I must confess,
I have offended three years now with thee.

Ray. But do you yet repent you of the same?

Mil. I' faith, I cannot.

Ray.   Nor will I absolve thee
Of that sweet sin, though it be venial;   110
Yet have the penance of a thousand kisses,
And I enjoin you to this pilgrimage:
That in the evening you bestow yourself

purpose, to be put in practice by Frank . . . and by its
means I was delivered to Sir Arthur Clare. (But the
passage is probably corrupt; 'Plotted by' will hardly bear
this weight of meaning, and it is crude to say that 'Fabell
. . . Plotted . . . by Fabell'. Warnke and Proescholdt (1844)
read 'Harry' for 'Fabell' in line 85 (cf. line 151), and
Tucker Brooke (1908) adds after line 84 a conjectural line
'Helped me to act the part of priestly novice.')   90
dream'd] in a dream.

Here in the walk near to the willow ground,
Where I'll be ready both with men and horse
To wait your coming, and convey you hence
Unto a lodge I have in Enfield Chase.
No more reply, if that you yield consent—
I see more eyes upon our stay are bent.   119

Mil. Sweet life, farewell! 'Tis done: let that suffice;
What my tongue fails, I send thee by mine eyes.

[*Exit.*

Enter Fabell, Harry Clare, *and* Frank Jerningham.

Frank. Now, visitor, how does this new-made nun?

Harry. Come, come, how does she, noble Capuchin?

Ray. She may be poor in spirit, but for the flesh,
'Tis fat and plump, boys. Ah, rogues, there is
A company of girls would turn you all friars.

Fab. But how, Mounchensey, how, lad, for the wench?

Ray. Sound, lads, i' faith; I thank my holy habit,
I have confess'd her, and the Lady Prioress   129
Hath given me ghostly counsel with her blessing.
And how say ye, boys,
If I be chose the weekly visitor?

Harry. 'Sblood, she'll have ne'er a nun unbag'd to
sing mass then.

Frank. The Abbot of Waltham will have as many
children to put to nurse as he has calves in the marsh.

Ray. Well, to be brief, the nun will soon at night
turn tippet; if I can but devise to quit her cleanly of
the nunnery, she is mine own.

Fab. But, sirrah Raymond,   140
What news of Peter Fabell at the house?

Ray. Tush, he's the only man;
A necromancer and a conjurer
That works for young Mounchensey altogether;
And if it be not for Friar Benedick,
That he can cross him by his learned skill,

133 unbag'd] unpregnant.   138 turn tippet] change
(especially from spinsterhood to matrimony).

The wench is gone;
Fabell will fetch her out by very magic.

   Fab. Stands the wind there, boy? Keep them in
     that key,
The wench is ours before to-morrow day.   150
Well, Harry and Frank, as ye are gentlemen,
Stick to us close this once! You know your fathers
Have men and horse lie ready still at Cheston,
To watch the coast be clear, to scout about,
And have an eye unto Mounchensey's walks:
Therefore you two may hover thereabouts,
And no man will suspect you for the matter;
Be ready but to take her at our hands,
Leave us to scamble for her getting out.

   Frank. 'Sblood, if all Hertfordshire were at our heels,
We'll carry her away in spite of them.   161

   Harry. But whither, Raymond?

   Ray. To Brian's upper lodge in Enfield Chase;
He is mine honest friend and a tall keeper;
I'll send my man unto him presently
T' acquaint him with your coming and intent.

   Fab. Be brief and secret!

   Ray.   Soon at night remember
You bring your horses to the willow ground.

   Frank. 'Tis done; no more!

   Harry.   We will not fail the hour.
My life and fortune now lies in your power.   170

   Fab. About our business! Raymond, let's away!
Think of your hour; it draws well off the day.

                             [Exeunt.

Act IV. Scene I.

   Enter Blague, Banks, Smug, *and* Sir John.

   Host. Come, ye Hungarian pilchers, we are once
more come under the *zona torrida* of the forest. Let's

159 scamble] struggle.   164 tall] brave and good-
hearted.   1 Hungarian] pun on 'hungry'.   pilchers]
thieves.

be resolute, let's fly to and again; and if the devil
come, we'll put him to his interrogatories, and not
budge a foot. What? 'Sfoot, I'll put fire into you, ye
shall all three serve the good Duke of Norfolk.

Smug. Mine host, my bully, my precious consul, my
noble Holofernes, I have been drunk i' thy house
twenty times and ten; all's one for that: I was last
night in the third heavens, my brain was poor, it had
yeast in 't; but now I am a man of action; is 't not so, lad?

Banks. Why, now thou hast two of the liberal
sciences about thee, wit and reason, thou may'st serve
the Duke of Europe.   14

Smug. I will serve the Duke of Christendom, and do
him more credit in his cellar than all the plate in his
buttery; is 't not so, lad?

Sir John. Mine host and Smug, stand there; Banks,
you and your horse keep together; but lie close, show
no tricks, for fear of the keeper. If we be scar'd, we'll
meet in the church porch at Enfield.   21

Smug. Content, Sir John.

Banks. Smug, dost not thou remember the tree thou
fell'st out of last night?

Smug. Tush, an 't had been as high as the Abbey,
I should ne'er have hurt myself; I have fallen into
the river, coming home from Waltham, and scap'd
drowning.

Sir John. Come, sever, fear no spirits! We'll have
a buck presently; we have watched later than this
for a doe, mine host.   31

Host. Thou speak'st as true as velvet.

Sir John. Why then, come! Grass and hay, &c.
[*Exeunt.*

Enter Harry Clare, Frank Jerningham, *and* Millicent.

Harry. Frank Jerningham!

4 put ... interrogatories] cross-examine him.   19
close] hidden.   33 Grass and hay, &c.] *sc.* the Priest
speaks his usual tag.

Frank. Speak softly, rogue; how now?

Harry. 'Sfoot, we shall lose our way, it's so dark; whereabouts are we?

Frank. Why, man, at Potter's Gate; the way lies right: hark! the clock strikes at Enfield; what's the hour?   40

Harry. Ten, the bell says.

Frank. A lies in's throat, it was but eight when we set out of Cheston. Sir John and his sexton are at ale to-night, the clock runs at random.

Harry. Nay, as sure as thou liv'st, the villainous vicar is abroad in the Chase this dark night! the stone priest steals more venison than half the country.

Frank. Millicent, how dost thou?

Mil.   Sir, very well.
I would to God we were at Brian's lodge.

Harry. We shall anon; zounds, hark! what means
    this noise?   50

Frank. Stay, I hear horsemen.

Harry.   I hear footmen too.

Frank. Nay, then I have it: we have been discover'd,
And we are followed by our fathers' men.

Mil. Brother and friend, alas, what shall we do?

Harry. Sister, speak softly, or we are descri'd.
They are hard upon us, whatsoe'er they be;
Shadow yourself behind this brake of fern,
We'll get into the wood, and let them pass.

Enter Sir John, Blague, Smug, *and* Banks, *one after
    another.*

Sir John. Grass and hay! we are all mortal; the
keeper's abroad, and there's an end.   60

Banks. Sir John!

Sir John. Neighbour Banks, what news?

Banks. Zwounds, Sir John, the keepers are abroad;
I was heard by 'em.

42 A] he, *sc.* the bell.   in's] in his.   46–7 stone
priest] compare IV. ii. 48–50.

Sir John. Grass and hay! where's mine host Blague?

Host. Here, Metropolitan. The Philistines are upon us, be silent; let us serve the good Duke of Norfolk. But where is Smug?   68

Smug. Here; a pox on ye all, dogs; I have kill'd the greatest buck in Brian's walk. Shift for yourselves, all the keepers are up. Let's meet in Enfield church porch; away, we are all taken else.   [*Exeunt.*

Enter Brian, *with* Ralph, *his man, and his hound.*

Bri. Ralph, hear'st thou any stirring?

Ralph. I heard one speak here hard by, in the bottom. Peace, master, speak low; zounds, if I did not hear a bow go off, and the buck bray, I never heard deer in my life.

Bri. When went your fellows out into their walks?

Ralph. An hour ago.   79

Bri. 'Slife, is there stealers abroad, and they cannot hear of them: where the devil are my men to-night? Sirrah, go up the wind towards Buckley's lodge!

I'll cast about the bottom with my hound.

And I will meet thee under coney oak.

Ralph. I will, sir.

Bri. How now? by the mass, my hound stays upon something; hark, hark, Bowman, hark, hark, there!

Mil. Brother, Frank Jerningham, brother Clare!

Bri. Peace; that's a woman's voice! Stand! who's there? Stand, or I'll shoot.   90

Mil. O Lord! hold your hands, I mean no harm, sir.

Bri. Speak, who are you?

Mil. I am a maid, sir; who? Master Brian?

Bri. The very same; sure, I should know her voice; Mistress Millicent?

Mil. Ay, it is I, sir.

Bri. God for his passion! what make you here alone? I look'd for you at my lodge an hour ago.

86 stays upon] scents.   98 make] do.

What means your company to leave you thus?   100
Who brought you hither?

Mil. My brother, sir, and Master Jerningham,
Who, hearing folks about us in the Chase,
Fear'd it had been Sir Ralph and my father,
Who had pursu'd us, thus dispersed ourselves,
Till they were past us.

Bri. But where be they?

Mil. They be not far off, here about the grove.

Enter Harry Clare *and* Frank Jerningham.

Harry. Be not afraid! man, I heard Brian's tongue,
That's certain.   110

Frank. Call softly for your sister.

Harry. Millicent!

Mil. Ay, brother, here.

Bri. Master Clare!

Harry. I told you it was Brian.

Bri. Who's that? Master Jerningham? You are a
couple of hot-shots; does a man commit his wench to
you, to put her to grass at this time of night?

Frank. We heard a noise about here in the Chase,
And fearing that our fathers had pursu'd us,   120
Sever'd ourselves.

Harry.   Brian, how happ'd'st thou on her?

Bri. Seeking for stealers are abroad to-night,
My hound stayed on her, and so found her out.

Harry. They were these stealers that affrighted us;
I was hard upon them, when they hors'd their deer,
And I perceive they took me for a keeper.

Bri. Which way took they?

Frank. Towards Enfield.

Bri. A plague upon't, that's that damned priest,
and Blague of the George—he that serves the good
Duke of Norfolk.   131

117 commit] entrust.   123 stayed on] scented.   125
hors'd] hoisted up.

A noise within: Follow, follow, follow.

Harry. Peace, that's my father's voice.

Bri. Zounds, you suspected them, and now they are here indeed.

Mil. Alas, what shall we do?

Bri. If you go to the lodge, you are surely taken;
Strike down the wood to Enfield presently,
And if Mounchensey come, I'll send him t'ye.
Let me alone to bustle with your father;
I warrant you that I will keep them play   140
Till you have quit the Chase; away, away!

[Exeunt all but Brian.

Who's there?

Enter the Knights.

Sir Ralph. In the king's name, pursue the ravisher!

Bri. Stand, or I'll shoot.

Sir Ar. Who's there?

Bri. I am the keeper that do charge you stand;
You have stolen my deer.

Sir Ar. We stol'n thy deer? we do pursue a thief.

Bri. You are arrant thieves, and ye have stolen my deer.

Sir Ralph. We are knights; Sir Arthur Clare, and Sir
    Ralph Jerningham.   150

Bri. The more your shame, that knights should be such thieves.

Sir Ar. Who or what art thou?

Bri. My name is Brian, keeper of this walk.

Sir Ralph. O Brian, a villain!
Thou hast received my daughter to thy lodge.

Bri. You have stol'n the best deer in my walk to-night.
My deer!

Sir Ar. My daughter!
Stop not my way!

Bri.   What make you in my walk?
You have stolen the best buck in my walk to-night.

139 Let me alone] trust me.   bustle] contend.

Sir Ar. My daughter!   161
Bri. My deer!
Sir Ar. Where is Mounchensey?
Bri. Where's my buck?
Sir Ar. I will complain me of thee to the king.
Bri. I'll complain unto the king you spoil his game:
'Tis strange that men of your account and calling
Will offer it!
I tell you true, Sir Arthur and Sir Ralph,
That none but you have only spoil'd my game.
Sir Ar. I charge you, stop us not!   171
Bri. I charge you both ye get out of my ground!
Is this a time for such as you,
Men of your place and of your gravity,
To be abroad a-thieving? 'Tis a shame;
And, afore God, if I had shot at you,
I had serv'd you well enough.   [*Exeunt.*

Scene II.

Enter Banks *the Miller, wet on his legs.*

Banks. 'Sfoot, here's a dark night indeed! I think
I have been in fifteen ditches between this and the
forest. Soft, here's Enfield Church: I am so wet with
climbing over into an orchard for to steal some filberts.
Well, here I'll sit in the church porch, and wait for
the rest of my consort.   6

Enter the Sexton.

Sex. Here's a sky as black as Lucifer, God bless us!
Here was goodman Theophilus buried; he was the
best nutcracker that ever dwelt in Enfield. Well,
'tis nine o'clock, 'tis time to ring curfew. Lord bless
us, what a white thing is that in the church porch!
O Lord, my legs are too weak for my body, my hair
is too stiff for my nightcap, my heart fails; this is the
ghost of Theophilus. O Lord, it follows me! I cannot

168 offer it] presume to do it.   6 consort] band.

say my prayers, an one would give me a thousand
pound. Good spirit, I have bowl'd and drunk and
followed the hounds with you a thousand times,
though I have not the spirit now to deal with you.
O Lord!   19

Enter Priest.

Sir John. Grass and hay! we are all mortal. Who's
there?

Sex. We are grass and hay indeed; I know you to be
Master Parson by your phrase.

Sir John. Sexton!

Sex. Ay, sir!

Sir John. For mortality's sake, what's the matter?

Sex. O Lord, I am a man of another element;
Master Theophilus' ghost is in the church porch.
There was a hundred cats, all fire, dancing here even
now, and they clomb up to the top of the steeple; I'll
not into the belfry for a world.   31

Sir John. O good Solomon; I have been about a
deed of darkness to-night: O Lord, I saw fifteen spirits
in the forest like white bulls; if I lie, I am an arrant
thief: mortality haunts us—grass and hay! the devil's
at our heels, and let's hence to the parsonage.

[*Exeunt.*

The Miller *comes out very softly.*

Banks. What noise was that? 'Tis the watch, sure;
that villainous unlucky rogue, Smug, is ta'en, upon
my life; and then all our villainy comes out; I heard
one cry, sure.   40

Enter Host Blague.

Host. If I go steal any more venison, I am a para-
dox! 'Sfoot, I can scarce bear the sin of my flesh in the
day, 'tis so heavy; if I turn not honest and serve the

27 of another element] doomed to leave this world
(Walker); or perhaps 'of a changed nature', 'reformed'.
40 one] some one.

good Duke of Norfolk, as true mareterraneum skinker
should do, let me never look higher than the element
of a constable.

Banks. By the Lord, there are some watchmen,
I hear them name Master Constable; I would to God
my mill were an eunuch, and wanted her stones, so I
were hence.   50

Host. Who's there?

Banks. 'Tis the constable, by this light; I'll steal
hence, and if I can meet mine host Blague, I'll tell him
how Smug is ta'en, and will him to look to himself.
                                                          [*Exit.*

Host. What the devil is that white thing? this same
is a churchyard, and I have heard that ghosts and
villainous goblins have been seen here.

Enter Sexton *and* Priest.

Sir John. Grass and hay! O that I could conjure!
We saw a spirit here in the churchyard; and in the
fallow field there's the devil with a man's body upon
his back in a white sheet.   61

Sex. It may be a woman's body, Sir John.

Sir John. If she be a woman, the sheets damn her;
Lord bless us, what a night of mortality is this!

Host. Priest!

Sir John. Mine host!

Host. Did you not see a spirit all in white cross you
at the stile?

Sex. O no, mine host: but there sat one in the porch;
I have not breath enough left to bless me from the
devil.   71

Host. Who's that?

Sir John. The sexton, almost frighted out of his wits.
Did you see Banks or Smug?

Host. No, they are gone to Waltham, sure. I would

---

44 mareterraneum skinker] 'skinker' = 'tapster'; the
adjective 'mareterraneum' perhaps conveys the idea that
he drew oceans of drink.   58 conjure] work spells.

fain hence; come, let's to my house: I'll ne'er serve
the Duke of Norfolk in this fashion again whilst
I breathe. If the devil be amongst us, 'tis time to
hoist sail, and cry Roomer! Keep together; sexton,
thou art secret. What! let's be comfortable one to
another.   81

Sir John. We are all mortal, mine host.

Host. True; and I'll serve God in the night hereafter afore the Duke of Norfolk.   [*Exeunt.*

Act V. Scene I.

Enter Sir Arthur Clare *and* Sir Ralph Jerningham,
        trussing their points as new up.

Sir Ralph. Good morrow, gentle knight.
A happy day after your short night's rest!
    Sir Ar. Ha, ha, Sir Ralph, stirring so soon indeed?
By'r Lady, sir, rest would have done right well;
Our riding late last night has made me drowsy.
Go to, go to, those days are gone with us.
    Sir Ralph. Sir Arthur, Sir Arthur, care go with those
        days,
Let 'em even go together, let 'em go!
'Tis time, i' faith, that we were in our graves,
When children leave obedience to their parents,   10
When there's no fear of God, no care, no duty.
Well, well, nay, nay, it shall not do, it shall not;
No, Mounchensey, thou'st hear on't, thou shalt,
Thou shalt i' faith!
I'll hang thy son, if there be law in England.
A man's child ravish'd from a nunnery!
This is rare!
Well, well, there's one gone for Friar Hildersham.

79 cry Roomer] as in a ship about to tack before the
wind.   Heading. trussing their points] tying their laces
(which often served where we use buttons).   13 thou'st]
thou shalt.

Sir Ar. Nay, gentle knight, do not vex thus, it will
but hurt your health. You cannot grieve more than
I do, but to what end? But hark you, Sir Ralph, I
was about to say something—it makes no matter.
But hark you in your ear: the Friar's a knave; but
God forgive me, a man cannot tell, neither; 'sfoot,
I am so out of patience, I know not what to say.

Sir Ralph. There's one went for the Friar an hour
ago. Comes he not yet? 'Sfoot, if I do find knavery
under's cowl, I'll tickle him, I'll firk him. Here,
here, he's here, he's here. Good morrow, Friar;
good morrow, gentle Friar.   30

Enter Hildersham.

Sir Ar. Good morrow, Father Hildersham, good
  morrow.

Hil. Good morrow, reverend knights, unto you
  both.

Sir Ar. Father, how now? you hear how matters go;
I am undone, my child is cast away.
You did your best, at least I think the best;
But we are all cross'd; flatly, all is dash'd.

Hil. Alas, good knights! how might the matter be?
Let me understand your grief, for charity.

Sir Ar. Who does not understand my griefs? Alas,
  alas!
And yet ye do not! Will the Church permit   40
A nun in approbation of her habit
To be ravished?

Hil. A holy woman, benedicite!
Now God forfend that any should presume
To touch the sister of a holy house.

Sir Ar. Jesus deliver me!

Sir Ralph. Why, Millicent, the daughter of this
  knight,
Is out of Cheston taken the last night.

Hil. Was that fair maiden late become a nun? 49

36 cross'd] thwarted.

Sir Ralph. Was she, quotha? Knavery, knavery, knavery; I smell it, I smell it, i' faith; is the wind in that door? is it even so? dost thou ask me that now?

Hil. It is the first time that I e'er heard of it.

Sir Ar. That's very strange.

Sir Ralph. Why, tell me, Friar, tell me; thou art counted a holy man; do not play the hypocrite with me, nor bear with me. I cannot dissemble. Did I aught but by thy own consent, by thy allowance, nay, further, by thy warrant?

Hil. Why, reverend Knight——   60

Sir Ralph. Unreverend Friar——

Hil. Nay, then give me leave, sir, to depart in quiet; I had hop'd you had sent for me to some other end.

Sir Ar. Nay, stay, good Friar; if anything hath hap'd
About this matter in thy love to us,
That thy strict order cannot justify,
Admit it be so, we will cover it.
Take no care, man:
Disclaim not yet thy counsel and advice,
The wisest man that is may be o'erreach'd.   70

Hil. Sir Arthur, by my order and my faith,
I know not what you mean.

Sir Ralph. By your order and your faith?
This is most strange of all. Why, tell me, Friar,
Are not you confessor to my son Frank?

Hil. Yes, that I am.

Sir Ralph. And did not this good knight here and myself
Confess with you, being his ghostly Father,
To deal with him about th'unbanded marriage
Betwixt him and that fair young Millicent?   80

Hil. I never heard of any match intended.

Sir Ar. Did not we break our minds that very time,
That our device of making her a nun
Was but a colour and a very plot

84 colour] pretence.

To put by young Mounchensey? Is't not true?

   Hil. The more I strive to know what you should
mean,
The less I understand you.

   Sir Ralph. Did not you tell us still how Peter Fabell
At length would cross us, if we took not heed?

   Hil. I have heard of one that is a great magician,
But he's about the university.   91

   Sir Ralph. Did not you send your novice Benedick
To persuade the girl to leave Mounchensey's love,
To cross that Peter Fabell in his art,
And to that purpose made him visitor?

   Hil. I never sent my novice from the house,
Nor have we made our visitation yet.

   Sir Ar. Never sent him? Nay, did he not go?
And did not I direct him to the house,
And confer with him by the way? and did he not   100
Tell me what charge he had received from you,
Word by word, as I requested at your hands?

   Hil. That you shall know; he came along with me,
And stays without. Come hither, Benedick!

Enter Benedick.

Young Benedick, were you e'er sent by me
To Cheston Nunnery for a visitor?

   Ben. Never, sir, truly.

   Sir Ralph.   Stranger than all the rest!

   Sir Ar. Did not I direct you to the house? Confer
    with you
From Waltham Abbey unto Cheston wall?

   Ben. I never saw you, sir, before this hour!   110

   Sir Ralph. The devil thou didst not! Ho, chamber-
    lain!

   Cham. Anon, anon.

Enter Chamberlain.

   Sir Ralph. Call mine host Blague hither!

85 put by] divert.   88 tell us still] keep telling us.

Cham. I will send one over to see if he be up; I think he be scarce stirring yet.

Sir Ralph. Why, knave, didst thou not tell me an hour ago mine host was up?

Cham. Ay, sir, my master's up.

Sir Ralph. You knave, is a up, and is a not up? Dost thou mock me?   120

Cham. Ay, sir, my master is up; but I think Master Blague indeed be not stirring.

Sir Ralph. Why, who's thy master? is not the master of the house thy master?

Cham. Yes, sir; but Master Blague dwells over the way.

Sir Ar. Is not this the George? Before God, there's some villainy in this.

Cham. 'Sfoot, our sign's remov'd; this is strange!

[*Exeunt.*

Scene II.

Enter Blague, *trussing his points.*

Host. Chamberlain, speak up to the new lodgings, bid Nell look well to the bak'd meats!

Enter Sir Arthur *and* Sir Ralph.

How now, my old jennets balk my house, my castle, lie in Waltham all night, and not under the canopy of your host Blague's house?

Sir Ar. Mine host, mine host, we lay all night at the George in Waltham; but whether the George be your fee-simple or no, 'tis a doubtful question: look upon your sign!   9

Host. Body of Saint George, this is mine overthwart neighbour hath done this to seduce my blind customers. I'll tickle his catastrophe for this; if I do not indict him at next assizes for burglary, let me die of

119 a] he.   3 balk] shy at.   8 fee-simple]
property.   10 overthwart] across the way.   12
catastrophe] end (as above, II. i. 8).

the yellows; for I see 'tis no boot in these days to serve the good Duke of Norfolk. The villainous world is turn'd manger: one jade deceives another, and your ostler plays his part commonly for the fourth share. Have we comedies in hand, you whoreson, villainous male London lecher?

Sir Ar. Mine host, we have had the moiling'st night of it that ever we had in our lives.   21

Host. Is't certain?

Sir Ralph. We have been in the forest all night almost.

Host. 'Sfoot, how did I miss you? Heart, I was a-stealing a buck there.

Sir Ar. A plague on you; we were stayed for you.

Host. Were you, my noble Romans? Why, you shall share; the venison is a-footing. *Sine Cerere et Baccho friget Venus*; that is, there's a good breakfast provided for a marriage that's in my house this morning.   32

Sir Ar. A marriage, mine host?

Host. A conjunction copulative; a gallant match between your daughter and master Raymond Mounchensey, young Juventus.

Sir Ar. How?

Host. 'Tis firm, 'tis done. We'll show you a precedent i' th' civil law for't.

Sir Ralph. How? married?   40

Host. Leave tricks and admiration. There's a cleanly pair of sheets in the bed in Orchard chamber, and they shall lie there. What? I'll do it; I'll serve the good Duke of Norfolk.

14 yellows] jaundice.   20 moiling'st] most troublesome.   29 a-footing] coming.   29-30 *Sine . . . Venus*] Love grows cold lacking food and drink.   36 young Juventus] alluding to an old moral interlude of *Lusty Juventus*, by R. Wever, plagiarized about this time in Anthony Munday's *Sir Thomas More*.   41 admiration] astonishment.

Sir Ar. Thou shalt repent this, Blague.

Sir Ralph. If any law in England will make thee smart for this, expect it with all severity.   47

Host. I renounce your defiance, if you parle so roughly. I'll barricado my gates against you. Stand fair, bully; Priest, come off from the rearward! What can you say now? 'Twas done in my house; I have shelter i' th' court for 't. D'ye see yon bay window? I serve the good Duke of Norfolk, and 'tis his lodging. Storm, I care not, serving the good Duke of Norfolk. Thou art an actor in this, and thou shalt carry fire in thy face eternally.

Enter Smug, Mounchensey, Harry Clare, *and* Millicent.

Smug. Fire, 'sblood, there's no fire in England like your Trinidado sack. Is any man here humorous? We stole the venison, and we'll justify it: say you now!

Host. In good sooth, Smug, there's more sack on the fire, Smug.   61

Smug. I do not take any exceptions against your sack; but if you'll lend me a pike-staff, I'll cudgel them all hence, by this hand.

Host. I say thou shalt in to the cellar.

Smug. 'Sfoot, mine host, shall's not grapple? Pray, pray you; I could fight now for all the world like a cockatrice's egg. Shall's not serve the Duke of Norfolk?   [*Exit.*

Host. In, skipper, in!   70

Sir Ar. Sirrah, hath young Mounchensey married your sister?

Harry. 'Tis certain, sir; here's the priest that coupled them, the parties joined, and the honest witness that cried Amen.

Ray. Sir Arthur Clare, my new created father, I beseech you, hear me.

Sir Ar. Sir, sir, you are a foolish boy; you have done

---

58 humorous] quarrelsome.

that you cannot answer; I dare be bold to seize her
from you; for she's a profess'd nun.   80

Mil. With pardon, sir, that name is quite undone;
This true love knot cancels both maid and nun.
When first you told me I should act that part,
How cold and bloody it crept o'er my heart!
To Cheston with a smiling brow I went;
But yet, dear sir, it was to this intent,
That my sweet Raymond might find better means
To steal me thence. In brief, disguis'd he came,
Like novice to old Father Hildersham:
His tutor here did act that cunning part,   90
And in our love hath join'd much wit to art.

Sir Ar. Is't even so?

Mil. With pardon therefore we entreat your smiles;
Love, thwarted, turns itself to thousand wiles.

Sir Ar. Young Master Jerningham, were you an
    actor
In your own love's abuse?

Frank.   My thoughts, good sir,
Did labour seriously unto this end,
To wrong myself, ere I'd abuse my friend.

Host. He speaks like a bachelor of music, all in
numbers. Knights, if I had known you would have
let this covey of partridges sit thus long upon their
knees under my sign-post, I would have spread my
door with old coverlids.   103

Sir Ar. Well, sir, for this your sign was removed,
was it?

Host. Faith, we followed the directions of the devil,
Master Peter Fabell; and Smug, Lord bless us! could
never stand upright since.

Sir Ar. You, sir, 'twas you was his minister that
married them?   110

Sir John. Sir, to prove myself an honest man, being

79 answer] answer for, i.e. justify.   104 for this] *sc.* so
that the runaway couple might spend the night at the true
George whilst the knights slept across the road.

that I was last night in the forest stealing venison—
now, sir, to have you stand my friend, if that matter
should be call'd in question, I married your daughter
to this worthy gentleman.

Sir Ar. I may chance to requite you, and make your
neck crack for 't.

Sir John. If you do, I am as resolute as my neighbour vicar of Waltham Abbey; ahem, grass and hay!
we are all mortal; let's live till we be hang'd, mine
host, and be merry; and there's an end.   121

Enter Fabell.

Fab. Now, knights, I enter; now my part begins.
To end this difference, know, at first I knew
What you intended, ere your love took flight
From old Mounchensey; you, Sir Arthur Clare,
Were minded to have married this sweet beauty
To young Frank Jerningham; to cross which match,
I us'd some pretty sleights; but I protest
Such as but sat upon the skirts of art;
No conjurations, nor such weighty spells   130
As tie the soul to their performancy.
These for his love, who once was my dear pupil,
Have I effected. Now, methinks, 'tis strange
That you, being old in wisdom, should thus knit
Your forehead on this match, since reason fails;
No law can curb the lover's rash attempt;
Years, in resisting this, are sadly spent.
Smile, then, upon your daughter and kind son,
And let our toil to future ages prove,
The Devil of Edmonton did good in love.   140

Sir Ar. Well, 'tis in vain to cross the providence:
Dear son, I take thee up into my heart;
Rise, daughter; this is a kind father's part.

Host. Why, St. George, send for Spindle's noise
presently: ha, ere 't be night, I'll serve the good Duke
of Norfolk.

    127 cross] thwart.   144 noise] band.

Sir John. Grass and hay! mine host, let's live till we die, and be merry; and there's an end.

Sir Ar. What, is breakfast ready, mine host?

Host. 'Tis, my little Hebrew.   150

Sir Ar. Sirrah, ride straight to Cheston Nunnery,
Fetch thence my lady; the house, I know,
By this time misses their young votary.
Come, knights, let's in!

Bil. I will go to horse presently, sir.—A plague a my lady, I shall miss a good breakfast. Smug, how chance you cut so plaguily behind, Smug?

Smug. Stand away, I'll founder you else.

Bil. Farewell, Smug, thou art in another element.

Smug. I will be by and by; I will be Saint George again.   161

Sir Ar. Take heed the fellow do not hurt himself.

Sir Ralph. Did we not last night find two St. Georges here?

Fab. Yes, knights, this martialist was one of them.

Sir Ar. Then thus conclude your night of merriment!   [*Exeunt omnes.*

FINIS.

155 a] of, on.   157 cut] strike.   158 founder] lame.
160–1 I will be Saint George again] Tucker Brooke points
out that this refers to an incident not found in the
play but recounted in a prose tract of the same name
by Antony Brewer, where Smug climbs upon the sign of
the White Horse Inn, thus converting it to that of the
George (St. George mounted on his charger), and baffling
his pursuers. There are other allusions to this episode in
lines 162–3 and perhaps in lines 106–8 and 156–7.

PRINTED IN GREAT BRITAIN
AT THE UNIVERSITY PRESS, OXFORD
BY VIVIAN RIDLER
PRINTER TO THE UNIVERSITY